Death _ 77

narr as both alliance + conflict
Reasons for vulnerability of comm's
Kinship as mask for exploit 48, 86
Attack on ideological reductionism 87
State + politics are part of econ's exploit 91, 92
Extra econ factors & supply + demand do not explain low wages 91, 92
+ international trade → suspended

Maidens, Meal and Money

Key - must explain the conds under which the elements for
reproducing labor are produced 93

Underdev results from overexploit of workers, therefore
polie action must take place among the exploited classes
not thru govt 93   econ rel's between modes of prod - classes
not between nation states 139
cause → of transfer between econ sectors w/ diff rel's of prod; the
domestic + capitalist sector 94, 95, 101 -
Capitalism + feudalism rely on Dom. mode of prod to
reproduce themselves 94, 138

Refutes dual econ model - cap. sector preserves the dom.
econ to extract value but in so doing, simultaneously
destroys it.   Focus on organiz of econ rel's between the
2 sectors - Dom sector undergoes various changes 97, 98, 110
BUT SEE PG's 117 - 123   Double labor market 115 - 129
Labor in integral vs. imperialist cap - Marx's theory of
surplus-value must be modified for latter form 99

Marx on primitive accumulation - the pt at which feudalism
dissolves + capitalism takes off 104, 105
His model does not take colonialism + imperialism into
account 105
Primitive accum is therefore, not a transitory moment as
Marx thought - It is inherent in cap 105
What has been ignored - the extended phenom. of the
rotating migration of labor 106 - 115
Labor power is transformed from non-cap → cap econ in 2
ways 1) rural exodus 102 - 109 2) organiz of rotating migration 107, 110
permanent migration 122
These pop. movement are the driving force of growth in
the cap sector 108, 109, 139
This permanent migration destroys the peasantry + the dom.
mode of prod 110, 115, 131, 139
labour rent extracted by feudal lord or cap 111, 112 -
This extracted labor power can be used to grow export crops
(cash cropping) to to prod. non agric goods (rotating labor
migration 112 - 115 extraction of labor rent requires rotating
labor migration
Labor rent vs. surplus value 115 (two forms of extraction)

see
neocolonialism
136, 137

[handwritten top margin:] peasant proletarians created by delib blocking of the extension of cap. To rural areas supplying cheap labor 117 - marginalized 132 -

[handwritten:] Distinct mode of exploiting peasant proletarians has emerged 3 ways: 1) Double labor market 2) rotation of rural labor force back to the domestic sector 3) racist ideology which supports these policies 120 -

[handwritten:] Double labor market; migrants/integrated workers 120 -
Immigrant workers 120 -
Profits from rotating migration 125 126
Appropriation of this profit parents take off 126

Themes in the Social Sciences

Editors: Jack Goody and Geoffrey Hawthorn

The aim of this series is to publish books which will focus on topics of general and interdisciplinary interest in the social sciences. They will be concerned with non-European cultures and with developing countries, as well as with industrial societies. The emphasis will be on comparative sociology and, initially, on sociological, anthropological and demographic topics. These books are intended for undergraduate teaching, but not as basic introductions to the subjects they cover. Authors have been asked to write on central aspects of current interest which have a wide appeal to teachers and research students, as well as to undergraduates.

[handwritten:] Contrast to Scott - prod. efforts to extract from peasantry must include measures to ↑ prod of land 127
Factors Scott ignored 129 - 132

Other books in the series

Edmund Leach: *Culture and Communication: The logic by which symbols are connected: an introduction to the use of structuralist analysis in social anthropology*

Anthony Heath: *Rational Choice and Social Exchange: A critique of exchange theory*

P. Abrams and A. McCulloch: *Communes, Sociology and Society*

Jack Goody: *The Domestication of the Savage Mind*

John Dunn: *Western Political Theory in the Face of the Future*

David Thomas: *Naturalism and Social Science: A post-empiricist philosophy of social science*

Jean-Louis Flandrin: *Families in Former Times: Kinship, household, sexuality*

David Lane: *Leninism: A sociological interpretation*

Anthony D. Smith: *The Ethnic Revival*

Jack Goody: *Cooking, Cuisine and Class: A study in comparative sociology*

Roy Ellen: *Environment, Subsistence and System*

John Dunn: *The Politics of Socialism: An essay in political theory*

S. N. Eisenstadt and L. Roniger: *Patrons, Clients and Friends: Interpersonal relations and the structure of trust in society*

Martine Segalen: *Historical Anthropology of the Family*

Tim Ingold: *Evolution and Social Life*

David Levine: *Reproducing Families: The Political Economy of English Population History*

Robert A. Hinde: *Individuals, Relationships and Culture: Links between Ethology and the Social Sciences*

[handwritten bottom margin:] Consequences of necessity to import subsistence foods (this is due to need to maintain low prices of sub foods - must be imported because of migration to urban areas) 129 -

Insecurity of worker's positions → high birth rates as attempt to insure future 130

Food aid / dependence on world powers 130

Maidens, Meal and Money

Dividing the internat proletariat 133–

Capitalism and the domestic community

neo colonies – exploit laborers in their own countries rather than as immigrants 136, 137

Contradictions facing cap. arise from its dependence on dom. comm for labour 138

by Claude Meillassoux

1st Internal contradiction is that it both relies on main of dom comm (for labor) & yet also destroys it 138–

2nd contradiction – by destroying family, also destroys free labour power 141–144

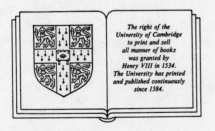

The right of the University of Cambridge to print and sell all manner of books was granted by Henry VIII in 1534. The University has printed and published continuously since 1584.

Cambridge University Press

Cambridge
New York New Rochelle
Melbourne Sydney

Published by the Press Syndicate of the University of Cambridge
The Pitt Building, Trumpington Street, Cambridge CB2 1RP
32 East 57th Street, New York, NY 10022, USA
10 Stamford Road, Oakleigh, Melbourne 3166, Australia

Originally published in French as *Femmes, greniers et capitaux* by
Librairie François Maspero, Paris, 1975
and © Librairie François Maspero 1975

First published in English by the Cambridge University Press 1981 as
Maidens, meal and money
English translation © Cambridge University Press 1981
Reprinted 1984, 1986, 1988

Printed in Great Britain at the University Press, Cambridge

British Library cataloguing in publication data

Meillassoux, Claude
Maidens, meal and money. – (Themes in the social sciences).
1. Economic anthropology – Africa, West
I. Title   II. Series
301.5'1   GN 652.5   79-42615

ISBN 0 521 22902 2 hard covers
ISBN 0 521 29708 7 paperback

Contents

Contents

Preface to the English translation

In 1964 I devised a long term project to identify and characterise the different modes of production which existed in pre-colonial West Africa and to analyse both their reaction to each other and to the colonial impact. It was then the era of independence. But the policy underlying development, as it went along with decolonisation, had quite a different outlook on the problem. Plans for cash-cropping and mining were conceived without regard for the existing social structures, which were considered as the remnants of a superseded archaic past. French anthropology could not have been of a great help anyway, since it had treated economics, in so far as it had been concerned with it at all, in a completely ethnocentric way. When 'primitive' people were not considered as living off myth and religion, they were sparsely granted some sort of backward 'primitive capitalism'. The only categories used for analysis were those of liberal economics. Furthermore, the effects of the imperialist economy – which, within this framework, should have been considered as relevant to these categories – were ignored or hidden. Anthropological tradition, too intent on discovering savages preserved from civilisation, was more prone to idealistic reconstruction of past paradises than to a materialist approach.

When in 1957 I embarked on my first field work under Georges Balandier, he was setting up, together with Paul Mercier and Gilles Sautter, one of the first French curriculum on Africa. At that time there was no training in anthropology available in Paris except a very short course at the Institut d'Ethnologie of the Musée de l'Homme. Through a research project on the impact of techniques on social organisation, Balandier introduced me to the best of current anthropology – that is to British anthropology – which provided me with some of the best research on this topic, particularly on the effect of massive migrations undergone by peoples from eastern and southern Africa (somewhat earlier than in the francophone countries). Anthropologists such as Isaac Schapera

vii

and Max Gluckman, Monica Hunter-Wilson and others in the 'forties had the courage to expose the appalling exploitation of the Africans in the racist states of southern Africa. Functionalism however, while very descriptive and stimulating, was based more on a sort of legalistic empiricism than on a thorough analysis of the content of economic and social relationships. The notion of kinship invaded all the field and glutted the analysis of family households, cloaking the concept of relations of production. It is on the basis of this material and analyses, anyway, that Balandier and Mercier renovated French anthropology and threw a new light on African societies by setting them back into their historic realm, and by pointing at the situation of 'crises' induced by the policy of 'development' to which they were exposed. In other words by exposing exploitation.

It was thanks to Balandier that I was able to orient my first field-work toward an examination of the problems related to the transformation of African peasants into commodity producers. Although Balandier was always reserved towards historical materialism he was most interested in my work on the Guro (1964) and was very instrumental in promoting it.

With regard to my theoretical and field orientation, I had worked until then in relative isolation. No one was then interested in France in economic anthropology, except Pierre Bessaignet (1966) with whom I had little contact. In the field of historical materialism the Communist Party was holding a monopoly by which nothing could be done except along the line of official orthodoxy. I wrote *Anthropologie économique des Guro de Côte d'Ivoire* while reading *Capital*, which I had discovered a few years before as a militant in a leftist group. Not that it provided me with ready-made schemes; but Marx's approach, his way of arguing and analysing, of uncovering hidden truth, his subtle dialectic gave me an unequalled intellectual stimulus. In my confinement, Marx became an interlocutor and a master. I thus learned to distinguish between, and at the same time to link together, empirical field-work and theoretical thinking. It is along this line that I produced my first two works: an analytical description of historical transformations that have taken place in a population of peasants converted into cash croppers and, in 1960, a theoretical essay on self-sustenance.

Balandier was not only a researcher and a teacher; he was also the promotor of African studies in France. Most French Africanists today owe their career to him, even those who now work in different schools of thought. He almost invariably recruited people of great talent so that from the 'sixties onward I was joined by a new generation of researchers whose theoretical, methodological and political concerns were close to mine. This coincided with the development in France of a research policy which opened up greater prospects for field investigation. After 1965, unfortunately, bureaucracy gained a growing control over the administration of French research and it has now reached the point where the original impetus is lost and the results of the last fifteen years are in jeopardy. In spite of the present obstacle, French anthropologists remain of considerable quality and they have started to produce high-grade original work. It is in these stimulating surroundings that I have had the chance to follow up my research.

Since 1963 my fieldwork has carried me among peoples of Mali and Senegal. The ancient tradition of their civilisations induced me to give a larger part to history as a means of gaining knowledge on present societies and to the analysis of present societies as a means of understanding the past. From my research among the Soninke, the Bamana, the Maninka, the Pular of Fuuta Tooro I have brought back a large amount of material that I am trying to treat theoretically and historically in order to build up a *theory of social practice* as it seems to fit best Marx's intent. Given the extension of French anthropological research in the 'seventies my data could now be brought together and tested against that of my colleagues working in the same socio-cultural area, namely West Africa. From village or ethnic monographs which have been predominant for the last 20 years, we were able to move towards research covering whole historic and geographical areas within which each people is organically related. It is in this context that research on trade, slavery or war was attempted.

It was also on the initiative of this group that French Africanists were led to take a stand on the great Sahelian famine of the 'seventies and to expose the political and economic background of this disaster which was too easily put down to climatic fatality. A large demonstration, an exhibit of documents, films, discussions, a book and a manifesto were produced on the problem. It had such an impact that it resulted in several of the signatories being subject to administrative sanctions and considerable professional difficulties.

Finally it was through our acquaintance with the world of the African migrant workers in France that the problem of their exploitation was posed in a critical way. Our research, which had begun in African villages, led us to the squalid and overcrowded dormitories of Paris suburbs where the very same men that we met in their places as proud peasants were converted into anonymous proletarians.

Should not such a situation lead the anthropologist to associate the analysis of the domestic economy where these people came from with that of the problem of labour in the capitalist economies, as I have tried to do in the present volume? Colonisation has brought capitalism and the domestic economies into direct contact; the in-between modes of exploitation and their related classes of masters and lords vanished amidst this encounter. The abrupt transition between the first part of the book, which deals with anthroponomic societies, and the second, which jumps to modern conditions of labour, was forced down upon me as it is forced down on African peasants by the callousness of the colonial relationship.

Indeed my first intention was to proceed in a more academic way and to deal successively with the modes of production in their presumed historical order. But it seemed to me important at this point of my research that I should use my results to support an argued exposition of the specific mode of exploitation that it revealed. This might be an unorthodox way to proceed, but it is one that may contribute further to free anthropology from an outworldish attitude and demonstrate its relevance to current affairs. This discipline should cease to be a pretext for exotic fantasies and become an instrument of freedom.

Introduction

If the notion of kinship has pervaded the field of anthropology it is because it refers to a widespread institution – which regulates a function common to all societies, the reproduction of human beings, both as productive agents and as reproducers and (mostly in the domestic economy) social reproduction at large. Yet, through kinship, classical anthropology has only grasped the institutionalised expression of reproduction without investigating its basic function. Being unable to connect kinship to the other levels of social reality it has considered it as a sort of a postulate and dealt only with its normative and formal sides. 'According to the materialistic conception, the determining factor in history is, in the final instance, the production and reproduction of the immediate essentials of life. This, again, is of a twofold character. On the one side, the production of the means of existence, of articles of food and clothing, dwellings, and of the tools necessary for that production; on the other side, the production of human beings themselves, the propagation of the species.' (Engels, [1884], pp. 1-2)

Was Engels wrong to put on the same level the reproduction of the means of existence and the reproduction of men? This is the contention of the Marxist editors of the French translation (Editions Sociales, 1954) according to whom it would be a mistake. But I believe these critics of Engels are, here, getting away with a production essential among others, namely the production of human energy, or, in the capitalist context, of labour-power. The reproduction of human beings is, in terms of economics, production of labour-power in all its forms. But in spite of this foreview of Engels, little attention was given by historical materialism to this problem. Instead of granting to the production of this essential good the importance which could be expected from a theory of labour, it gives only partial attention to it.

It is true that the historic and economic conditions under which

xi

capitalism arose did not point at the reproduction of labour-power as to an urgent matter. Through the process of primitive accumulation it was solved straight off and the peasants migrant from European hinterlands contributed to rid the theoreticians of this extra worry. Neither Marx nor the other economists were really concerned with it.

In spite or maybe because of Malthus, the study of human reproduction has nearly been, since then, the exclusive concern of demography, a statistical technique whose extrapolations are often viewed as the effects of a causal theory. If historical materialism rightly rejected demography as a determination, and the Malthusian notion of poverty as resulting from the proliferation of unchaste brutes, it rejected also but, wrongly, the problem of reproduction.

Marx was undoubtedly right to think that every mode of production has its own laws of population. This statement, which he never explicitly argued, implies above all that questions about population cannot be considered apart from the dominant relations of production. Strictly speaking there is no such thing as 'demographic causes'. The growth of population is governed by constraints other than the fertility of women. In all societies the biological capacity for procreation is far above the birth rate. Poverty, illness, starvation, rites, beliefs, or in our societies, 'well-being', have always set the rate of reproduction below that of fertility.

In the analysis of the nineteenth-century capitalism, the lack of a theory of the reproduction of labour-power did not undermine Marx's theory of labour in a critical way. In Marx's model, everything happens as if a non-specified part of the labour-power used by the capitalist sector is given as being produced and reproduced outside the capitalist sector (a historically and conjuncturally correct hypothesis for this period). To reintroduce the process of reproduction of labour-power into the model requires only a readjustment of the argument, not a reassessment. The reasoning applied to the equalisation of the rate of profit can be applied equally to the phenomenon. So doing, it gives to the theory of Marx a wider historical relevance and a larger scope by connecting it with the problem of the expansion of capitalism (as raised by Rosa Luxemburg).

If we are to understand how the domestic society operates, reproduction must be taken into central consideration. The domestic community is indeed the only economic and social system which manages the physical reproduction of human beings, the reproduction of the producers and social reproduction at large through a comprehensive set of institutions, by the ordered manipulation of the living means of reproduction, that is: women.

Neither feudalism, nor slavery, even less capitalism, know such regulating and correcting built-in mechanisms governing the process of reproduction. On the contrary, in the last analysis, we find that all modern modes of production, all classes of societies depend, for the supply of labour-power, on the domestic community. As for capitalism, it depends both on the domestic communities of the colonised countries and on its modern transformation, the family, which still maintains its reproductive functions although deprived of its productive ones. From this point of view, the domestic relations of production can be considered as the organic basis of feudalism, slavery as well as of capitalism or bureaucratic socialism. None of these forms of social organisation can be said to represent an integrated mode of production to the extent that they are not based on homogeneous relations of production and of reproduction. It is not therefore strictly accurate to look at the modes of production which developed on the domestic community, which dominated and exploited its productive and mostly its reproductive capacity, as being in every way superior to it. In terms of their productive potential they are superior, but not in terms of the reproduction of human beings. Marx's argument, which states that the key to inferior forms is found in more advanced ones, does not quite apply to the evolution of human societies and the naturalistic analogy with the anatomy of the man and of the ape is, like all analogies, faulty and insidious. Our knowledge of capitalism, when it remains linked to other relations of production vividly maintained as necessary elements of its development, is not enough to enlighten us on the mysteries of the domestic economy. But the recognition in this last mode of production of a problem of reproduction, leads to an understanding of this function in the capitalist system. If it is true, as Marx argued, that the hierarchy of institutions does not reflect their order of emergence, and that in this respect family has a subordinate position in the capitalist society, it remains that its function is crucial in that it is the family which produces, not only the physical worker, but also this social ingredient essential to the functioning of capitalism and which Marx has called 'the free labourer', freed from lasting servitude (as the slave, the serf, or the junior members of the lineage).

Introduction

The maintenance of functional domestic relations within the capitalist system raises the problem of the characterisation and classification of the social systems. We know that history cannot be perceived as a succession of modes of production totally exclusive from each other. But it is not only that each mode of production contains the germs of future relations of production or the relics of ancient ones, it is that, up until now and for an indefinite future, the domestic relations of production have been organically integrated into the development of each and all of the subsequent modes of production. Is it the evidence of the fact that we are still in the pre-historic phase of the development of humanity and that only communism, the real one, will be able to rid humanity of the archaism of kinship and re-invent at the same time affective relationships?

PART I

The domestic community

The agricultural domestic community, through its organised capacity for production and reproduction, represents an integrated form of social organisation which has existed since the neolithic period, and upon which still depends an important part of the reproduction of the labour-power necessary to the development of capitalism. This social formation has been the object of some attention by students concerned with economic history and the theory of pre-capitalist societies. Marx and Engels both tried to define its characteristics. In the *Formen*[1] Marx's ideas on this still appear to be influenced by bourgeois ideology. He viewed the community as being constituted 'spontaneously', the family, or tribal community, as being 'natural', and kinship as being 'consanguineous'. By formulating it this way, he by-passed the historical and material conditions which contributed to the development of this particular form of social organisation, and therefore tended to regard the family as an extra-social given.

However, in other texts and in the work of Engels, there are elements of a more relevant approach. This could be summarised as follows: the domestic community is composed of individuals who (a) practice self-sustaining agriculture, (b) produce and consume together, on common land, access to which is subordinated to membership of the community, and (c) are linked together by unequal ties of personal dependence. Within this community only use-value emerges.[2]

Marx and Engels attached considerable importance to common ownership of the land, which they contrasted to the private ownership of the means of production characteristic of capitalism. Elsewhere (1972a) I have criticised this retrospective approach to history which, although it undoubtedly demonstrates the radical evolution of social structures, does not provide concepts which can be applied to all societies.

It is interesting to note that few of the features in this description relate to the level of productive forces. They refer rather to norms (the division of labour, common ownership of land) or to traits which are not specifically defined (like self-sustenance and use-value) which, at this level of the productive forces, are implied by the process of agricultural production. Also, the idea that such communities are self-sufficient is only true as far as production is concerned, for their reproduction depends on their being one of a group of similar communities.

However, in *Capital* (Vol. III, p. 831) Marx does recognise that the problem of reproduction of communal society is 'its ultimate purpose': this refers not only to phyisical reproduction of individuals but to the social reproduction at large.

Thus, in contrast to some of his other propositions by which he seems to consider the community as 'natural' and 'spontaneous', Marx emphasises here, as does Engels in *The Origin of the Family*, the position occupied by the relations of production in the constitution of the domestic group.

German and British sociologists of the second half of the nineteenth century did not, however, choose to define the domestic community in this way, but rather made a distinction between trading and non-trading societies. Rodbertus (1865) took up the idea of the self-sustaining community again, using the term 'oikos' to designate an autonomous productive unit, whose main feature was, in his view, that it did not trade. This he related to a specific form of economic organisation within which the categories of political economy did not operate: there was no selling or buying, and no transfer of 'national dividend' or property. Production, consumption, investment, etc. were all undertaken without resorting to trade. Although he recognised their inadequacy, Rodbertus started from the categories of liberal economics (production, distribution and consumption), and thus remained imprisoned within a negative view of the domestic community in that he could describe it only in terms of what it was not.

This approach, thinking of economic phenomena *a contrario*, and using the notions of classical economics negatively, not only deprives the latter of their eventual operative capacity – in so far as they have one – but confines itself to the limited statement that pre-capitalist societies are different from capitalist societies only in being their opposites. It provides neither elements for a positive clarification of the relations of production, nor the means to distinguish qualitatively between different social systems.

4

For the nineteenth-century German and British schools of sociology, the distinction between use-value and exchange-value was perceived in terms of its juridical implications. H. Maine (1861) distinguished between societies in which social relations were established on the basis of status and those in which contract or bilateral agreement prevailed. Morgan (1877) made a similar distinction between the 'societas' in which personal relationships were dominant, and the 'civitas' based on territorial possession and property – a distinction to which Marx and Engels returned in their exploration of primitive society (Krader, 1972). Tönnies (1887) used the term *Gemeinschaft* to describe those societies in which relations of kinship and neighbourhood were predominant and *Gesellschaft* for those societies in which individuals, through exchange, confront one another as strangers. These distinctions, taken up by Max Weber, contain certain positive analytical elements. The drawback is that they are only juridical, or argue that the juridical distinction is determinant. In fact, they do not express social change, only the norms which societies adopt to perpetuate themselves.

For Polanyi (1957/1968) and his school the rise of exchanges was the major distinction – 'the great transformation' which separates the antique from the market economies. Two forms of circulation dominate in the former, both inseparable from the status of the parties concerned: reciprocity between peers and redistribution between the central authority and its subjects. In the market economy, in contrast, commodities are exchanged for each other. Despite the relevance of these distinctions, which point at a qualitative difference between the market economy and those that preceded it, they are still descriptive and structural and do not touch upon the phenomena of production, although it is from production, however, that relations which operate at the level of circulation develop.

What Polanyi did show was that in ancient societies the economy was subordinate to a unified political endeavour and not to the varied individual decisions of entrepreneurs. He found that in a status-based society the movement of goods was subordinate to hierarchical structures and their renewal; these were the channels through which goods had to flow if circulation was to reinforce rather than to disrupt established social relations. Consequently, the economy seemed to him to be embedded in the social fabric and did not, as it seems in a market economy, to occupy its own exclusive place, constrained by its own laws. In fact, the economy

5

is integrated into capitalist society just as it is in other societies. Polanyi here is confusing economics as a discipline, the product of an intellectual division of labour, with its object. Marx showed that what appeared to the liberal economists to be purely economic and material, for example commodities or capital, was, in fact, the crystallisation of social relations, in particular those which dominate the wage earning process.

Through reading ancient philosophers, Polanyi and his collaborators clarified a few mysterious aspects of the ways in which these ancient societies functioned. But the focus of their research moved to trading societies, to slavery, and to the manorial economy. So that, as a whole, Polanyi treated more of the antique economy in general than, as I intend to do here, the domestic economy on its own.

More recently, Marshall Sahlins (1972) attempted to define what he called the domestic mode of production by emphasising the characteristics of production rather than those of exchange. For Sahlins, the main features of the domestic mode of production are the following: the sexual division of labour, based on the minimum family: a man and a woman; a man–tool relationship deriving from the individual manipulation of tools; production geared to satisfy basic needs, from which it follows that, according to Chayanov's law[3] (1925), productive capacity is limited; rights over things exercised through rights over people; an 'introverted' circulation of domestic products and thus the predominance of use value.

Still, this domestic economy in this form would be as unreliable as it is apparently functional. The irregularity of production, the effects of Chayanov's law (which states among other things, as does Sahlins, that the productivity of labour varies in inverse proportion to the number of active labourers in the peasant family), the underproduction and underpopulation which is inherent in this mode of production, the ecology, are all factors which require reciprocity between communities, at the same time as they explain the simultaneously anarchic and independent nature of this society.

Following Marx, Sahlins specifies the *individual* nature of the means of production in the domestic economy and recognises a more subtle form of appropriation through the creation of personal ties. He raises the problem of a double level of the social structure, the community and the association of communities, a contradictory organisation which according to the author could be

6

explained by this specific mode of production. On the other hand, as opposed to Marx and Engels, but like almost all other contemporary writers, Sahlins' weakness remains that he nowhere specifies the historical period to which this 'mode of production' applies. Although several of the characteristics he proposes are related to the productive forces, he never specifies what level of knowledge has been acquired, what techniques of producing energy, or what mode of exploitation of the land exists.

The characteristics that he delineates apply just as well to hunter-gatherers and to fishermen, to pastoralists or to agriculturalists. The title of his book leaves one to conclude that all these activities are part of the same 'stone age'[4] economy, although his argument on the 'domestic economy' seems – without its being very clear – to be uniquely concerned with agricultural communities. I have been similarly unclear myself in the past (1960) and these criticisms could be levelled equally well at me. They derive from the fact that up to now we have not known how to distinguish the characteristics of the level of the productive forces from traits that derive from them. Therefore, despite an attempt at rigour, Sahlins' approach remains to a great extent empiricist. The model of exchange and the generalisation of the idea of reciprocity that he puts forward in the same book demonstrate all the drawbacks of his analysis. His model in fact incorporates data from *all kinds of societies* without taking account of their historical specificity which his analytical method is unable even to distinguish. But generalisations dealing with highly diverse societies can only be applied after each of the systems considered has been analysed and identified. They can only incorporate *elements explaining historical change* and not scattered traits belonging to different periods.

From the outset, then, our job is to discover which of those societies known to us belong to similar economic systems, and in what way they can finally be reduced to distinct modes of production, the 'models' of which will serve to guide and demarcate our progress.

1. *Locating the domestic community*

Initially I had meant to limit my research to 'the domestic mode of production' which I will later define in terms of the historical level of the productive forces to which it corresponds (Part 1, Ch. 2, § 1). As a first approximation the domestic mode of production overlaps with the 'segmentary' agricultural societies, composed of productive social units which are generally named lineages, although more appropriately identified with households. In a previous work (1967), I tried to show how these societies are based on a mode of exploition of the land which, because of its social, political and ideological implications, sharply distinguishes them from those societies which practise extraction/production activities (in particular hunting and gathering). However, I realised during the course of this work that to achieve an appropriate definition of the domestic community I would have to pursue my analysis further if I wanted to get really close to the subject of my research. To clarify some of the distinctions I wished to make between the domestic economy and other forms of social organisation of production and/or reproduction, I was led to reject certain erroneous notions about the latter and to undertake, in order to justify the specificity of the subject of my research, at least a trial analysis of forms of social organisation which are *not* domestic but usually assimilated with it.

The object of this first chapter is to establish how at least three types of society have positive characteristics distinguishing them from the domestic community. This is demonstrated through implicit comparisons with the domestic economy which is not defined until later in the book: reference to Chapter 2 will allow the reader – I hope – to follow the argument which underlies the present chapter.

It is evident that in order to situate the domestic community properly among all social and economic systems, a definition of each of them should also be given. My aim is less ambitious. It is simply to show, taking cases with which I am most familiar, that the notion of primitive or traditional economies is unduly applied to distinctive forms of social organisations each with their own laws. It is also to show that it is possible to discover relevant and scientific criteria for the characterisation of social systems, to which specific concepts apply. Assimilating these systems to modes of production is a question of judgement which one may make about each case, judgements which may eventually allow us perhaps to refine the notion and give it operative value.

All writers in this field, particularly Marx and Engels, attempted to establish how the 'primitive community' differs from captalism and, in a less convincing way, from slavery and feudalism – that is, in every case, from the forms of organisation which came of it. Few have been concerned to distinguish it from other forms of social organisation that are presumed to be anterior or inferior to it. As we have seen, the 'primitive economy' remains a relatively vague category within which only some dominant *activities* appear distinctive. We therefore talk of hunting, fishing and pastoral societies, etc. This initial approximation should not be rejected altogether. It shows that for researchers production plays a determinant role. However, the logical relationship between these different activities (which are not necessarily exclusive) and the types of social organisation, has not been established. Can we properly accept that this distinction is an *a priori* one through which 'modes of production' can be defined? Marx teaches us that what men produce matters less than the way in which they produce it.

In fact Engels himself was mistaken, as is shown in a famous letter (Engels to Marx, London, 8 December 1882 in Marx and Engels, 1846–95): 'The similarity [between the Germans of Tacitus and the Red Indians – C.M.] is indeed all the more surprising because the method of production is so fundamentally different – here hunters and fishers without cattle-raising or agriculture, there nomadic cattle-raising passing into agriculture. It just proves how at this stage the type of production is less decisive than the degree in which the old blood bonds and the old mutual community of the sexes within the tribe have been dissolved.'

We know that it was on the basis of this statement of Engels that Claude Lévi-Strauss (1968, 336ff.) could claim to be Marxist. If in fact one affects to understand by what Engels wrote that historical materialism does not apply to primitive societies, the true Marxist is he who excludes Marxism from the field of anthropology and substitutes for it a 'method' more appropriate to the study of these 'old ties of consanguinity'. The betrayers of Marxism are those who stubbornly try to apply Marxist analysis to subjects outside its scope. But what Engels really means is that the relations of production are not 'decisive'. He implies, without here being explicit, that beyond the relations of production 'consanguinity' covers the relations that bind people together for reproduction of life. In saying this he does not deny historical materialism as a means of analysing primitive societies as his work on the *Origin of the Family, Private Property and the State* proves decisively. Lévi-Strauss' pirouette does not destroy the fact that these societies are obliged to produce – under conditions determined by the level of the productive forces – in order to exist and perpetuate themselves. Even though they do not all fall within the same scientific categories, they all are encompassed by historical materialsm.

In addition to Lévi-Strauss' deliberate confusion here, there are other confusions which are more important. Engels' letter betrays the weakness of the concept of 'mode of production', even for those who coined the notion, for it is here reduced to a simple productive activity. Moreover, the theoretical analyses concerning anthropology were still too crude to enable a distinction to be made between all the kinds of relations subsumed under what was called 'consanguinity'. This distinction in fact still has to be made in relation to 'kinship', and in the following pages I will try to show how the confusion persists relative to the nature of social relations which are conflated in this category.

Fishing, hunting and agriculture are each multiform activities to which no simple determinism can be applied. Each of these activities involved numerous labour processes (Terray, 1969),[1] some collective, others individual, requiring more or less investment of labour. The relations which unite producers depend on the means they employ, the labour processes and the nature of the product and its use. Analysis should start from the relations that develop between the producers and their means of production (particularly the land) and the social relations which are necessary for setting these means of production to work.

Why incest?

In classical anthropology, the whole problem of reproduction is superseded by kinship theory. It is explicitly assumed, both by functionalists and structuralists, that the universal prohibition of incest is the primary cause of exogamy[2] and the exchange of women,[3] therefore accepted as the basis of kinship theory. Before we embark on any discussion we must remove the assumption that there is an ideological *primum mobile* behind the socialisation of marriage relations as observed in agricultural societies.

Lévi-Strauss (1969, 29) assumes that the incest prohibition, 'which has its roots in nature' – how otherwise could its supposed universality be explained? – can nevertheless have a sociological

10

explanation in the need to exchange women. This is stated in such a way that it is not clear whether he believes this prohibition relates to law and morality (which derive from the general conditions of society) – in which case I would agree with him – or whether it is a natural given, over which men have no control.[4] Though he persistently claims to be Marxist, Godelier (1973b), faithful to his structuralist options, accepts this latter premise, seemingly without reservations, as an ideological postulate. Robin Fox (1967, 31) makes it one of the four basic axioms upon which, according to him, kinship is based: 'primary kin do not mate with each other'. Members of a 'kinship' group, being unable because of this prohibition to have sexual relations with each other, should look, in order to mate, for a partner outside their group. In this way the 'exchange of women' which takes place even when kinship groups are large enough to allow members to mate with each other, is explained. The universality of the incest prohibition is, however, far from being proved and remains too doubtful to serve as the basis for the whole of kinship theory.[5] Furthermore it is unnecessary to explain matrimonial mobility.

If incest is taken to mean copulation between offspring of the same genitors, or between genitors and their offspring (without extending this idea even to classificatory kin), we know that such relations are practised and sometimes institutionalised in a certain number of societies. Incest has been legitimately practised among brothers and sisters in Hawaii, within the Pharaonic dynasties, between Azande fathers and daughters, Mbuti mothers and sons, and even among commoners in Roman Egypt, etc. (Middleton, 1962). Other cases could probably be found, but presumably, as with other practices which Christianity considered 'shameful', they were quickly suppressed. All anthropological fieldworkers know how it becomes difficult wherever missionaries and colonial administrators have penetrated, to get information about practices which offended the latter's morals (human sacrifice, the killing of the old, certain sexual practices, cannibalism and even slavery) (Meillassoux ed., 1975). It is also well known that when anthropologists and travellers discover these facts, they tend to censor their own information for fear of vilifying peoples who have won their sympathy. Because of the extreme repulsion which surrounds incest in our Christian societies, it is probable that information on this subject is even less available than on others.

In societies with relatively unelaborated matrimonial controls

11

and not very strict rules of filiation, incest (especially incestuous birth), since it would have no effect on the forms of social organisation, could well be a matter of indifference. The relative infrequency of incest in practice results from the fact that there is a greater difference in age between the possible sexual partners within a relatively restricted group than between those in different groups. In particular, there is a greater probability that members of a restricted family will find partners outside that group before they have the opportunity of sexual relations within the group itself. In spite of this difficulty, we know that incest is prescribed, for example in dynastic societies, for positive reasons. Incest does not involve, any more than do other sexual practices that are claimed to be 'abnormal' or deviant, 'natural' feelings of revulsion among the majority of people; on the contrary it seems to have exercised such a powerful attraction that wherever social conditions (such as the extension of the domestic group) facilitated its practice the resources of religious terrorism had to be enlisted to control it.[6] As we shall see, far from being inscribed in nature, the incest prohibition is the cultural transformation of endogamous prohibitions (a social proscription) into a sexual prohibition (i.e. a 'moral' or a 'natural' and absolute one). *It arises when control over marriage becomes one of the elements of political power.* In other words incest is a moral notion produced by an ideology which is tied to the extension of power in domestic communities, as one of the means used to control the mechanisms of reproduction. It is not an innate proscription, (if it were it would in fact be the only one of its kind). What is presented as a sin against nature is in fact only a sin against authority.

Resorting to the notion of incest to explain matrimonial mobility stems from a narrowly demographic vision of social growth. Thus Robin Fox (1967, p. 54) can write that 'the mother–child group could . . . be totally self-sufficient for the purposes of reproduction'. At least three presuppositions are contained in this statement. The first assumes that constituted social groups inevitably coincide with genetic groups; the second that their growth depends only on their natural reproductive capacities; and the third that nothing but fecundity limits their size. All three of these assumptions must be rejected.

At this point we will limit our discussion to the question of group size and return later to the question of growth and reproduction.

It is clear that in a society organised for survival the constituent

12

groups are those that are capable of providing for their material and, more particularly, their nutritional needs. From this point of view the mother–child group left to the vagaries of fecundity is not a functional constituent group. It is not necessarily composed of individuals who are able to produce and satisfy the material needs of the whole group. Its physical existence depends on its incorporation into a productive cell of a different size and composition, economically and socially determined by the general conditions of production. The conditions for reproduction of the mother–child group and its reproductive capacity are subordinated to the nature of the productive cell of which it is part. The only constituent cells which can be considered functional are those built up round the relations of production as such. In an economy using only individual means of production the number of people in each of these cells, if they depend exclusively on the requirements of production, is always lower than that which is necessary to ensure endogenous reproduction. Since the proportion of reproducers (i.e. women) in relation to the whole population is always lower than the number of producers, there is less chance that a cell which is organised strictly round the activities of production will, *at any given time*, count enough fertile women for their progeny to replace the active members of the group as far as number, sex and age are concerned. Neither the band nor the agricultural community is demographically self-sufficient. Therefore, to ensure that structural reproduction takes place, mobility of individuals between productive cells is necessary.

According to Washburn and Lancaster (in Lee and Devore, 1968; 303). 'about 100 couples are needed to produce enough children to ensure that the sexual balance reaches about 50/50, and that social life continues without unevenness. This requires a population of about 500 people.' These figures were also arrived at by Professor Sutter (according to Françoise Héritier, verbal communication). This estimate, however, presupposes monogamy and leads us back to the problems of mating. It is not, however, the equal distribution of women among men which decides reproduction, but the fecundity of pubescent women in the group concerned.

For Leroi-Gourhan, calculating group size depends upon the relation between 'available food resources, the number of individuals composing the group and the surface area of frequented territory (at a given stage of technical–economic evolution), (Leroi-Gourhan, 1964, 213–14). He deduces that among hunters and gatherers 'the primary group is composed of a limited number of individuals of both sexes' (*ibid.*, p. 216) whose lives are 'linked to neighbouring groups by a network of exchange which corresponds to their *reproductive needs*.[7] Of the two levels of grouping, food collection is particularly important for the primary group (the couple of domestic family) and the acquisition of wives is dominant in the larger (kinship and ethnic) group.[8]

The clustering of such constituent cells and the alliances between them depend less on the requirements of production and exchange than on the imperatives of reproduction. The relationships established to ensure reproduction are of a different kind from those formed around production, so that, as Leroi-Gourhan noted, there are always at least two different levels of social organisation: that of the productive cell, and that of the reproductive group. If there is to be a 'mode of production', it is here, in this gathering of productive units, organised for reproduction, that it is to be found.

(ii) The band and the relations of adhesion

Following a suggestion of Marx (1867, vol. 1, pp. 178–9), two primary types of economy associated with land can be distinguished, according to whether land is 'subject of labour' (as in hunting and gathering) or 'instrument of labour'. The social implications of using the land as instrument of labour (as in agriculture) are analysed later when we look at the domestic community. Here I want to look briefly at extraction economies based on exploitation of land as subject of labour, and at various intermediate cases only in so far as to distinguish them from the domestic community.[9]

Land[10] is subject of labour when it is exploited directly, no human energy being invested previously in it. The productive activity consists of taking from the soil products which it has produced on its own, with no further alteration of environment by man. Hunting and gathering are representative of this mode of exploiting land.[11] Compared with agriculture, which requires an investment of labour in the land, and a delayed return on this investment, the extraction economy gives instant returns: the productive gesture furnishes the product at once. Nuts, grubs, honey or meat are available following each hunting or gathering expedition. If the returns are instantaneous, however, they are not necessarily immediate because production requires the use of mediating instruments and tools, on which some energy expended. According to the amount of investment needed for this (making

14

tools, weapons, traps, etc.) and according to the individual or collective character of these investments, co-operation between producers is more or less frequent and more or less long-standing. Some activities can be managed by a single person (hunting or trapping small animals); these seem to make an important contribution to production. Others demand the co-operation of a greater number, whether to ensure that the instruments used (such as hunting nets for example) are employed collectively, or in constructing and then operating larger artefacts (big traps, beating game towards pits, etc.), or simply to ensure the mutual security of group members even when each one is operating separately or individually (as in gathering).

When the collective enterprise only requires individual investment (for example if it is undertaken by producers each with their own, or with no tools), sharing the produce between the producers concludes the enterprise. This sharing releases each person from obligation to the others, and from the point of view of production, nothing demands that the same producers work together in the same group in the future. Other relationships formed within the band and independent of productive activities can certainly encourage the same groups to re-form, but the material conditions of production and distribution do not make this form of regrouping compelling. Each team recruits on a voluntary basis. If communal enterprise requires making a collective means of production which can be used repeatedly, group members will be encouraged to remain together while it is in use. However, the ties created in this way are not binding. They may last only for that time during which the collective object is used; producers who leave the band before this time do not break any productive cycle as in agriculture where the product of one season is essential to carry out the work of the next. The cycle for the reproduction of human energy is short. Subsistence foods from hunting and gathering do not keep well and must be consumed shortly; there is hardly any accumulation of the product. The cycle of the transformation of food into energy is a daily one: virtually each day the producer exploits the energy he absorbed in the past few hours to produce what he needs to subsist for the hours to come. The product is invested as a means of producing human energy only for a short period. Thus the average time spent on daily labour is not very long – about four hours according to studies undertaken in several different societies (Lee and Devore, 1968). In contrast the repetition of productive tasks takes place

15

almost daily and productive and unproductive periods follow each other with only a few hours' interval between them. There is no dead season during which no productive activities take place.

The social relations of production resulting from this short-term mode of production are themselves precarious. The low level of investments, and their short duration, the fact that produce cannot be accumulated, and the daily repetition of dissociated activities, favour neither the formation of organic and comprehensive cells, nor the emergence of a managerial authority. In fact these productive cells, these bands, are known to be unstable, with changing membership. The mobility of individuals between bands is today a recognised fact, although until recently this de facto institution was regarded as of incidental significance.[12]

There are no rules of virilocality nor of gynecolocality. Active males and females move freely and peacefully from one band to another, either because of disagreements, or because another group is more appealing, or to get a sexual partner. Unions between men and women are fragile. After weaning, and sometimes before, children are adopted by members of the band as a whole and do not necessarily follow their genitors' movements.

Social reproduction reflects this mode of production which is so intimately tied to the present. In contrast to agricultural societies, each band gains its complement through the movement of adults between several different bands, which together represent the reproductive group, the constitution of which is not necessarily constant. The producer is most often included in a band because of his *present* rather than his future productive capacities. Institutions associated with social reproduction (pairing, welcoming of strangers) aim to attract adults and keep them in the band rather than anticipate the filiation of its members' offspring. *This free and voluntary movement between bands of adults of both sexes is the key mechanism of social reproduction.* Biological growth only supplies its basic material. The social distribution of individuals is not decided at birth by ties of filiation pre-established by their elders' marriages, but during each individual's own active life. Under these conditions procreation does not give rise to strict social control, it is merely the by-product of sexual relationships. Age- and sex-spread tends to be random. Social reproduction of the band, and the balance between productive and non-productive members, thus depend above all on its ability to retain or attract adults of both sexes. If we take the case of the Mbuti (Turnbull, 1965), the only institution that seems linked to the reproduction of the band is the little welcoming ceremony during which new-comers are accepted, or after honey has been collected, when the elders express the wish that the band will not disperse. There are in contrast no ceremonies for marriages, funerals or baptisms, apart from those introduced in imitation of their Bantu neighbours and exploiters.[13]

J. H. Steward noted (1968, 333–4), as have other writers, that war does not seem to be an activity which characterises the relations of hunter-gatherers. The Guayaki, whom Clastre (1974, 89) describes as being exclusively hunter-gatherers, would be an exception. Since they practise female infanticide, a permanent deficit in the number of women would force them to turn to war to obtain wives. But some features which emerge from the literature (ancestor worship, subordination of women) suggest, as Clastre admits, that these people were originally proto-agriculturalists. Contrary to what he thinks, it seems that these groups have continued to practise warfare in a socio-historical environment (proximity to proto-agriculturist warlike groups) which encouraged it, with the effect of maintaining the situation of male dominance, and not because of their hunting activities.

Because of the instability of its constituent cell, and its mode of social reproduction, social relations within the band are initially defined in terms of its *present membership*. Membership is expressed by participation in the common activities of production and consumption. Members of the band do not place themselves in reference to a common ancestor, nor do they classify themselves according to a formal genealogy. Whether some or all the members are biologically related is a matter of secondary importance: such ties *in themselves* create no permanent reciprocal obligations, nor do they define the status or even the rank of individuals.

Under such circumstances it is unlikely that the generic terms used by the members of such a group to refer to each other are associated with real ties of consanguinity, which are far less important than *relations of adhesion*. It is unlikely that we will be dealing *a priori* with *kinship* terms, if we mean by that terms based upon *filiation*. They are more likely to refer to the demarcation of age, sex, and functional categories connected with participation in productive activities (non-productive children, adults, old people), and to sexual unions. In this way all nubile women in the group may be 'sisters' without reference to filiation; 'brothers' are those who belong to the same generation of active men; 'fathers' may refer to the old men who no longer take part in collective hunts or beating. Lineage patterns have so permeated the minds of most anthropologists, however, that even the most perceptive of them see social relations first of all through kinship

17

categories.[14] This is true, for example, of Lorna Marshall (1957). In the same way Turnbull (1965) mentions a marriage by 'sister exchange' among the Mbuti pygmies, even though in the same work he tells us that unions form when the boys seduce the girls during certain festivities at which the bands meet. These two statements being contradictory, Turnbull, when asked to explain them, admitted that 'brother' and 'sister' mean no more than men or women of the same generation belonging to the same band. So it is clear that the notions of 'preferential marriage' or 'sister exchange' have in this context no relevance in terms of kinship.[15]

Steward's observation (1968, 321ff.) according to which the minimal groups of which hunting and gathering bands are formed are themselves made up of consanguines and affines, in no way implies, if true, that kinship dominates their social organisation. Similarly in capitalist society, even though the family remains the unit within which social reproduction takes place, and even though each individual is involved in family relationships, the dominant principle of social organisation is not kinship but the system of contract which connects individuals to each other by the exchange of commodities and money. When Washburn and Lancaster (in Lee and Devore 1968, 301), following the same line of thought as Steward, underline that family organisation has its origins in the hunting way of life and that, since the problems in agriculture remain the same, the family therefore continues, they make the same mistake and in fact compound it. It is also the error of Moscovici (1972).

Thus two very distinct kinds of relations are manifestly being confused: adhesion and kinship. In the band an individual's position depends on voluntary, unstable and reversible relationships in which he is involved for the limited period during which he actively participates fully in common activities. Kinship relations, on the other hand, are imposed by birth; they are lifelong, statutory and intangible, and it is on their basis that the individual's position in productive and reproductive relations are defined at the different stages of his life. In the former case society is constantly being reconstructed around the free movement of individuals between the different bands; in the latter, individuals are subject to established norms of social reproduction within the limits of the lineage into which they are born. In the one, social membership is an individual affair, in the other it is transmitted from one generation to the next.

The confusion which exists about these two very different kinds of social relations still dominates all kinship theory.

Needham noted with dismay that none of the notions proposed by kinship theory has any content. 'The word kinship . . . does not denote a discriminable class of phenomena or a distinct kind of theory . . . it has an immense variety of uses . . . In other words, the term 'kinship' is . . . an 'odd job' word, and we only get in trouble when we assume that it must have some specific function . . . The word has in fact no analytical value . . . There is no such thing as kinship, and it follows that there can be no such thing as kinship theory' (1971, 5). Further on Needham adds: 'Very similar considerations apply to the concept of marriage.' As a whole his book is a demonstration by the functionalist school of the failure of the functionalist (and structuralist) theory of kinship. Barth (in Goody, 1973a, 18) reaches the same kind of conclusions: 'the very extensive debate on descent and filiation . . . has not produced adequate generalizations or a comparative understanding of descent system . . . Attempts to clarify and refine the anthropological concept of descent as a central analytical concept will hardly meet success since it straddles so many analytical levels and encloses so diverse feed-back effects'. Needham concludes by observing that the comparative method, as it has been used – that is by being limited to the notion of 'class' of phenomena (a notion borrowed by analogy from mathematics) – has yielded no results. Barth (*idem.*, 19) calls for the construction of 'models which capture more of the dialectical relation between concepts and norms and social reality.' Both critique and programme are in fact already contained in historical materialism, until now confidently ignored by both functionalism and structuralism alike.

By forcing band societies into the kinship models anthropologists have inverted the historical logic of semantic transformations by attributing to peoples who had not developed the notion of kinship a vocabulary borrowed from other societies who had already progressed in this direction.[16] It is more likely that terms which in the band indicate adhesion to the same group, have acquired, in lineage societies, the more *restricted* meaning of membership of a same *segment*. What, in the former case, would indicate a relationship between functional *age groups*, in the latter becomes a relationship between *kin-linked generations*. By making the lineage society their referent, anthropologists have managed to invert this by applying the more restricted notion to the wider meaning.[17] In so doing, they transformed the nature of their subject. In this instance it might be suspected that anthropology had undertaken to interpret history backwards rather than discover its real movement.

(iii) Mating and filiation

This tendency to excessive generalisation can also be found in another confusion between norms related to *mating* or to *filiation*. The former specify possible partners, the latter – through marriage and the births which follow from it – the relations of dependence which an individual has to preceding generations. In other words the quest for a wife has been confused with the quest for off-spring. Kinship as a category only applies in the latter case. It is filiation which leads to the notion of kinship between people whose relationships are defined by their lifelong, permanent and intangible ties to a shared, near or distant, real or putative father. (Part I, Ch. 2, § ii).

The Elementary Structures of Kinship is entirely devoted to the problem of the choice of a spouse, in other words, with mating.[18] Lévi-Strauss (1967) only discusses filiation (Chapter 8) in relation to the problems raised by matriliny or patriliny concerning the choice of a partner, without considering the central problem of kinship, which is *the destination of the offspring*. Under these circumstances 'kinship' seems to be universally relevant because it deals only with the universal phenomenon of *mating* to which it is thus restricted without procreation being taken into account. All societies can therefore be lumped together whatever their social organisation and their underlying drive. Certainly, kinship also regulates mating with reference to the position of individuals in a *genealogical* framework, but the opposite is not true. Norms which only order *mating*, where these exist, refer to simpler categories permitting the recognition, from one generation to the next, of possible partners, without involving the destination of the offspring. The so-called moiety systems[19] confine their criteria to these. Here moieties replace genealogies as means of identification. The notion of filiation ends as soon as the cycle of matrimonial restrictions is closed – after one or several generations according to the number of subsections in the system – but always within the single perspective of helping to identify possible spouses. The rules which govern mating, in opposition to filiation rules, are geared much more to the past and to the present than to the future: *ego*'s matrimonial relations are defined by his relations to the preceding generation, but concern with posterity, shown by true kinship societies, is ignored.

Restricting the study of kinship to the problem of mating in itself postulates that the main if not the single purpose of marriage is to allow individuals of different sexes to live together. Lévi-Strauss, in this instance oddly materialist, believes in fact that there are economic reasons *sufficient* to explain mating (1967, 46), in particular the complementarity of male and female labour. But this is not an economic cause. The sexual division of labour – is it still necessary to point this out? – is a 'cultural' not a 'natural' phenomenon. If it is possible to observe the formation of a division of labour (often variable according to culture) between men and women – or at least between those who answer to the social definitions of 'man' and 'woman' – a division which makes the woman (or the slave) a servant of men, this division is the effect of an anterior and socio-political subjugation of women and is not due to any imaginary distinct capacities. The only activities that women alone are able to undertake are those of birth and breast feeding. This natural specialisation would explain mating only in terms of reproduction, although once they have been impregnated women can operate economically and socially on their own. In fact nothing in nature explains the sexual division of labour, nor such institutions as marriage, conjugality or paternal filiation. All are imposed on women by constraint, all are therefore facts of civilisation which must be explained, not used as explanations.

Lévi-Strauss' *Elementary Structures of Kinship* generalises the rules of mating to all kinship societies. But here the generalisation works in reverse. We have already seen how terms that express membership through adhesion have been confused with terms expressing kinship through filiation, and how this transposition turns the band into a proto-lineage. Now, in contrast, the kinship rules of lineage societies are reduced to the mating norms which predominate in bands, and tend to describe lineage societies as composed of exogamous proto-moieties.

It thus seems that neither functionalism nor structuralism provides theoretical ways of differentiating between two distinct modes of social organisation, one ordered through adhesion, the other through filiation: in one, the individual's social position is a function of his actual and present participation in communal activities; in the other of his development within a productive cell and of his position in the reproductive cycle established through genealogical reference. These features, as well as the radical difference between them in terms of their mode of exploiting the land, contribute to distinguishing two basic economic and social systems whose fundamental principles are not reducible to the same categories.

Although Serge Moscovici (1972) suggests that a distinction should be made between relations of adhesion (which he calls affiliation) and kinship relations, in many other respects we do not agree. In the first place Moscovici employs this distinction to differentiate hominids and hunters, whereas for me the division is between hunter-gatherers and agriculturalists.[20] So doing, he re-introduces, like most writers, a serious confusion between these two kinds of civilisation, assigning, without caution, characteristics of one to the other. On the other hand he does establish a critical difference between gathering and hunting, whose relations of production are, according to him, radically different. Thus the relations established in gathering would be individual and would require neither special knowledge nor physical training. Hunting relations, on the other hand, would be collective, requiring training and apprenticeship. In the first case society would therefore remain individualised, in the second, organised relations and paternal kinship ties would appear. Now what we know about the reality of social relations of production (cf. in particular the contributions in Lee and Devore, 1968) does not confirm this imaginary reconstruction. Gathering often requires wandering over long distances. It takes place *in groups* so as to provide protection against wild animals. It therefore requires not only some physical training but also precise knowledge of plants, places, of dangerous animals and means of protection from them, and of raw materials useful for cutting, carrying and curing. The hunting and trapping of small animals, in contrast, usually takes place in the immediate vicinity of the camp, by hunters, men and women, young and old, who keep the produce for themselves without sharing it. It requires little skill, no physical training and does not create solidarity. Moscovici is actually referring to a very specific kind of *collective* hunting or tracking, but he does not make this clear and does not analyse the relationship these activities have to the others. In the same context, he links the introduction of kinship with that of hunting activities which would thus be the basis for 'long-term ties'. However, as we have seen, the opposite is true: hunting societies are inherently unstable. According to Moscovici, kinship would base itself on paternity, which itself would arise through the father hunter's desire to 'reproduce men' by transmitting his knowledge to his son. To think that blood should suddenly make itself felt at this moment is a remarkably naïve and 'naturalist' view. In these societies paternity is not yet individual: it is the concern of the whole group. Moreover, why choose a boy rather than a girl for this apprenticeship? Moscovici himself shows that once apprenticeship is institutionalised - as occurs in societies of a different kind - it is most often left not to the father but to distant relations or allies, which reduces the force of his argument. Also, the time of apprenticeship in the techniques of survival is relatively short, and is more often achieved through imitation; it does not tend to support long-term ties (Meillassoux, 1960). Furthermore, when the power of adults over the young is achieved through knowledge, it is based not on the transmission of practical knowledge but of *artificial, esoteric, irrational knowledge* which, having no empirical or rational foundation, *can never be rediscovered*. The invention of this kind of 'clerical' knowledge as a means of domination probably took place well after the paleolithic period.

(iv) Protected women, abducted women

Although individual mobility is the rule and contributes in all cases to social reproduction, its form and scope are different in bands and in agricultural societies. In the former, where relations of adhesion predominate, reproduction is achieved randomly by the flux of adults of both sexes, physical reproduction being the by-product of the mating which follows this movement. In the latter, mobility of one sex or the other is the object of either peaceful or violent political action, with the purpose of bringing together, for procreative reasons, pubescent adults whose offspring will from birth be located within relations of filiation. As we have seen, for functionalism as for structuralism, matrimonial mobility

22

is confined to the problem of the choice of a spouse; it can be dealt with and resolved in a formal way. For us, because this mobility acts both upon the sex- and age-composition of the active population, on its growth, on the social distribution of individuals, and finally on the functioning of power, it embodies all the means by which a society organises production and the reproduction of the relations of production – mechanisms which are not universal but subject to the historical conditions of production.

I show below (Part I, Ch. 2, § § ii and iii) how by exploiting the land as an instrument of labour, agricultural production, under given circumstances, encourages the formation of permanent and indefinitely renewed social ties, and how the circulation of goods between consecutive generations and the solidarity it subsequently creates between them, arouses concerns linked to the physical and structural reproduction of the group. When there are such concerns, related to the reproduction of organic relations that connect through time members of the productive group, women are then sought as child-bearers as much as companions. Given that mating usually requires the association of individuals whose social membership is different (Part I, Ch. 1, §i), the problem which is raised in societies concerned with long-term reproduction is that of the social membership of their offspring.

According to classical ethnography, filiation is established around two main axes, matriliny and patriliny.[21] In the former, the progeny are filiated to the community from which the genitrix originated. Filiation is established through the mediation of the sisters or daughters of the men of the community. The mother's brother (the mother's 'oldest' brother) has authority over the children of his sister or sisters. In patriliny, a woman's children are filiated to the community of her recognised husband, generally through his mediation. This is the father–son relationship with which we are familiar. Anthropology has recognised intermediate forms between matriliny and patriliny, those called bilineal for example, in which both families of husbands and wives share rights over their children or where inheritance passes through both lines.

Nevertheless, this terminology does not express a real symmetry. If, according to this classification, patriliny creates ties between the 'father' and his wife's sons, matriliny is not established between a mother and her daughters (this would be a matriarchal system), but between the mother's brother and her children. (It is only because no known societies have a mother–daughter filiation that this use of language is not ambiguous.)

If classical terminology always presupposes institutional and genealogical filiation (in other words one which upholds the structures of society through time), residential rules are given in relation to the kin with whom the couple live, without reference to progeniture. In this way distinctions are made between *patrilocality*, when the couple lives with the husband's father; *avunculocality* when they live with the husband's uncle. *matrilocality* (which is often replaced by the more accurate term *uxorilocality*) when they live with the wife's family; *virilocality* when they live in the husband's home, etc. But it seems equally important to specify the *residential rules regarding the couple's children* in relation to the communities from which the couples originate. Their residence usually decides that of the mother since she must stay with the child through the weaning period which extends the work of child-bearing. This residence can vary according to whether the marriage lasts for one child or for several. In the former case, for example, children can be taken by the genitor's community after weaning while the genitrix remains in or returns to her own. The most common mode of residence for women is that by which she remains in the community in which she gave birth and to which her offspring is affiliated.[22]

As we have noted, classical anthropological terminology concerning this problem relates exclusively to kinship-based societies in which kinship relations are institutionalised and genealogical. Their content is thus more juridical than functional. Generalising its use to all forms of social organisation is a source of confusion. In societies in which relations of filiation are not institutionalised, in other words where they remain to some extent subject to choice, the problem of the offspring's destination is usually linked to that of the mobility of nubile women: where mothers are kept, so are their children. This means that *present filiation* is decided by the mother's residence (at least until weaning), either in her community or in that of her husband. At a strictly functional level and independently from the rules of filiation or residence, there are two kinds of mobility affecting pubescent adults (rules which are also often compelling norms since they are relatively incompatible) and whose demographic, social and political implications may be critical. In the first case, women live in their original communites, to which men are invited to procreate and eventually live. Such a system could be classified as *gynecostatic:* the *reproduction of the group rests entirely on the reproductive capacities of the women born within the group*. In the second case, women, exchanged on a reciprocal basis, do not procreate within their community but in an allied community which recovers the progeny. *Reproduction depends on the political capacities of the communities to negotiate an adequate number of women at all times.* These two kinds of circulation are not equally efficient since they play on the different reproductive functions of the two sexes: man's ability to inseminate is practically unlimited, but any man can do, while woman's procreative potential is only equal to the length of her fertile period divided by the length of the periods of gestation and breast-feeding – frequently extended by cultural restrictions. During this gestation period, the symbiosis between the mother and her child creates an entity which is strictly *sui generis.* In other words, in terms of procreative capacities, men are expendable; each pregnant woman is unique in her kind.

If the woman's offspring are the stake, it is evident that whenever one type of mobility is operative it tends to exclude the other, since the simultaneous mobility of both sexes allows no organised distribution of women and therefore of the benefit of their procreative capacities. Either all women are kept, or they are all exchanged for others. Mobility, according to the sex, has practical and logical implications on residence and filiation, as observed in all so-called 'harmonic' societies, that is, in the great majority of cases. The most frequent relation is between gynecostatism, matrilocality and matriliny on the one hand and between gyneco-mobility, patrilocality and patriliny on the other. The social effects of these two solutions are important since, as we shall discuss below, gynecostatism offers less opportunity to correct such accidents as morbidity, sterility, premature deaths, etc. which threaten the reproduction of small demographic units.

The criterion of mobility introduces into our analysis the possibility of connecting the mode of filiation to general conditions of production in agricultural societies.

Residential and descent rules proposed by classical ethnography refer to the normative or juridical sphere. They are not linked to any apparent necessity, and can only suggest that 'society' makes an arbitrary 'choice' in favour of one or another body of rules. However, in fact we see that matrimonial mobility, which has direct effects on residence and filiation, is roughly associated with distinct agricultural practices.

The German anthropological school has for a long time recognised the apparent correlation between the agriculture of plantage-bouturage[23] and so-called matrilineal forms of social organisation. Gynecostatism and filiation through daughters or sisters is most common in areas where this kind of agriculture predominates (the forest regions of Africa and the Amazonian jungle for example), while gynecomobile and patrilineal societies are found more often in cereal-producing zones. A brief consideration of the conditions of production which dominate in planting agriculture reveals elements which make the correlation fairly logical and which permit us, through two different modes of matrimonial circulation, to see the correlation of domestic relations of production and reproduction.

It should be stressed that this correlation only denotes a tendency and not an absolute determination, for the relations of production are essentially the same whatever sort of agriculture is practised. They always serve to support the institutional relations of reproduction. As we shall see, what determines a society's mode of patrilineal filiation is its *political* capacity to organise the peaceful exchange of women between its component cells. This political capacity is able to develop more easily in the context of cereal agriculture, for reasons which will be explained later, than in planting agriculture. Patrilineal forms are, however, not impossible in these latter societies for they depend partly on the total social space occupied by planting agriculture in relation to other activities and on the political capacity to alleviate the specific contradictions which this kind of agriculture seems to entail. On the other hand matriliny is not incompatible with cereal agriculture for the same reason.

Planting agriculture is practised either by replanting part of a tuber (yam, manioc, taro, etc.) or a shoot (bananas, for example). This vegetative reproduction does not therefore need seed. The productivity of, and returns on this kind of agriculture are relatively high (Rivière, 1974). However, produce cannot be stored for long (less than a year), and being heavy and bulky is usually kept in the fields, where it lasts longer. Above all, before it is edible it has to go through a low-productivity process which is long, tedious and tiring, preparation absorbing a good deal of the total social energy.

The fact that the produce cannot be preserved for long makes this kind of agriculture vulnerable to climatic hazards, for it is not possible to accumulate reserves for several years. Non-agricultural activities like hunting, fishing and gathering therefore remain necessary to compensate for the ever-present danger of deficit. Furthermore, since according to Sauer (1969, 26–7) and Rivière (1974) planting-produce does not provide a balanced diet, it must

26

necessarily be supplemented by protein from hunting and gathering. The association between planting agriculture and extraction economies is therefore widespread but variable. Their relative importance is to be judged not so much in terms of time spent, or amounts produced, as by the influence which either activity has on the social structure.

In all cases agricultural practice involves the constitution of productive cells adapted to a process of delayed production requiring investment of energy in the land (here as an instrument of labour); it requires continuity, concatenation of successive tasks over several months, and a waiting period while the produce ripens. The slow rhythm of production keeps the producers together throughout the agricultural cycle and beyond it.[24] On the other hand agriculture does not require large number of people and can be undertaken by teams of a few individuals. With this kind of repetitive and cyclical activity, comprehensiveness and cohesion of the constitutive cells develop along with an organisation for reproduction and production, so that, in contrast to the band, the household (genitors, spouses plus the latter's immediate progeny) within which relations are both associated with agricultural activity as well as with reproduction, acquires social and functional existence. It represents the constitutive cell of a larger gathering. Relations between households differ according to whether hunting or agriculture is dominant at the level of the larger association: households tend to bond through relations of adhesion when hunting is the structuring factor, and by matrimonial relations when agriculture dominates.

In the former situation (hunting is the structuring factor between households), which has been called by some writers proto-agriculture, households – associated with agricultural activities – remain small. They gather, in varying numbers, through the mediation of the hunters from each household who collaborate over hunting, fishing or gathering activities and in case of war. This kind of association is unstable for the same reasons as among individual members of a band, but here the instability is between households and not between individuals. The political organisation of such proto-agricultural societies dominated by hunting activities does not find the bases of a strong cohesiveness either in agriculture or in collective activities. None of the productive activities seems capable of materially supporting a continuous and coercive authority likely to extend beyond or to influence the household. (Part I, Ch. 2, §iii) Since a civil, conciliating power does not

27

develop within this form of social organisation, based on groups in precarious association which can only support temporary alliances, matrimonial problems tend to be regulated through procedures which involve minimum contestation. The solution which is simplest and most compatible with this situation is to allow each household to retain the progeny of its own women. Reproduction is thus based upon the immediate reproductive capacities of each cell. Gynecostatism would thus represent a peaceful solution to matrimonial circulation within such a gathering when political power is too weak to withstand the tensions and conflicts that reciprocal exchange of women would entail.

The relations of adhesion between households in a collectivity may therefore be supplemented, within the limits set by the number of partners available, by peaceful marriage relations. Women, who ensure the continuity of agricultural tasks and of the productive cells, are the poles towards which men gravitate. Male mobility is thus dominant within the collectivity of households. However, this mode of male circulation, the corollary of which is the immobilisation of women in their original household, limits the capacity for social reproduction to the fertility of present pubescent women born into each unit. If the number of such women, or their fertility, falls below a given level, the household's ability to reproduce is threatened.

If differential fertility results in a deficit of female births (a frequent occurence in small units which do not obey the statistical laws) the household will be forced to import women in order to perpetuate itself. But the female mobility necessary to correct this deficit inevitably puts into question the principles of filiation based on the immobilisation of women in their groups of origin. The deficit can only be corrected by introducing women taken from outside the household, in other words by contravening the rules of matriliny which govern the collectivity; if the latter is surrounded by others equally concerned to keep their women, this inevitably leads to violence. Hence, a permanent tendency to abduction and warfare.

When hunting plays a decisive role in social organisation, hunting techniques, generally the best mastered, tend to be used to correct the haphazard allocation of women – with the difference that since women are not animal game but human beings incorporated into complex social structures which ensure their protection, other tactics have to be employed to capture them. The hunter, attacking not animals but other human beings, becomes a warrior. In this situation woman is a prey. But to capture her she has to be put in a situation of tactical inferiority. Abduction encapsulates all the elements of the enterprise of the inferiorisation of women and anticipates all the others. Groups of armed men organised and in league, acting according to pre-established plan, attempt to capture a woman by surprise, preferably one who is isolated, unarmed, unprepared and unwarned. Whatever her physical strength or intelligence, she is from the beginning doomed to defeat. Her safety lies not in resisting but in immediate *submission* to her captors. Her protection does not depend on herself but on the other members of her group, moreover on the men rather than the women. This dependence on men as fighters does not arise because they are naturally more fitted but because they are relatively useless as reproducers. Men are more expendable and less coveted. Thus women are thrown into a situation of dependence as much in relation to men of their own group who protect them as to men of other groups who abduct them in order to protect them in their turn. Made inferior because of their *social* vulnerability,[25] women are put to work under male protection and are given the least rewarding, the most tedious and, above all, the least gratifying tasks such as agriculture and cooking. From the outset excluded from war or hunting activities on which the society's values are built,[26] women are devalued to such an extent that female infanticide is sometimes practised more frequently than male, in spite of their essential gift of child-bearing.

In addition to its functions of regulating and sanctioning the circulation of women, war also becomes the means by which adult men affirm their superiority over all the other social categories: women, the aged, and the young. As a result war occurs more frequently than is strictly necessary to carry out its corrective functions. When war is semi-permanent, it supports a class of 'men'; the warriors. It eulogises strength and courage, it favours the emergence of a forceful, brutal, often cruel but personalised, arbitrary and obtuse authority. Such an authority is unstable however, since it is constantly challenged by rival men, an authority rarely transmitted in an orderly way from the man who possesses it to someone else since it is based on personal exploits which the incumbent must constantly be able to repeat, and not on any institutionalised mechanism. In the absence of an institutionalised political power a personal power emerges, an authority sought after, and coveted, an object of rivalry.[27] Despite Jaulin's claims (1974), this authority depends upon war, that is on violence, force, strategems, feats, and frequently on murder, which is characteristic of all warlike or military rule. Helen Valero's descriptions of her life among the Yanoáama of the Amazon (Biocca, 1968) are more informative in this respect than a good deal of the anthropological material available. Because it arises from war, that power is simultaneously arbitrary, brutal, and unstable.

Although households (but not individuals) can freely leave the collective house (Pinton, in Jaulin, 1973: 149), their gatherings are more cohesive than the bands because of the enlargement and the stability of the masculine core (reinforced by war), the upbringing and education of children in the group, and the need for defence and protection. Relations of filiation, albeit confused, endure for more than one generation. The nature of the power held by the dominant social category, the warriors, is in contradiction with the peaceable regulation of the circulation of women, on the one hand, because the preeminence acquired by adult males depends on perpetuating violence and war, and on the other hand because the hostility between collectivities prevents the kind of alliances necessary to regulate the circulation of women. The system tends to perpetuate itself.

Sociologically, this type of society is heterogeneous, meaning that social relations within it do not derive from uniform principles of organisation. We have seen that relations of adhesion predominate between households which are part of the same collectivity, sometimes supported (but not organically) by marriage relations. Within households, two kinds of relations of filiation and conjugality develop, depending on whether the spouses come from the collectivity of allied households or whether the wives come from outside as a result of war and abduction. In the former situation, the wife's offspring stay in her household of origin (marriage is uxorilocal, tending to matriliny); in the latter the offspring remain in the husband's household (marriage is virilocal tending to patriliny). It can be seen that the formal categories proposed by anthropology hardly fit such social systems *as a whole*.

When agriculture is or becomes more important to the survival of the social group than hunting, and when men participate more in it, if war becomes too frequent it poses a threat to the conditions of production because of the death and absence it causes. The necessity to mantain the labour-force entails a regulation of marriage relations if possible non-violent, or allowing only controlled violence. In order to manage a sufficient number of women

and eventually exchange them on a reciprocal basis, *civil power,*
based on alliance and conciliation, must take the place of power
based on war.[28]

Although there may be for this reason, a tendency for kinship
to extend beyond the household and for affinity to replace the
relations of adhesion which link them,[29] this development
towards the constitution of a civil lineage power is hampered in
planting societies. Difficulty in storing produce as well as the
absence of seed, make the manipulation and control of subsistence foods and the organisation of a managerial power less
likely. Furthermore, because it is not an obstacle to segmentation, planting agriculture does not favour extended kinship groups.
The storage of subsistence foods in the fields allows parties of
individuals separated from the mother-group to supply themselves
with stolen plants, cuttings and food during the dead season and
to initiate a cycle of agricultural production of their own. Just as
the man separated from the community is obliged to snatch away
from the fields the ingredients necessary for the reproduction of
plants and for his own immediate reproduction, he also has to
steal the means for his social reproduction – a woman. Thus
abduction[30] tends to perpetuate itself in these societies, along
with a state of hostility between communities which is un-
favourable to the peaceful circulation of women, and which
re-assigns the reproduction of each unit to the reproductive
potential of its daughters.

The effects of immobilising women become increasingly acute
as procedures of conciliation and alliance which govern uxorilocality and matriliny are practised at the expense of war (a
demographic compensation but which tends towards patriliny).
Demographic accidents become more difficult to correct as
society, in the observance of matrilineal rules becomes more
organised, policed, and ordered. Mobility of women becomes more
and more urgent as relations between communities become more
peaceful. Gynecostatic systems, which seek to keep women and
their children in their original households, are inflexible, unstable
and turbulent, because they are unable to adjust within their own
norms. They produce complex and multiform social practices
designed to contain this permanent contradiction which leads them
either to disappear peacefully or to the risks of violent reproduction. Hence a latent tendency either to maintain war and abduction, or eventually, to introduce patriliny; and, if conditions for an
alliance between the different groups are present, to the adoption

31

of a peaceful mode of <u>circulation of women</u>. Such intricate processes make the study of 'matrilineal' agricultural societies so difficult that I leave to those more qualified than myself the task of formulating a general theory for such societies.[31]

2. Domestic reproduction

Environmental conditions, associated with the level of acquired knowledge, the nature of the product and the objective conditions of its production, contribute to link decisive relations of production with variable capacity for control of the mode of social reproduction. This control over social reproduction depends in turn on the built-in political capacities of the society, in other words on the strengthening of civil power which, in the last analysis, is based on the relations of production it seeks to maintain.

In the advanced form of the domestic community which we will now consider, the progeny of the wife is granted to the husband's community. Peaceful circulation of women replaces both peaceful circulation of men and violent circulation of women. Alliance decisively supplants violence as a means of regulating matrimonial relations, through generalising the procedures of conciliation that authorise the consolidation of civil authority, which is itself linked to the new conditions of production.

This scheme offers one considerable advantage over gyneco-statism on account of the fact that the reproductive capacities of the sexes are unequal. Thanks to the mobility of pubescent women, a group's reproductive capacity does not depend on the number of pubescent women of the group, but on the political capacity of its leaders to negotiate them into the group. The number of pubescent males is, from the point of view of reproduction, unimportant (as long as it is not zero), since one man can make a practically unlimited number of women pregnant. We will see later on how this scheme, with patrilineal effects, is the most likely to ensure a better distribution of women *in time and in space* and to best exploit their reproductive potential, even though, in the long run, each community only disposes of as many women as it produces. It is furthermore a stable system, able to readjust and correct itself, while remaining within its own norms.

33

We must now examine the functioning and perpetuation of such an historical advance.

(i) The level of the productive forces

In order to define the domestic community as we consider it, we must specify the historical period to which it relates, not only as one dated moment in a possible evolution, but as characterised by a given development of the productive forces.

The domestic community is the basic cell in a mode of production which is formed by a collection of such communities organised for the economic and social production and the reproduction of the, specifically domestic, relations of production (Marx 1866, 257). The level of the productive forces to which development of the domestic community corresponds can be given as dominated by the following characteristics:

(1) Knowledge of agricultural and craft techniques to allow the practice of an *agriculture in which productivity is high enough to satisfy the basic nutritional needs required to maintain and reproduce its members as well as to repeat the agricultural cycle.* All other subsistence activities, even those indispensable to a balanced diet, are complementary. They are never undertaken at the expense of agricultural activities.

Repetition of the agricultural cycle (in an economy based essentially upon this activity) entails conservation of a volume of agricultural produce sufficient to cover two kinds of period: one, the annual shortfall; the other (achieved by replenishing stocks), a period long enough to face climatic variations and other accidents (drought, locusts, or other catastrophes) likely to interrupt production for a year or more. The ability to keep enough in reserve to cover a period roughly equal to the greatest length of probable catastrophe indicates the minimum productivity that agriculture must reach. In this respect, it is clear that cereals, storeable for a period much longer than the agricultural cycle, lend themselves to the development of the domestic community far more than do root crops or fruit. The domestic mode of production reaches its fullest development in cereal agriculture.

Other characteristics are:

(2) Use of *land as an instrument of labour*, whose delayed production is the end result of an investment of energy.

(3) Use of *human strength* as the major source of energy in agriculture and craft work.[1]

(4) Use of *individual means of agricultural production*, which only require individual investment of labour to be made.

34

Domestic reproduction

Activities other than agriculture may be the objects of collective investment, at the level of several domestic communities, for example, grouped into villages. This is so for certain hunting or fishing activities, when the construction of traps involves the work of several producers. These collective investments only have a secondary effect on the social system because the activities to which they relate are themselves subordinated to social relations determined by the dominant activity, agriculture. Such forms of cooperation cannot be analysed in isolation, as so many 'modes of production' (Terray, 1969), but as *labour processes*.

In the agricultural domestic community, agriculture is dominant, not only because it receives most of the producers' energy inputs, but above all because it determines the general social organisation to which other economic, social and political activities are subordinate. In this way, relations established through certain other activities, such as war or hunting, predominate only for so long as they last and only within their own field of action. They dissolve when they are completed; on their return to the village, those who led the war or the hunt are once more subject to the relations of filiation and precedence which dominate domestic society.

The above characteristics define a model which is very different (a) from economies where animal traction or the application of collective or social means of production[2] are involved; (b) from peasant communities subject to exploitation and obliged to hand over a portion of their product to an exploiting class; and (c) from those organised to sell their agricultural produce on the market. In other words, this model is to be located in a historical context where communities formed in the conditions outlined *have relations only with similar communities*; their possible relations with other social formations being but superficial and unlikely to transform them qualitatively.

Relations between similar communities define a specific form of free access to the land, water and raw materials needed by each community to carry out its various activities. Access to these natural means of production should not be confused here with any form of 'property' or ownership of the land. For an individual, access to land as a means of agricultural survival is necessarily associated with access to subsistence during the whole period of crop preparation and to seeds, without which 'property' in land would have no content. *Access to land is thus subject to the existence or creation of previous social relations – such as filiation or affinity[3] – through which these materials are obtained.* A man excluded from the community is not forbidden access to land so

35

much as access to means of cultivating it. Land, being indissociable from the relations of production and reproduction which allow its exploitation, cannot in itself be the object of an 'appropriation', through which it would be separated from the social context which gives it economic existence and use-value. In their own representations, cultivators do not dissociate land from the ancestors, in other words, from the past and present social ties that underlie its productiveness. The analysis of the relations of production confirms that there cannot be individual 'ownership' of land, a point which is now generally recognised. Nevertheless, since *membership of a collectivity is the condition for access to land*, the collectivity is generally considered to have 'common ownership' of the land. In reality, a conscious notion of 'appropriation', that is, of an exclusive relationship to a piece of land, does not arise from the process of exploring and occupying land, nor from the labour invested by past and present members of the group. It only arises if the use of the land is threatened by another collectivity. But in fact, we find that territorial conquest plays virtually no part in relations between *domestic societies*, even when population density is high. On the whole, domestic societies do not make it difficult for outsiders, whether individuals or families, to join them once the social relations which will link them to the collectivity have been defined. 'Conquests' often prove to be the effect of long-term infiltration by immigrants incorporated in this way, either through the sheer weight of numbers or because specific activities have enabled them at a given moment to dominate their hosts. Even if we accept that land may be coveted and conquered by military societies, its protection does not *ipso facto* involve the construction of such a sophisticated law as to create the concept of *property* independently of definite historical conditions. *Property*, which in its full meaning contains the rights of *usus*, *fructus*, and *abusus*, is linked to the market economy which allows *products to be alienated and transformed into commodities*, i.e. which draws it into contractual relations of production different in kind from those prevailing in the domestic community. The term 'property' is thus inappropriate even when it is said to be 'common', which in this respect does not alter its meaning. The most relevant category, to be substituted for 'property' is that of *patrimony*, that is to say a good which belongs indivisibly to members of a community and is transferred by inheritance, gift or donation between its members, in other words, *without counter-claim.*[4] The patrimonial relation to land arises from domestic relations of production, that property, far from reinforcing, contributes to undermine.

Associated with the historical conditions outlined above is *self-sustenance*, that is the ability of the community to produce the subsistence goods it needs to maintain and perpetuate itself, from resources which are within its reach and obtained through direct exploitation. Self-sustenance is not an exclusive characteristic of the domestic community – it is also found in the band, but under different social conditions of production. In the domestic community self-sustenance is directly tied to a specific mode of distributing produce that works against social division of labour[5] and which eliminates *equivalent* exchange in favour of identical *exchange* (see below Part I, Ch. 4, § iii).

Although it is not a determining factor, self-sustenance can be considered to be a *critical* feature, for its disappearance eventually causes the breakdown of the domestic relations of production.[6]

Self-sustenance should not, however, be confused with the notion of autarchy. It does not imply that there are no relations outside the community, nor trade as long as its effects are neutralised and do not reach the critical point beyond which it causes irreversible changes in the relations of production. I have shown elsewhere (1964, 1968, 1971) how, for example, commodities and currency are neutralised by being transformed into 'treasure' or patrimonial goods within the domestic or manorial economy, and how exchanges are centred around the elder or the sovereign and do not pervade domestic or affinal relations.[7] Furthermore, self-sustenance is not incompatible with the existence of *specialists*, associated with the practice of techniques such as iron working. Having a *speciality* does not, in this context, imply *specialisation*, that is the exclusive practice by an autonomous productive unit, of a non food-producing activity that implies continuous transfer of subsistence goods to the specialised unit. Practising a *speciality* does not necessarily imply relinquishing agricultural work. When this does happen, and often it only partially occurs, the subsistence of the specialised party is ensured through the extension of the redistributive mechanisms. In this case the specialist group acts as *client* to one or more agricultural communities which provide it with subsistence in return for which it satisfies its patrons' needs for the products in which it specialises. In this way the immediate effects of the social division of labour are forestalled, and the basic structures of the domestic community are preserved even though these transfers may eventually influence the social conditions of subsistence production (Meillassoux, 1973). The model I am proposing applies to such situations insofar as these protective institutions still operate.

The level of the productive forces, therefore, is not defined solely by the practice of a particular technology, but by the socially accepted effects of its use. It is for this reason that use of a new technology does not revolutionise society immediately, as the latter may accommodate to it, sometimes for a long time, offering institutional resistance to the social effects of specialised production, and to the restricted exchange to which it gives rise.[8] Changes more often occur at the level of consolidated political formations rather than at the level of communities.

The social organisation of the domestic agricultural community is built (simultaneously and indissolubly) both upon *the relations of production*, in so far as these emerge from the economic constraints imposed by agricultural activity - undertaken under conditions defined by the level of productive forces – and upon the *relations of reproduction* necessary to perpetuate the productive cell. Although the need to explain this process entails separating these two kinds of relations, in fact they interact continuously due to the simultaneity of the requirements of production and reproduction on the one hand, and to the necessity to fulfil them within their area of interaction. It is evident that reproduction is the dominant preoccupation of these societies. All their institutions are organised to this purpose. The emphasis placed on marriage, matrimonial and paramatrimonial institutions, filiation, fertility cults, representations associated with maternity; the change in a woman's position according to her place in the fertility cycle; anxieties regarding adultery and illegitimacy, and sexual prohibitions – all indicate that reproduction is a central concern. Kinship relations resulting from marriage (as an institution) even more than from birth (which is only an event regulated by rules fixed at marriage) are clearly relationships which form around the reproduction of individuals.[9]

In the domestic society, the reproduction of individuals and the places they occupy from birth throughout their lives are the object of careful social control which dominates social relations as a whole. Rather than being, as in the band, a brief act whose effects are immediate (incorporation, mating), the process of reproduction in the domestic community is achieved by means of very-long-term commitments (vows, engagement, marriage, dowry, etc.). It is within this context that the notion of filiation develops. It is filiation, and therefore succession, which are sanctioned by the most important ceremonies like funerals and, less often, baptisms and marriages, which, unlike mating, regulate not only the cohabitation of the married couple and their respective tasks, but the future position of their anticipated offspring. Still, the process of reproduction, although it appears to dominate political and social concerns and does inspire the core ideological and juridical concepts, remains subordinate to the constraints of production.[10]

(ii) The constitution of the relations of production

We saw above that the fundamental difference between the band and the agricultural community lies in the fact that the former exploit the land as a *subject of labour* and the latter as an *instrument of labour*.

Using the land as an instrument of labour means that a certain amount of human energy[11] is invested in it in the prospect of an eventual return. The accumulation of this energy, which is involved in this kind of exploitation of the land, leads in turn to *the accumulation of the product*. For both climatological and botanical reasons, production is delayed until the end of the labour process, and of the ripening of the harvest.

Agriculture, very generally, is not a continuous but a seasonal process. The agricultural cycle is divided into successive productive and non-productive periods. It begins, inevitably, with a non-productive agricultural period, during which human energy is invested in the land, preparing, clearing, seeding, maintaining, weeding, etc. This is followed by a productive period when the crop is harvested. For the cycle to begin again, what was produced in the productive season must be consumable during the non-productive period, to maintain the 'producer's' life and energy.[12]

Thus, the agricultural cycle can only be undertaken if the producer has enough stock of subsistence goods to survive through the period of preparation, and while his crops ripen. Historically, therefore, agriculture can only arise when it is linked to an economy of immediate return (fishing, hunting and gathering). These activities will keep their importance for so long as agricultural productivity is still unable to meet the nutritional needs of producers during the non-productive periods or in periods of scarcity. Modes of production based on the exploitation of land or water as subjects of labour thus fulfil the functions of primitive accumulation for agriculture.

Socially, the same process is as it were repeated in agricultural societies when a group decides to separate by segmentation from the mother-group. The segment will have to rely on activities with immediate returns, like hunting, to last through the first non-productive period. But as agriculture becomes more sophisticated, segmentation becomes increasingly difficult. We have seen that planting agriculture imposes fewer material constraints on segmentation, for it is easy throughout the nonproductive period to steal plants or cuttings from the fields as well as some food. Under cereal agriculture, on the other hand, the crops are stored, centralised and kept in the village. It is necessary furthermore to conserve relatively large quantities of *seed*[13] from one season to another. Therefore. segmentation is subordinated to the maintenance or creation of social bonds with an agricultural cell formed around the granary of a common ancestor, a maternal kinsman, an affine or a friend, from which to obtain seeds. As far as food is concerned, the group which does segment is also compelled to resort to comparatively primitive forms of production – hunting, fishing, gathering, or planting. Such obstacles, encountered in segmentation, are probably one cause of the stability and spread of domestic communities.

When agriculture becomes the dominant activity, storing and *managing* the agricultural produce gradually replace resort to the extraction economy to provide for periods of scarcity or prime again the agricultural cycle. Storing allows the produce to be shared and distributed among producers over the *time* that covers the non-productive period. From then on, hunting, gathering and fishing, even if they make up for shortfall, are subordinate to agricultural social organisation.

As mentioned above, I shall now consider the case where agricultural productivity permits this management. From that point onward we can see the main features of the domestic agricultural economy: *delayed production resulting from investment of human energy in the land, accumulation, storage, and organised and managed distribution of the produce.*

Agriculture practised with the means of production we have described above does not require a large group of labourers.

40

Technically, all jobs may be done by a comparatively restricted workforce, members of which vary in strength and capacity, a group which could correspond to the nuclear family. However (leaving aside work that has to be completed within a limited time period, but which can be done with the participation of allied groups), a different kind of concern is operative here. It relates to the random nature of the productive capacity of cells counting few members and to which the statistical law of large numbers does not apply. The concern is to have enough workers to ensure that illness or accidents do not prevent the productive unit from functioning. Illness, which is a constant source of worry in such societies, has immediate economic repercussions on production. It has to be averted by all means, magical, medical and statistical (Retel-Laurentin, 1974).

The number of active workers which will enable the production unit to maintain itself in face of the uncertainties of death and illness will therefore tend to be greater than the number necessary from a purely technical point of view. The constitution and perpetuation of the agricultural team and its workforce is subordinate to its ability to recruit, which depend in turn on its belonging to an organic unit of *reproduction*, as we shall see below.

Because production is delayed, agricultural co-operation between members of the productive cell is long-lasting if not permanent. Agricultural activity creates links between individuals on two accounts: firstly, there are links between those who have worked together from the moment preparatory work was undertaken through to the time of harvest – it is in the interests of these individuals to remain together so as to benefit from their common labour; secondly, and this is even more important, it creates links between the successive workers who, at each season, depend for their survival through the non-productive period and for the preparation of the next cycle on the subsistence food produced during the previous productive period. Seen from this perspective, the agricultural cycle generates a mode of distribution by which an endlessly repeated series of *advances and returns* of the product between the productive groups which operate from one season to the next. It is as if the workers of one season would advance subsistence food and seed to those who will work the following season whose product they would consume and store in the next season. Of course from one season to the next, the majority of workers remain the same, but over time the work-team changes: the older workers disappear while young ones take their place.

41

This progressive transformation of the composition of the group leads in the end to a *change of generation*.

The changing composition of the producing team is reflected in the evaluating hierarchy which dominates agricultural communities, and which divides those 'who come first' from those 'who come after'. This hierarchy relies on positions of *anteriority*. The 'first ones', the elders, are those to whom the seed and subsistence goods are owed; the oldest among them in the productive cycle owes nothing to any living person, only to the ancestors, while he concentrates on himself all that junior people owe to the community, which he therefore comes to embody.

Because of his position at the apex of the community, the elder is logically appointed to store and centralise its produce. He is also in a good position to manage it. So the need for management to ensure reproduction of the productive cycle creates a function, while the structure of the productive cell points at the person to fill it. The cycle of *advances and returns* described above operates between the elder and his junior partners. Formally, it is revealed in the cycle of *prestation and redistribution* which is the dominant mode of circulation in communities of this kind.

Here, therefore, we have the essence of the relations of production: *they create lifelong organic relations between members of the community; they support a hierarchical structure based on anteriority (or 'age'); they constitute functional coherent economic and social cells which are organically linked through time; they define membership, as well as a structure and a power of management which fall to the eldest in the productive cycle.*

(iii) The constitution of the relations of reproduction

Beyond the reproduction of the productive cycle, cultivators must solve the problem of reproducing the productive cell and its relations of production. The continuation of the distributive cycle ensuring that each member of the community may benefit in the future from past and present work, is subordinate to the ability to reproduce the relations of production and to recreate the social organisation according to a repetitive scheme and in the same structural form.

One of the requirements related to this reproduction is to maintain a satisfactory balance in the community between the number of productive and non-productive members: there must be enough people of appropriate age of each sex to reproduce the productive unit, in numbers and in structure. We already know that there is no necessary correspondence between the numbers needed for agricultural production and for genetic increase. We have also seen that technically and theoretically the minimum size of the productive cell could be reduced to the size of the nuclear family and that it is the necessity to face the hazards of illness and premature death which tends to enlarge it. A unit constituted solely for production functions is too small to guarantee its own continuous and regular reproduction. Access to other communities which together form a body large enough to ensure this genetic and social reproduction is therefore indispensable.

The elder who, by virtue of his position in the circulation of subsistence goods, is responsible for the management of the community, also controls the group's reproduction. This kind of managerial, civil and gerontocratic power encourages peaceful alliances and regulation of the matrimonial relations between similar communities, through the organised mobility of pubescent women. This mobility makes it possible, whatever the number of pubescent men and women born into each community, to ensure an optimal reproduction rate, by means of a better distribution of the genetic capacity of the women.

Given our hypothesis that the mobility of women is preferred to that of men, reproduction is achieved by incorporating the wife's offspring in the husband's group, in other words by institutionalising *male filiation*, or, anthropologically speaking, by patriliny. It is the procreative powers of a woman that are the subject of negotiation when she is taken into another group for a period generally held *a priori* to last as long as her fertility. An agreement is reached which decides the devolution of the woman's offspring since, due to the circumstances cited above, a woman does not procreate for her community of origin (the identity of the family which will benefit from her procreation must be made public while the claims of the other community are restricted) and also because, since the woman does not procreate for her own benefit, jurally constituted patrilineal filiation must replace self-evident maternal filiation.[14]

The agreement which regulates the conditions under which the producer is produced and devolved is *marriage*; as an institution, marriage defines the wife's position in the community she joins and the relationships she will maintain with its members and which her children will have with their father's community and her own: in other words, rules of filiation.[15]

43

It is obvious that *nothing can replace a pubescent fertile woman in her reproductive functions except another pubescent fertile woman*. Whoever gives up a young woman expects another in return. But for the reasons which make this transaction necessary, as outlined above (in particular the small size of the productive cell), immediate reciprocity accompanies the exchange of women only in exceptional cases. As a result of the exchange of women is usually a delayed affair. Among some populations it remains based on bilateral agreements which allow for delayed reciprocity; the group that has given a woman waits for a woman in return from the group which acquired her. But such agreements tend to extend over a population large enough to count marriage partners in proper numbers to ensure continuous reproduction. In the process bilateral agreements develop into multilateral ones.[16]

Although in the long term, as a result of multilateral exchange, no community possesses more women than it produces, it is not, as in a matrilineal system, subject to demographic hazards, because exchanges can extend over time. Women acquired now either replace women given away previously or are a claim on women to be returned in the future. Multilateral exchange therefore allows reproduction to be spread over time and managed more flexibly. The betrothal of very young girls, engagement and arranged marriages, all reveal this concern for long-term adjustment.

Thus *matrimonial areas* are formed by allied communities usually turned towards themselves, depending on the intricate changing network of marriage agreements arranged by community elders.[17] However complex such a network is, only those individuals who are in a position to return a woman in the foreseeable future can in principle take part in these transactions.[18] To maintain their power to negotiate, elders must ensure that the girls of their community are available for exchange and hence must maintain control over the latter's fate.

If the social cell was to be strictly limited to the size of a productive unit it would be unnecessary to impose a prohibition on endogamy. Beyond the fact that the opportunity of mating between brothers and sisters within such small units is always less than with outsiders of more suitable ages, such a prohibition would be unnecessary to maintain the elders' authority if this relied only on the management of subsistence goods. When the cell, however, in order to reproduce itself, must open itself to the outside world in order to secure wives, the elder's power tends to shift

44

from control over subsistence to control over women – from the management of material goods to political control over people. As I have already noted elsewhere (in Seddon, 1978, 144), political authority gained through the control of women can be extended to a larger community than can an authority gained through the material management of subsistence. As the group grows, food management becomes burdensome while matrimonial politics is demonstrably more efficient. The community can expand and integrate several productive cells by decentralising control over subsistence goods (i.e. over hearths and granaries).[19] Segmentation can now take place at the economic level of production and distribution by the formation of autonomous productive cells, while cohesion is maintained and reinforced at the matrimonial level which defines a larger exogamous political cell (the extended family, the lineage, the clan). When this happens the elder's authority depends less on material than matrimonial management and on his ability to deal with similarly constituted communities. Since marriage and social reproduction are the main reason for these external relations, marriage, in order to maintain the elder's authority, must be prohibited within the group so that nubile girls remain available as subjects of these transactions. Paradoxically, this restriction on marriage becomes increasingly necessary and rigorous in that the group, by expanding, could grow through endogamouse intermarriage. When reproduction becomes statistically possible through the mating of members of the community, the power of the elders, rebuilt on matrimonial management, is threatened by the very effects of this management which makes expansion of the community possible. *Thus political authority depends on a circumstance which it tends to abolish when it reinforces itself.* The authority must, to be preserved, devise and develop a coercive and authoritarian ideology. Religion, magic ritual, and a terrorism based on superstition is inflicted upon dependants, young people and above all on pubescent women; sexual prohibitions become absolute and punishment for transgression increase (Isichei, 1973). Endogamy becomes incest, and sexual prohibition a taboo.

Preferential marriages[20] between members of the same social unit do reveal, however, a tendency towards self-reproduction which could permit the community to acquire the same autonomy in reproduction that it has in production. In fact, for the political reasons given above, endogamy is never an absolute rule even in the largest domestic communities. It is most prevalent in aristocratic lineages, where it is involved in class relations which subject the dynasty to different reproductive norms; and also in patrimonial societies among families anxious to preserve their wealth.[21]

If we suppose at this point of the argument that pubescent women do circulate and are distributed evenly among the pubescent male members of the community, a balanced reproduction of the population is still not guaranteed. Differential fertility (by which some lineages will grow faster than others, while some will disappear), uneven sex-ratio, premature deaths, illness and casualties will all be causes of imbalance between the productive and the unproductive members. Genetic reproduction is unable by itself to guarantee the reproduction and stable growth of a functional agricultural community. If indeed genetics is enough to ensure the natural reproduction of a population on a large scale, as in our modern society, under optimal statistical conditions, it does not guarantee the reproduction of the demographic structures of small scale functional units. As I have observed and described in writing about Guro communities (1964), natural reproduction must continually be corrected by redistributing individuals among constituted productive units and by co-opting members born outside the community. Many methods are used to correct the ever precarious equilibrium: the children of one lineage are adopted by another, as are prisoners of war, clients, and debtors; sometimes wives are received as gifts or women are abducted; weak families combine together, etc.[22]

Expanding the domestic community, or regrouping several constituted cells organised for production into a larger collectivity constituted around the *political* functions of reproduction, facilitate this redistribution of producers and dependants within the latter. As we shall see, this redistribution is one condition for the organic functioning of the expanded community and for the social production of human energy.

We have observed the logical development of the domestic organisation from its origins in the production of subsistence goods, upon which the authority of the elders is based, to the social reproduction which is organised and ordered around this authority, itself changed in the process. The domestic community's social reproduction is not a natural process, nor is it, as in earlier social systems, the result of war abduction and kidnapping. It is a political enterprise.

The relations of production and reproduction have shown themselves to underlie the juridical-ideological relations of kinship. Co-operation in agricultural work leads to *lifelong* relations between partners, as family relations are. Reproduction of the agricultural cycle involves a necessary and practically permanent *solidarity* between the producers who succeed each other in the cycle. The notions of *anteriority* and *posteriority*, which define the positions of producers in the agricultural cycle, preside over the social hierarchy between *elders* and *juniors*, protectors and protected, adopters and adopted, hosts and strangers from the moment that they are placed in these relationships. The management and redistribution of the product establishes the eldest man in the productive cycle at the apex of the productive community. In this position he acts as the provisioning 'father' of all the younger men to whom he redistributes the subsistence goods necessary to continue and re-prime the agricultural cycle. 'Father'[23] does not in fact mean *genitor* but *he who nourishes* and protects you, and who claims your produce and labour in return. In fulfilling his functions of regulating social reproduction the 'father' is also *he who marries you*. If such relations of production and reproduction between the parties are broken, this breaks the kinship ties between them.[24] Adoption, on the other hand, creates those same material and social relations between the parties involved.

The family, the cell of production, becomes the locus of the development of an ideology and ritual in which respect for age, cults of the ancestors and fertility, all in different ways celebrate the continuity of the group and strengthen its hierarchy.

If the domestic community emerges from the relationship established between the producers within a specific economic structure, once this is established it becomes the institutional framework into which future producers are received. The relations of dependence linked up and realised in production must therefore be re-created by filiation or adoption within a kinship framework. In order to achieve the reproduction of the domestic community, filiation relations have to correspond to relations of dependence and anteriority established in production. *Relations of reproduction must become relations of production.* Now, since constraints on production (given that the level of the productive forces remains constant) are intangible, it can only be at the level of the reproductive process that rules, adjusting reproduction to the material demands of production, may be applied. Reproduction can be manipulated by political decisions and the actions of the

authorities to achieve this adjustment.[25] If reproduction is therefore the dominant preoccupation because it is the locus of social
reconstruction, it is still subordinate to the constraints of production, which remain determinant.

The respective importance of productive and reproductive relations is revealed in different institutions. Succession through the
transfer of the doyen's prerogatives to the producers who succeed
each other in the cycle of advances and returns is widespread in
this kind of society. This kind of succession, which takes the institutional form of collateral filiation from 'brother' to 'brother' is
closely associated with the productive cycle which supports this
continuity. It clearly reveals a relation of production.[26] The determination of the relations of production is also demonstrated, as
we shall see, by the redistribution of children or by their being
allocated to the whole group (Part I, Ch. 3, §iii); both these
institutions reaffirm the dominance of man as producer over man as
reproducer.

But the place occupied by the relations of reproduction in social
organisation and management explains the importance acquired by
their juridico-ideological representation, i.e. kinship – even more
strongly in that, as we have seen, the material foundations of
authority tend to be undermined as authority increases and resorts
more and more to ideology as a means of coercion. As this goes
on, the relations of reproduction, although they remain subordinate to the relations of production, tend to dominate at the
political level and to revamp the essential 'values' of the community towards a non-equalitarian class society.

The relations of production and reproduction in fact overlap,
but are not co-extensive. The former encourage *lateral* filiation,
from elders to juniors, from 'brother' to 'brother' according to the
order of access to the productive cycle. Relations of reproduction
on the other hand, tend to establish *vertical* filiation, from one
generation to another, from 'father' to 'son'. Lateral succession
implies continuity between people of neighbouring age, the producers' physical strength being an important factor in the constitution of small communities in which agricultural labour is predominant. However, once the conditions of social inequality have
appeared, and a dominant aristocratic class emerges, reproducing
itself according to its own norms (and preoccupied with political
succession and with the conditions of reproduction of its dominance), vertical succession tends gradually to be imposed upon
collateral succession. Vertical succession, which implies a wider

48

age divide between 'father' and 'son', can only occur once p.., cal strength is less important for the continuity of the group than political acumen, something which may be retained into old age.[27]

Classical ethnology, hastier to grasp notions at the level of native representations, than to analyse the underlying bases of social organisation, thought that kinship was the key to anthropology. This illusion has been shared by proto-Marxist structuralists who, going even further, have attributed to kinship the double role of both infra- and superstructure (Godelier 1970, 1973b), the alpha and omega of all explanation regarding primitive societies; kinship in some way is seen as generating its own determination. It follows from this that the economy is *determined* by social evolution (as Garlan, one of Godelier's disciples, understands it, 1973, 126), and that historical materialism is left without scientific basis.[28] However, we have seen that the infrastructure does not give rise to kinship ties but to relations of production. The necessity to reproduce these relations of production, which are linked through the production of the producer, squeezes them up into individual ties, within an institutional framework designed to manipulate them and shape them to the requirements of the organisation and management of production.

The above analysis shows that historical materialism is also valid for 'primitive' society and that 'the production of material life conditions the general process of social, political and intellectual life' (Marx, [1859], pp. 20–1).

Still – and this is important – in contrast to capitalism, *power in this mode of production rests on control over the means of human reproduction – subsistence goods and wives* – and not over the means of material production.

This latter distinction invalidates proto-Marxist interpretations, which see non-capitalist societies merely as precursors of capitalist societies, social systems in which the relations of production can only be created through juridical ownership of the material means of production. This narrow interpretation of historical materialism can only lead to endless repetition of a few vulgar materialist schemata.

Social control through the means of human reproduction survives in all societies where sociologists have observed the predominance of 'status' over 'contract', as can be seen both in the rise and fall of slavery and in the different kinds of servitude in West Africa which are associated with it (Meillassoux, ed., 1975).

3. The alimentary structures of kinship

The foregoing is only a descriptive outline of the ways in which the domestic community functions. Production and reproduction are achieved through circulation which, as Marx has taught us, is only analytically separable from the process of production.

The circulation of the product is based on precedence in the productive cycle. It appears, at this stage in our analysis, not in its juridical-ideological form of a cycle of prestations and redistributions, but in the form of a cycle of advances and returns of the product. In this cycle there is no *equivalent exchange*, that is transfer of objects, goods or services against equivalents. Thus goods are never in fact compared (1960), and conditions under which exchange-value can arise do not occur. The product circulates from the producer to the manager and returns to the first one eventually in the form of an *identical* commodity. But behind its apparently unchanged material form the product undergoes a series of transformations through which reproduction is achieved. 'There is in every social formation a particular branch of production which determines the position and importance of all the others, and the relations obtaining in this branch accordingly determine the relations of all the other branches as well.' (Marx, [1859], p. 212).

In the domestic community the 'determined' production is that of agricultural goods whose transformation into 'human energy' ensures the continuity and reconstitution of the community.

The concept of 'human energy' which I use here is more comprehensive than that of 'labour-power'. It covers all the energy produced by the metabolic effects of foodstuffs on the human organism. In capitalist society only a fraction of this energy is used in the form of labour-power, when it is sold on the market either directly to an employer, or indirectly though being incorporated in an object sold by the producer himself. Labour-power is only that portion of human energy with exchange-value. Energy spent on leisure activities is not counted as marketable. For the worker it only has use-value, even when it is used to reconstitute labour-power. In the domestic community,

50

where all human energy has use-value, this distinction does not exist. Therefore when dealing with such a society, the argumentation must encompass the whole of the human energy that is produced and redistributed between different activities.

The production of energy and of food are two aspects of the same productive process; one is transformed into the other and *vice versa*. This process is of course universal, but though its analysis in the domestic cycle would be relatively straightforward, it has yet to be done, in order to uncover the social mechanism of the transformation by which the community perpetuates itself as a comprehensive and organic unit of production.

(i) The reproduction of human energy or the process of production: energy – subsistence – energy

Economic reproduction takes place by producing subsistence goods – the means of producing human energy – and distributing this energy in the productive cycle, i.e. between the past, present and future producers

As we shall see when we discuss the cost of reproducing labour power in the context of imperialism (cf. Part II), the calculation of labour time on an hourly basis is specifically linked to capitalist exploitation. This means of calculating in fact excludes the cost of training and of reproducing labour-power (See Part II, Ch. 2). An economy like the domestic economy, in which labour power is not a commodity, cannot be analysed in terms of hourly calculation. In order to understand the mechanisms of production and circulation that operate over several successive generations in their own logical terms, we must replace hourly calculation by calculation in terms of the life span.

Although, in this kind of economy, control over human energy is inseparable from control over the producer, energy does not remain tied to the individual: it takes material form in the product and circulates with it. It is transferred and reproduced both by the producer's maintenance of himself and by his investment in future producers. The reproduction of the producers and the reproducers appears as a demographic phenomenon, but in fact it is entirely subordinate to the economy, to the production of the volume of subsistence goods necessary for the biological growth of future producers. 'Production of the means of subsistence', Marx wrote, 'is a condition of all production in general.' (Marx 1867, III, p. 315). In particular it is the pre-condition for the production of the producers. Demographic growth is dependent on a given society's capacity to produce enough to subsist, and on the share devoted

51

to reproduction. Since subsistence is the element by which producers are both produced and reproduced, it is through its appropriation that production and its composition should be analysed.

In the domestic community, the food product can be divided up as follows: one part is devoted to reproducing the product, by forming a reserve of seed; one part is reserved for social activities (parties, ceremonies, rituals etc.);[1] and the largest portion (which alone will be examined in my analysis) is consumed by members of the community. The food that is consumed has the following functions: to reconstitue the energy of producers (the portion consumed by productive adults); to produce future producers (the portion consumed by non-productive children); and finally the portion consumed by the old, who were once producers.[2]

The above can be expressed in the following simple formula:

let it be (in years).

A: The pre-productive period of childhood
B: The productive period of adulthood
C: The post-productive period of old age

and (in quantity)

α: Annual consumption per head[3]
β: Annual production per productive individual (in B).

αA, representing the amount an individual consumes during his pre-productive years,[4] it therefore also represents that portion of the social product invested in producing a future producer.

αB is that portion consumed by the producer during his productive period, and equals the proportion of social product which is devoted to reconstituting his energy.

αC is the portion of the social product which returns to the aged producer during his post-productive period, and corresponds on average to the proportion of his own production devoted in its own time to feeding elders of the previous generation. In αC we are including the portion devoted to other infirm people (the ill, handicapped, etc.), αC does not therefore produce useful energy, unlike αA and αB.

βB is the amount of subsistence food produced by an individual during his productive period.

Within the context of our definition of the domestic community, in order for the functional productive unit to reproduce itself, the volume of subsistence goods produced by each producer must equal or surpass the amount needed to maintain the producer himself, to bring up future producers, and to service the retirement of those who are no longer producing.

The conditions for reproduction are:

Simple reproduction (the producer reproduces himself by one replacement)

$$\beta B = \alpha(A + B + C)$$

Expanded reproduction (the producer produces more than one replacement)

$$\beta B > \alpha(A + B + C)$$

(It is supposed that αA which has been invested in bringing up the producer concerned was taken on the social product of the preceding generation.)

The rate R_d of domestic reproduction (i.e. the number of dependent minors, that a producer can feed during his active life until they reach productive age) is:

$$R_d = \frac{\beta B - \alpha(B + C)}{\alpha A} = \frac{S}{\alpha A}$$

(S = gross surplus-product)

The above formula represents the gross rate of reproduction, still supposing the proportion αA which was invested in bringing up our producer was taken on the social product of the previous generation. R_d thus includes among the producer's dependants, his replacement, the child who will replace him as a producer. Net reproduction, including only the number of additional children and expressing domestic growth is:

$$R_n = \frac{\beta B - \alpha(A + B + C)}{\alpha A}$$

The formula is valid for each producer (male or female). Reproduction of a household sums up the rate of reproduction of each of its active members.

As far as the wives who enter an already functioning community are concerned, we assume that each community eventually receives as many women as it gives away, so that transfers of αA cancel out. This hypothesis is consistent with the logic of the system (cf. Part I, Ch. 3, §iv).

53

The lifelong production of a producer may be stated in terms of the distribution of produce, as follows:

$$\beta B_1 = \alpha B_{11} + x\alpha A_{10} + \frac{1}{x}\alpha C_{12}$$

where x = the number of dependants who can be fed by the labour of the same producer and will feed together their common elder and indices 0, 1, 2 – depending on whether they are in first or second position, indicate the origin and destination of produce.

0: the future, still unproductive, generation (the young)
1: the present productive generation (active adults)
2: the previous non-productive generation (the old).

During his life the producer consumes $\alpha A_{21} + \alpha B_{11} + \alpha C_{10}$.

The community constitutes itself around the transfers of αA and αC, i.e. through the circulation of subsistance between the three successive producing generations.

If we take the quantities αA and αC to be identical among themselves, by subtracting the lifelong consumption of each producer from his lifelong production, we will obtain his lifelong surplusproduct.

$$S = \left(\alpha B + \frac{1}{x}\alpha C + x\alpha A\right) - (\alpha A + \alpha B + \alpha C)$$

$$S = \alpha C\left(\frac{1}{x} - 1\right) + \alpha A(x-1)$$

At the level of the entire community, the surplus-product at a given moment is represented by the volume of available subsistence goods above the amount needed for simple reproduction of the population.

For this surplus product to permit demographic growth of the domestic community, further conditions must be fulfilled. Given the fact that agricultural production is subject to the hazards of climate which may reduce output for several consecutive years, the first condition for demographic growth is, as we have seen, to command a stock of food large enough to last for periods at least equal to the duration of the longest calamities. If this is so, the average volume of the surplus-product must reach a constant level for a period at least equal to the length of time A during which one generation of producers is raised. One good harvest is therefore not enough to expand the population. For 15–20 years, extra children born at one moment must be sure of receiving the amount of food αA they need to grow up to productive age.

Thus, if we suppose that food can be stored for long enough to provide against calamities in order that a constant demographic level is maintained, we must have:

$$\frac{A(V)}{\alpha} = P$$

while an increase of population requires that:

$$\frac{A(V + \Delta V)}{\alpha} > P$$

Where: V = the annual volume of production of the community
ΔV: the increase in V, or surplus-product
P = the size of the community's population

The stocks which communities accumulate never represent 'surpluses', since they are intended to extend over time the community's capacity to reproduce and eventually expand.

Thus, whenever the exploiting classes take away some portion of the surplus-product, it is always done at the expense of growth and when at the expense of simple reproduction, it leads to the premature death of part of the population. (Premature death caused by poverty has never been accounted as an economic loss in the calculations of liberal economics.)

(ii) Surplus-labour

Even more than a surplus-product, the domestic community is susceptible to the production of surplus labour.

The division of agricultural activities into productive and non-productive seasons brings out quite clearly agriculture's ability to supply a volume of subsistence $\Sigma\beta$, the consumption of which produces an amount of energy ΣE superior to the amount needed to reproduce $\Sigma\beta$. This can easily be estimated in terms of the labour time needed to produce a crop. In general it is shorter than a year. To this period should be added the labour-time needed for auxiliary operations, particularly those relating to manufacture of agricultural tools, and the labour time taken up in the preparation of food, manufacturing cooking equipment etc. During the slack seasons tasks necessary to maintain the producers' energy are carried out: housebuilding, making clothes and furniture, etc. These minimum operations – which are essential for production and reproduction – do not usually occupy all the producer's energy during the slack season. Though the period of shortfall can often be difficult, a residue of energy is available which may be expended on supplementary productive activites (hunting, gathering, etc.), on social and political activities (debates, competitions, wars, etc.) or on production of non-productive craft goods.

Thus, E being the amount of energy annually produced by each active producer (male or female):

a proportion E_b of E is used to produce a volume of agricultural subsistence goods needed to reconstitute the producer's strength and bring up future producers (cf. Pt. I, Ch. 3, §i); a proportion E_i is allocated as investment necessary to manufacture means of production, such as tools, cooking equipment, etc, and to maintain the producer (housing, clothes); a proportion E_d is expended on other economic activities which, like social and political activities, are not strictly necessary to produce E. The remainder is E_r.

Hence $$E = (E_b + E_i) + (E_d + E_r).[5]$$

The difference between the amount of produced energy E, and the amount of expended energy, $E_b + E_i$ to produce E equals $E_d + E_r$. The difference between amounts of produced and expended energy reflects the difference between the labour time strictly necessary to produce the energy E and the length of time this energy is used, a length which always equals at least one complete agricultural cycle, in other words, one year.[6] That is, surplus-labour is the amount of energy available over and above the amounts of energy expended on producing the subsistence goods necessary for the simple reproduction of the community.[7]

For the community, $E_d + E_r$ is represented by the *free time* which it enjoys as a result of its own efforts and the exploitation of its physical and intellectual abilities; this time, used by the community for its own ends, is indispensable to all forms of growth and progress.

To take part in the productive cycle – *in order*, in other words *to belong to the community* – and also to ensure his own survival, each producer must; (1) return to the community the proportion αA_{21} that he consumed during the age of non-productivity, so that it may be re-invested in bringing up a future producer; (2) advance to the community the portion αC_{01} which he will consume when

56

infirm; (3) produce the portion αB_{11} which he needs to maintain himself in the present as a producer.

S, if it exists, is normally spent on the expanded reproduction of the producers, in other words in expanding the community to improve its capacity to reach the objectives discussed above. The circulation of the product between generations, which is essential for the reconstitution of human energy, means that each person, producer or future producer, depends on all the other members of the community. Each producer's ability to produce surplus-energy is subordinate to his membership of the community. Each producer's energy is the social and temporal product of the community and of the relations of production and reproduction linked over three successive generations.

From a strictly economic point of view the portion of produce expended on feeding non-producers, in particular the elderly, would seem unnecessary. But to say this is to forget that the conditions of production themselves cause the aged to be placed at the apex of the relations of production and contribute to their authority, to the concentration of managerial positions in their hands, and to the development of a gerontocratic ideology. All these structures define the teleology of this mode of production: survival and multiplication of its members. From this point of view, the domestic community represents progress over the band, which cannot support the ill and the infirm or ensure the survival of the elderly when they no longer have the strength to produce.

Now in the domestic community, the survival of those who are no longer productive is only possible because during their productive years they invested energy in bringing up future producers. A lone worker who did not invest in a productive or reproductive cell would be unable, as soon as he ceased working, to survive on his own for a period longer than he could preserve the subsistence goods he could have accumulated before retiring, thus no more than a few years. Without access to a means of exchange which would permit him to save over a long period by transforming his perishable agricultural produce into lasting valuables, re-exchangeable over time – like money, for instance – investment in the future is only possible through producing and reproducing the labour energy of immediate dependants and in constituting and reconstituting the domestic productive cell.

(iii) The circulation of offspring

One condition for the structural reproduction of the community is that future producers should receive a portion αA of the subsistence they need for their breeding. Given that the volume produced by each producer βB is about the same, but that individual procreative capacity is not linked to productive capacity, a mode of redistribution able to harmonise production and reproduction is required. In fact, though it may look paradoxical, balance is reached through redistributing offspring rather than produce.

This is generally achieved through commensality: the common produce is transformed and the food is equally distributed among all the community's members. But it is not so much the redistribution of produce which is brought about by this institution; rather it is offspring that are pooled, each one being considered to be equally the child of the senior elder. For this reason polygyny is more accentuated in societies which are very centralised economically (where the senior elder manages all the produce) than in decentralised communities. In the former, the senior elder may possess many wives and have numerous offspring, and this state of affairs will not effect redistribution of subsistence foods in any significant way, since everyone is equally the child of the senior elder.

But if the community is divided into households each of which disposes of all or part of its own produce, redistribution is necessary to correct their variation in fertility. In a decentralised community, therefore, the distribution of pubescent wives, of producers *and* of children must, come what may, agree with the distribution of produce. Within the limits of the produce available, this distribution between productive cells tends to balance out, since the present produce of each household only gains 'value' if it is consumed and thus transformed into a future product. Households which do not have enough children to absorb their produce do not realise its 'value'. Accumulating subsistence goods (over and above the reserves that are needed to cope with chance variations in production) is equivalent to wastage. On the other hand, households with too many mouths to feed will not realise the productive potential of their progeny.

Under the historical conditions in which the community functions, given that it only has very limited opportunities to recruit additional members from outside (unlike slave societies), the adjustment of the social product to consumption-requirements is achieved by moving individuals rather than produce between productive cells. Since the number of children born in each household is bound to vary more often and more rapidly than does production, the redistribution of dependants allows human energy to be shared more equally between productive cells, and balances the proportion between productive and non-productive individuals. This strategy of redistributing people according to the needs of production is revealed in various institutions – for example, the adoption of nephew and nieces. It can be observed in the movement of individuals between households in the same community. These institutions, by manipulating kinship relations, encourage permanent reconstitution of the relations of production (see Meillassoux, in Seddon, 1978, 289ff.; Pollet and Winter, 1971, 185, J. Schmitz, 1975, etc.).

If, instead of reallocating children through the mechanism described above, the produce was to be redistributed, this would concentrate proportionately a larger number of children in the most fecund households, enabling them at this stage, to gain access to more of the social product – taken from the community's production as a whole – than they produced on their own. This would already grant such households privileged rights over the future production of their offspring, whose growth would have been initiated by having benefited from the productive output of other households in the community. If the product of these children's labour remains afterwards in the households, there would be a break in the cycle of advances and returns and a definite appropriation of that proportion of the social product which was used to raise their extra productive members. However, the initial surplus-product appropriated in this way could be reproduced only in definite social circumstances, such that it could be socially invested independently of strict genetic increase. In other words, the surplus-product emanating from producers bred in a household as a result of having been supplied with produce from other units, must, in the next generation, meet a corresponding number of children; otherwise this surplus-product is wasted. Hence, to take advantage of it, the household must recruit people from outside itself – and from outside the community whose redistributive obligations it has breached – into whom its surplus-product may be invested. Differential accumulation of the produce assumes the possibility of such a recruitment of *outside* dependants (strangers). But the historical conditions under which the *domestic community* functions restrict this option to circumstantial and singular instances, which do not occur regularly and which are therefore neither institutional nor organic. Were it to be so, the initial redistribution of *produce* would set off a process of differential accumulation, but at the cost of a break in the relations of domestic production and reproduction, hence, of a radical change in the social structures.

Due to constraints on production, it is therefore logical to redistribute people rather than produce. It is the relatively even productive capacities of the household which are taken into account,

59

rather than their unpredictable reproductive potential: the social system is managed along its most relevant features. By redistributing the dependants, no producer is deprived of the product of his labour except in cases of early death. His surplus-product returns to him however many natural children he has begotten. It will allow him to feed the same number of children $S/\alpha A$ (whether these are his own or children belonging to the community).

The notion of family, extended to that of *classificatory kinship* prefigures this institutionalised circulation of people. It thus fits these conditions of production and circulation of subsistence goods which, quite logically, attach more weight to productive labour than to the hectic generative capacity of the male.

4. *The dialectic of equality*

The circulation of the progeny within the domestic community is not matched by any material counterpart. The circulation of wives between different communities does, however, sometimes involve a counter-movement of objects, and it is this kind of circulation whose modes, development and effects we are now to examine.

(i) The circulation of wives and of bridewealth[1]

In the matrimonial collectivity constituted by the alliance of several communities, the reproduction of each is ensured by an even distribution of available pubescent women among them.

The basic purpose of this redistribution is reproduction, of which women are the means. The devolution of women is not the ultimate aim of this exercise, however, as much as the redistribution of the progeny. In the following pages, 'the circulation of women' is to be understood as including the idea of 'devolution of children'. Given that women do not procreate in their own communities (except in cases of preferential marriage), they move to other communities; but this transfer can only take place on conditions of absolute reciprocity, *since the only functional equivalent of one pubescent woman is another pubescent woman.* Under these conditions, if this rule is respected, each community may only acquire from others exactly the same number of women as it has generated. Through the exchange of women a community cannot acquire more women than were born within it, but this number may be spread over time by making commitments in advance: thus one group will receive a nubile girl on the understanding that she will be replaced later by a girl who is still too young or even unborn. By this manouevre, communities which find themselves short of nubile girls at a particular time, can enter into immediate possession of those they receive against the promise of a future bride or of the future girls born from this operation, or as a counterpart of a girl given in the past. No community is therefore doomed to extinction simply because of accidents in fertility which might deprive them of women (they disappear paradoxically, for lack of pubescent men). On the other hand the possibility of an *equal* distribution of women among all communities is preserved. The organised mobility of women has the practical advantage over endogamy and matriliny in that it distributes pubescent women not only in space but in time.

The counterpart of this mechanism is *polygyny*, which allows the number of women in a community to be independent of the number of men (provided there is at least one).

The exchange of women, as we have seen, is either bilateral or multilateral. Bilateral exchange takes place between two allied communities and, because their numbers are few, on delayed terms. Giving away one woman entails the promise of another. Bilateral exchange limits the number of transactions to the number of pubescent women of whom the two communities dispose, and spreads them over a long period. Extending bilateral exchange to a greater number of communities partly overcomes this inconvenience and allows transactions to be more flexible.

But communities involved in what has become such a multilateral exchange network must be perfectly informed at all times of the situation regarding matrimonial transactions and the circulation of claims in wives, so that no community gets more wives than it has given or promised. When the number of transactions is limited, it is possible simply to memorise them all, but beyond a certain point an increase in their number makes it more difficult, if not impossible to remember the circulation of claims. When this point has been reached the claims tend to be given conventional material form through representative objects. Indeed such circulation of material objects may be observed when there is passage from bilateral to multilateral exchange of women (as in Douglas, 1963).

The nature of these objects is closely linked to the functions and specificities of marriage transactions. The discussion which follows will demonstrate how they reflect this function and how simultaneously they are likely to undermine it.

(ii) Bridewealth as wives' claims

Since the circulation of women may be regulated through sheer memory, the nature of objects intended to fulfil the same function may be just as abstract as memory itself. Their material form, representing only the claim and *not the object* of the claim, will therefore be independent of the latter's content. As in all other claim systems, matrimonial claim may be represented by any object, which may have *no intrinsic value*, merely a fiduciary value, based on that which derives from the unanimous agreement of the parties involved and the trust they have in each other.[2]

Through multilateral exchange, any pubescent woman who belongs to the matrimonial circuit may, if she is so designated by the debt cycle, be accepted as a counterpart of a woman previously given to another community. Within the limits of their kinship ties, pubescent women become fungible, and they lose in the marriage circuit part of their identity. A wife is chosen not because of her own qualities but as a result of an opportunity which is created by the network of alliances to which her community belongs, by previous obligations that community has entered into, and by the stage in the matrimonial cycle to which her age corresponds.[3] Fungibility of pubescent women is also indicated by the sororate, which exists within the confines of the donor group itself, and which may offer a 'sister' to replace a deficient or dead wife. Fungibility is limited, however, for women do not circulate within a system of 'generalised exchange' – as a mistaken structuralist formulation suggests – but within a network of multilateral circuits within which a woman's membership of her community of origin is never nullified. In contrast to what takes place under conditions of generalised exchange, in multilateral exchange the woman is never acquired by the husband's community: *she cannot be yielded again by the latter to a third party*. She moves only between her own community and another one, *never between third communities*.

Within these limits the fungibility of women may be reflected in the fungibility of things. They can be represented by sortings of objects which can be substituted for each other. All women being considered *a priori* identical in their reproductive functions, bridewealth portions, which are each a claim on a single woman, remain equivalent among themselves whatever their nature, content or volume, and whatever the quantity, quality, or scarcity of the matrimonial goods of which they are made up. All the same, a certain number of circumstances do affect the nature of bridewealth goods which, to be acceptable, must have certain specific attributes.

First of all, it is essential that bridewealth goods are intrinsically distinctive, not of women, since they are not distinguished from one another, but of the men who control them and who must have specific qualities. Bridewealth goods must demonstrate the social prerogatives of those who control them and their capacity to undertake matrimonial transactions. A bridewealth portion should be associated in kind and in composition with the social qualities of the elder, who, at the apex of the circulation of goods produced by the community, has, alone the social and rightful capacity to accumulate. Matrimonial goods will therefore usually be products that testify to the concentration of the human energy that, either in quantity or in quality, only an elder – because of his social position – can acquire. (Meillassoux, 1970, in Seddon, 1978, 127ff.)

But if, by its composition, bridewealth differentiates the elder from the other members of the community, it does not differentiate him from other elders whose prerogatives in matrimonial affairs are *a priori* identical. Therefore, if on the one hand bridewealth payments are abstract representations of pubescent women who are all seen alike, and on the other hand concrete representations of elders equal among themselves, they tend towards uniformity.

Finally, because bridewealth goods have the double function of representing both a *promise of a woman* and the *rank* of an elder, they can be non-productive goods, an attribute which is again accentuated by the fact that they are only used for circulation. Such goods, idle and symbolic, may have only *conventional and fiduciary value*. If this is so they will circulate as matrimonial goods only within societies constituted around these conventions – in other words within the group of allied communities belonging to the same matrimonial area.

In these circumstances it is therefore possible within this area to agree upon general conventions for the volume and composition of the bridewealth portion. The conventional and uniform rate of bridewealth portions expresses the fact that claims and partners are, in principle, equal. If the volume of bridewealth is allowed to vary, this does not modify the nature nor the content of the claim. He who chooses to give a more generous bridewealth portion will not gain extra-matrimonial rights. In other words, the quality, volume and content of the bridewealth portion remain independent of its 'legal tender' capacity.

Bridewealth goods may be either perishable or durable. Modes of circulating these goods will vary accordingly. In our hypothesis – whereby the bridewealth system allows an extention of matrimonial relations to larger areas – the circulation of bridewealth goods tends to encourage the use of durable goods.[4]

(iii) Identical exchange

An examination of the circulation of subsistence goods and of pubescent women reveals a crucial fact which distinguishes it from all forms of market exchange: *exchanges are made between goods which are identical*: subsistence goods against subsistence goods in the cycle of advances and returns of agricultural produce, and a wife for a wife, in the matrimonial cycle. The circulation of subsistence goods and of wives depends on the fact that their use is *deferred over time*. Goods which enter into these circuits, such as those which make up bridewealth in the matrimonial cycle, are intermediate between two moments of an exchange of identical elements. *Delayed exchange of identical goods* explains another oddity of exchange which has been observed by many anthropologists from Firth onwards: that is, the existence of restricted and exclusive spheres of exchange in which only specific products, related to a given level of circulation, can be *substituted for one another*, and that these products cannot be compared to other products being exchanged in different spheres. This circulation does not obey market laws, since substitution goods (such as matrimonial goods) have no 'value' except in terms of the ultimate exchange of goods they represent and which are always identical. So that variation in volume or content of intermediary goods is without accepted or acceptable influence on the final transactions.[5]

Through such *delayed* exchange the means of reproduction tend to be spread evenly over time: subsistence goods between the members of the community, offspring between the cells which form the community, pubescent women between communities. This whole process is the condition of a permanent reconstruction of the relations of production.

The mechanisms which we have examined reveal both the extent and limitations of this equalisation. Though the concern to maintain equalitarian relations dominates the ideology of domestic communities, it relies upon a long-term trend which history sometimes frustrates (cf. Pt. I, Ch. 6). The above mechanisms certainly do contribute to achieving a balance in each community (over a shorter or longer period depending on the case) between subsistence goods and consumers, between producers and non-producers, and between pubescent women and the population as a whole. If however, they tend toward the constitution of homologous or similar communities, these mechanisms do not ensure that the population is at all times *equally* distributed between all the communities which compose the social whole, which may be in different and changing positions in relation to each other as far as population-size is concerned.

The egalitarian ideal which exists *between communities* reflects the requirements of social reproduction. It is further reasserted when pressure from the outside brings threats of inequality. The case of the Lugbara (Middleton, 1974), among whom each community claims to be identical to all others, is a remarkable illustration of this, as is the collapse of the same ideal among the present-day Soninke, as described and discussed by Pollet and Winter (1971).

Structuralism viewed this egalitarian ideology through the concept of 'reciprocity', which Lévi-Strauss believed to be the driving force of the social system. Because it has not been applied scientifically, however, this intuitive notion has been deformed to refer to all movement or intention, which acts in the opposite direction (or which seems to do so). Despite Polanyi's attempt to give the notion a more rigorous definition, some writers have applied it to societies in which reciprocity does not operate and have even extended the notion to relations of exploitation such as the giving of tribute 'in exchange' for the lord's protection, or of tithe 'in exchange' for prayers from the priest.

Limited to the domestic economy, the notion of reciprocity can ideologically account for the egalitarian and equivalent mode of circulation of identical goods, which I have tried to define here. In such societies this ideology is indeed extended, beyond social relations, to the relations between man and land. For a peasant nothing comes from the land unless something else is given in exchange for it: he invests his labour and seed and draws his subsistence food in return. In this respect, activities which are predatory or merely extractive disturb him: they must be compensated by 'sacrifice' which re-establishes equilibrium since extracting resources from nature infringes the principle of advances and returns which dominate the domestic *agricultural* economy. Beliefs and rituals of this kind do not develop to the same extent in hunting and gathering societies, where land is merely the subject of labour. The necessity of a restitution is less obvious to a hunter who has no experience of investment in land. In aristocratic class societies, on the other hand, the ideology of reciprocity is maintained and used to justify relations of exploitation, though in fact it has no organic basis (see on this subject Vilakazi's very good criticism of the article by E. E. Ruyle, 1973).

66

(iv) Incipient value

When matrimonial transactions are checked both by a circulation of bridewealth and by memory, each leader of the community knows who owes or who is owed a wife. The function of bridewealth as a claim of debt dominates. As long as the partners remain within the close, neighbouring relations that enable each to see that matrimonial obligations are carried out, the prescribed functions of bridewealth do not alter, and its circulation remains subordinate to the need to reproduce the relations of production. The bridewealth circuit is contained within social relations which limit its effects to a level the system can support. Furthermore, the composite character of bridewealth and the labour prestations which often accompany it do not favour this simple, straightforward use that would make of the matrimonial goods some means of exchange, although exchange-value is latent within them.

The possession of a bridewealth portion does not by itself allow its possessor to negotiate a bride. The principles underlying these negotiations must first be accepted and the partners' qualifications recognised. It is because a woman is being negotiated that a bridewealth portion is transferred and not the other way around. Circulation of bridewealth only duplicates the primary and necessary circulation of the productive and reproductive agents; the circulation of bridewealth does not allow the modification of this distribution but only its ratification.

Other circumstances, in addition to these conventional and institutional limitations, also restrict bridewealth to its strict function of claim. If, as we have already seen, the size of the bridewealth portion does not alter the terms of the transaction, what happens when the number of bridewealth portions increases, when they are produced in quantity? Two cases are possible: either there are no limits to the amount of goods that constitute one bridewealth portion, and it is impossible to determine at what given amount any one begins to multiply itself; or the amount of bridewealth constituting a portion is fixed by custom, and an increment of the number of portions will not proportionately increase the number of available nubile women! A bridewealth portion only fulfils its function if there is a chance of using it for a marriage transaction. Over-production of bridewealth goods therefore ought not to give its producers any long or short term advantage.

To summarise, given that bridewealth portion is composed exclusively of non-productive goods which cannot enter directly into production or reproduction; that it mediates between the two sides of an identical exchange, a bride (now) for a bride (later); that it represents not a woman but her transfer; that this transfer only lifts a prohibition (that of unrestricted intercourse) and therefore only liberates latent reproductive functions without actually creating them; that its circulation does not increase the number of adult women nor their fertility; that its only function is to record the distribution of pubescent women in time and space, a function which is entirely abstract, bridewealth seems incapable of entering a circuit of equivalence which would give it exchange-value.

In spite of this, the entry of material and durable goods into marriage transactions – *objects which because of their conditions of production and distribution are different from the women and the goods that they come to represent* – entails contradictions which contain the potential for change.

If each bridewealth payment were identified with the woman for whom it had been transferred, it would be held in custody by the person who handed over the bride until, on receipt of a wife as a counterpart, he returned it to the debtor. Bridewealth would merely be a pledge. It would ratify bilateral agreements but not permit their extension. There would be as many bridewealth payments in custody as there were brides who had been handed over without immediate replacement. However, we have seen that, properly speaking, the bridewealth system exists only in so far as it allows women to be distributed over time through a circuit enlarged to an optimal number of communities belonging to the same marriage area and accepting the same conventions. Through this enlargement of the circulation by which it is acceptable to all the communities, the bridewealth payment is not merely a pledge but a claim of debt.

But if bridewealth is to fulfil this function, it cannot circulate exactly as brides do. In effect brides only circulate between their groups of origin and those of their husbands. They cannot be transferred from the latter to a third party. If the marriage breaks down, they may return only to their original community. Women therefore enter a reversible circuit, while bridewealth goods move in an open circuit.

In addition the two objects, bridewealth and women, have opposite fates. Through their marriage women are taken out of circulation, 'consumed' and used until their reproductive capacity is exhausted; while bridewealth, when made of durable, idle objects, exists indefinitely and can always be put back into circulation.

If marriage transfers succeeded one another over time in the order of the need that communities had for wives, a single bridewealth payment would suffice to ensure the circulation of all the brides. In reality this clearly does not happen and numerous factors encourage the production and circulation of new bridewealth goods. Several betrothals may take place simultaneously within the matrimonial area; a family to which a wife is returned may have no other daughter to offer in her place, nor bridewealth to hand over in compensation; others, in contrast, may hold on to the bridewealth they have been given. The number of bridewealth payments in circulation is the greater the fewer nubile girls available. Now the burden of producing a bridewealth portion falls on the community which has no available bride when it negotiates with a family from whom they covet a girl. In this way, an object with a public function moves into the private sphere. Bridewealth portions appear as objects of private appropriation whose creation and material fate are left to the owner's discretion. Moreover, the same community which produces a given portion will in the end receive it back in circumstances which change the effects of its circulation. When this community in its turn provides a woman to replace the bride it has received, it will nevertheless receive a bridewealth portion in return. But since this portion is returned to a community which owes a bride to the collectivity, this transfer closes the circuit and should cancel the claims: the goods composing the bridewealth portion should be immediately destroyed. But because they are material objects made of prestigious and durable substances, bridewealth goods last beyond the abstract claim which they represent and can enter another circuit. If bridewealth is accepted to have 'tender value' after the marriage circuit is closed, the system is biased; exchange of a *bride* for a *bride* no longer operates. In other words, when the original producer of the bridewealth receives a bridewealth portion in return from a bride whom he owes to the collectivity, he does not receive this portion under the same conditions as someone who advances a woman. In his hands, instead of opening a claim, the transfer of bridewealth cancels it. Although it is received on apparently the same conditions as a claimant who advances a woman, he has not in fact introduced any new bride into the matrimonial circuit but only restituted the one he owed. Nevertheless being in possession of an object which retains the physical and conventional appearance of a claim of debt but one which is actually effaced by virtue of its being returned, he is placed in the apparent position of a claimant. The very nature of bridewealth is inverted when, after directly or indirectly completing its cycle of advancing and returning women, it is put back into circulation. What should represent a cancelled debt becomes again an active claim.

The increase and extension of marriage transactions and the interchangeability of bridewealth goods, make it increasingly difficult to keep track of the marriage transactions which underlie bridewealth exchange, and to distinguish between bridewealth returning to a debtor, and bridewealth which initiates a new claim.

Now the continuous cycle of bridewealth transactions transforms a community issuing bridewealth payments into a claim-holding community every single time the circuit of advancing and returning women is completed. As new bridewealth payments come into circulation and complete their primary cycle, the communities most lacking in daughters become the richest in wives and bridewealth. To enrich onself and attract a large number of wives into one's community, it is enough to have produced one bridewealth payment which lends the producer a new claim over a woman at each rotation. Lineages which issue bridewealth payments – originally the most disadvantaged – would therefore succeed in exacting a growing demand on women in the matrimonial area without having to provide similar numbers in return.

If, on its return to the producer, bridewealth allows the latter to acquire a wife without giving away a woman, it ceases to act as a *mediating* good. It acquires a value of its own by directly confronting the single remaining term of the identical exchange – *one* bride. It comes to express a fixed value equal to one conventional pubescent woman. Thus within the limits of the matrimonial circuit, bridewealth comes to acquire an exchange value.

The intervention of other factors leads to the possibility that this 'value' may vary and thus become able to measure equivalence. When the ultimate object of marriage exchange is not the wife but her progeny, then, in addition to its function of a fixed claim, the bridewealth payment sanctions the completion of marriage, in other words, of its expected procreative functions. Since a woman's procreative potential is tied to her period of fertility, marriage, and the amount of bridewealth normally cover the period stretching from puberty to the menopause, if a bridewealth payment is to sanction the completion of marriages, it should be in proportion to this period of time and to the number of births. In practice this is what happens when marriage goods are delivered gradually. The bridewealth payment tends in this way to become the counterpart of the wife's progeny as it is indicated in various ways: as when bridewealth is partly repaid on divorce if children go with the mother; or when, at every new birth, the husband may make supplementary gifts to his affines; bridewealth may also be lower for women marrying for the second time, etc. As it comes to vary with the number of children, so also the bridewealth reflects the affluence of the community. So when the bridewealth portion is divided into separate goods, *its value contaminates the objects that it is made of*. In this way bridewealth goods may be used in various settlements, such as fines in cases of murder or adultery.

All these phenomena are latent. The potential emergence of exchange-value is first restricted to one sector – of marital and paramarital transactions – which only involves bridewealth goods. Here equivalence remains blurred because there is no direct confrontation between the primary goods of the exchange, the women and their children. In this limited sector, exchange-value may not be able to overcome the obstacles which institutions put in the way of such a transformation.

As a result, however, the way is open for human energy (applied to producing marriage goods) to be put in equivalence with women as reproductive agents, therefore to affect not only the growth of the progeny but also the distribution and accumulation of children: those who produce bridewealth acquire a latent capacity to acquire spouses through their production of material goods. Besides, bridewealth, as having exchange-value, makes it possible to put as an equivalent to a woman a portion of human social energy which is otherwise unusable for the maintenance of productive agents. Since the durable goods which make up bridewealth may be manufactured during the non-agricultural season, part of the energy that could not be used in direct or indirect subsistence production acquires the quality of being the equivalent of a begetter, and thus to reincorporate the energy producing cycle.

To overcome all these latent contradictions in the bridewealth system, and prevent exchange-value from creeping into its circulation, it is necessary that either some central power produces bridewealth and regulates its circulation, or that the bridewealth payments be *destroyed* when their claims are extinct, that is, on their return to the person who put them into circulation. In the context of a domestic society with no centralised power, the first solution is impossible. So destroying or neutralising bridewealth in the hands of those who are at the same time at the beginning and the end of a matrimonial cycle is the only way to restore the original function of bridewealth. And destruction does in fact take place on various occasions in these societies (be it only at funerals, when an elder is buried with some of his wealth), although it is usually sporadic and haphazard.[6] But for lack of precise means of identifying bridewealth payments made up of fungible goods, and since the debtor may not readily be distinguished from the claimant, some bridewealth payments which have been honoured continue to exist and circulate. Indeed the communities which accumulate most goods are those suspected of recovering them after having issued them; some social pressure can be exerted to make these communities destroy or neutralise them in some way. But if this destruction does not take place exactly when the claim is extinct then there is still room to play upon their new and fantastic virtue as exchange-value. The destruction of wealth is thus the logical solution to a contradiction arising out of bridewealth circulation; to eradicate incipient value from objects expected to remain neutral and economically dormant.

As a means of reproduction, woman is the irreplaceable wealth, and her progeny the ultimate good in which individual energy can be invested. Reproducing the system, and perpetuating individuals (the rich ones as much as others) depends upon being able to produce and bring up a progeny. Gold, cloth, and ivory, metal anklets and cattle may well be desirable, and even look like treasure, but they are only able to produce and reproduce wealth if they are successfully reconverted into the instruments of life. The opportunities for social control through their manipulation are always ultimately based upon the real focus of wealth they represent – subsistence goods, fertile women and their progeny. Redistributing these means of production through these forms of wealth does not depart from the framework of relations organically linking producer and reproducer, nor from the limits set by the volume of subsistence production and the number of past, present and future producers. In other words, since using these representative goods is never necessary, they can never be actual wealth, only its representation. Putting them into circulation brings about effects so complex and so difficult to control that they are resolved by stockpiling or destruction. Social control always derives ultimately, not from the possession of wealth, but from management of reproduction – in most cases directly rather than indirectly. Hence the apparent generosity of elders for whom wealth is efficient only through their continuous circulation – in contrast to gold at the beginnings of market exchange, as noted by Marx. (See also Meillassoux 1968, 765, for a distinction between the destruction of productive and of non-productive goods.)

However, this latent contradiction in the social system is not in itself sufficient to transform it. In order that the haphazard emergence of value should lead to social change and structural inequality, which would allow for the confiscation of the value, the contradiction must be taken to its limit, that is to the point where its implications are understood and consciously exploited to the advantage of a minority group, with the effect of its being institutionalised and geared to the deeper structures of production and circulation. The will to dominate must interfere for history to be made.

The latent valorisation of bridewealth may in fact assist the emergence of a ruling class, whereby 'women's takers' dominate 'women's givers'. But, unless it is incorporated into a developed market economy, value can only maintain the pre-eminence of a class if bridewealth producers are defined *institutionally*. Nothing *a priori* distinguishes the bridewealth producers except that in the initial marriage cycle they are, paradoxically, those who have fewer girls to offer. In order that their dominance should assert itself, the marriage network must enlarge to the point where it can no longer be controlled by memory. Furthermore the parties concerned must be so convinced by the illusion of the symbol of trust inherent in bridewealth that they desire bridewealth for its fiduciary value, making it increasingly possible to use bridewealth goods as a means to free oneself from other obligations. Therefore, if bridewealth producers want to exploit 'value' as means of domination they must concentrate the production of bridewealth goods to themselves alone, then control their circulation. But prohibiting certain classes from producing bridewealth is not enough; care must be taken to see that by-pass circuits do not develop in which other goods would acquire the same conventional qualities in the regulation of marriage. Now unless it leaves the marital or paramarital circuits altogether, bridewealth never acquires a greater 'value' than that represented by all pubescent women belonging to the matrimonial area. If, in order to dominate the bridewealth system, the production of bridewealth goods should be centralised, the fact that these goods are representative and fiduciary would still not permit an exclusive control over marriages, for any groups may constitute themselves around their own marriage conventions and symbols. In other words, any group that might want to monopolise the bridewealth system would realise that this system must either be universal or disappear. The logic is then to replace the bridewealth system by centralised and direct control over women, as before the appearance of bridewealth, but this time, to the benefit of a class born from the contradictions inherent in the development of the domestic society.

The process of valorisation of bridewealth we have described occurs in domestic society within a delineated matrimonial group. The emerging value of bridewealth derives from the claim of debt system and therefore remains conventional. Hence the process is not identical to that which arises when bridewealth goods, circulating in a matrimonial area, acquire a market value outside it, as when, for example, it consists of ivory, gold or other precious materials desired by traders. In this situation, bridewealth producers find themselves able to obtain women from other matrimonial groups in exchange for merchandise circulating under the guise of bridewealth. By opening the matrimonial circuit in this way they may also expect to delay the final matrimonial settlement by propagating it to communities which are increasingly foreign.[7] When money (usually issued by an external economic system) replaces local matrimonial goods in marriage transactions, then for their keepers, women become equivalent to livestock and marriage to the lease of livestock by which women's reproductive abilities are loaned out for a period corresponding to the amount paid. Again, the phenomenon we are dealing with here is different from the one discussed above. This is also different from the way in which women manage to turn marriage relations against men (Waast, 1974).

5. Who are the exploited?

(i) Women

In the foregoing analyses, women, despite their crucial role in reproduction, never appear as vectors of the social organisation. They are hidden behind men, behind fathers, brothers and/or husbands. As we have seen, this is not a natural given condition but one which results from changing historical circumstances, and always linked to the exploitation of women's reproductive functions.

In the hunting band, in which the problems of membership and mating predominate, and in which long-term reproduction is of little concern, women are more sought after as companions than as reproducers. Very little abduction takes place. Wars seem to be rare and, when they do occur, women are not usually at stake. Unions are precarious. Many observers note that women play an influential role wherever the mode of existence is not altered by the influence of agricultural neighbours.[1]

In agricultural societies, where women are wanted for their reproductive capacities, they are more under threat. As we have seen, whatever their physical constitution or capacity to defend themselves, they are more vulnerable because they are permanently subject to the aggression of men who are organised to abduct them. Guarding and keeping them in their original group becomes a major preoccupation which requires the organised participation of everyone in the group - particularly of those who are not threatened by the dangers of abduction: the men. Men thus are led to protect and then to dominate women. Thus, both in relation to the men in their own group who protect them and to the men of other groups who abduct them to protect them in their turn, women are forced into dependent relations which leads on to their time-honoured submission. In societies in which matrimonial exchange is linked to war and abduction, women, made inferior by

75

their social vulnerability, are put to work under male protection. In return gynecolocality gives women the advantage of living permanently in the same group and thus of being *its most stable component, through whom all goods (and eventually all inheritance) are necessarily transmitted*, including, eventually, cultivated land.[2]

When the domestic community succeeds in governing reproduction peacefully through the orderly circulation of pubescent women, the latter are not to the same extent 'protected'. But their past history of alienation predisposes them to a submission which remains necessary if they are to accept the alliances and the exile imposed on them by marriage and above all if they are to give up their rights over their progeny. Because a married woman lives with her affines, *her descent relations are always subordinate to her conjugal relations*. It is traitorous to wish otherwise, and wives are always suspected of betrayal. However, the position of women does not necessarily deteriorate in every respect for, since her material production is less determinant than their capacity to reproduce (which is repressed and revered at the same time), women retain an area of autonomy associated with their role as mothers.[3]

The notion of 'women' in domestic societies thus includes a number of definite functions that vary with age. The social role of women begins at puberty with their potential reproductive capacities. Institutionally, however, this quality is denied to them, for men alone are able to reproduce social ties: filiation only operates through men. Pubescent women are therefore controlled and subordinated, and directed into alliances which are defined by their community's obligations, so that procreation takes place in the context of male relations of descent.[4]

Once married, and therefore potentially fecund, a woman's situation is subordinated to the rules which govern the placing of her children. In contrast, after the menopause, and even more so as a grandmother, she is freed from these constraints and socially she comes into her own, gaining an authority that was denied her as a wife and mother. When old and widowed, and no longer able to procreate, her position becomes closer to that of men, for whom she may sometimes eventually substitute if there is no 'brother' or 'father' in the lineage, and if, through her, it is necessary to establish a patrilineal line of descent which would otherwise, without her mediation be definitely broken. It is when women lose their physiological capacity of reproduction[5] that they are bound to gain a social capacity of reproduction.

76

Who are the exploited?

Women's subordination makes them susceptible to two different kinds of exploitation - the exploitation of their labour, in that they lose their claim to their produce, which is handed over to their husbands who take control of it or pass it on to the elder, and is never returned to them in its entirety; and the exploitation of her reproductive capacities, mostly since filiation (that is rights over the progeny) is always established through men. Direct exploitation of women in the domestic community is often alleviated by the fact that they are given allotments or gardens, all or part of whose produce is theirs. The degree of a woman's exploitation, however, cannot be measured only by the amount of time she works, without recompense, for the community. It is also to be measured by the labour-energy she receives back from her children, in other words, by the amount of time given by her children to supply her needs. It happens in domestic societies that women benefit from some of the agricultural labour of their unmarried sons and that their influence depends on the number and position of their children. However, being deprived of actual rights over their progeny, the relations women maintain with their children do not involve obligation, as do those between children and their fathers. If the children desert them, women have no redress; *if childless they cannot, as men can, adopt a descendant*; should they be infertile, in old age they are seen as witches; after death their funerals are often almost unnoticeable, for women do not die, they disappear, without ever reaching - except in rare cases - the status of ancestor.

The subordination of women's reproductive capacities to men, the fact that they are *dispossessed of their children* to the benefit of men, their inability to create descent relations, go along with *women's inability to acquire a status based on the relations of production*. In fact, despite the dominant place which they occupy in agriculture as well as domestic labour, women are not granted the *status of* producers. Subjected to conjugality which dominates their kinship relations, what they produce enters the domestic sphere through the mediation of a man.[6] Because of this, they are excluded from the productive cycle of advances and returns which alone establishes collateral relations. A woman is not, in her husband's community, an 'ingenue', one born within the community. Filiation between women, when accepted, is strictly genetic. It is acknowledged between mothers and daughters, not between sisters. The sororate, imposed by the elder to replace an inadequate spouse by her sister, is not, by any means, symmetrical with the levirate.[7]

77

Françoise Héritier (1974) shows very clearly that among the Samo, even at the level of myth and ritual, collateral inheritance between women is unheard of.[8]

Marx is therefore right to believe that women probably constituted the first exploited class. All the same, it is still necessary to distinguish different categories of women in terms of the functions they fulfil according to age by which they are not in the same relations of exploitation and subordination. We have already touched upon the difference in status between pubescent and post-menopausal women. Research in this field, which would reveal the mechanisms and variations of women's exploitation, has yet to be undertaken. Engels' thesis concerning 'the historical defeat of the female sex', which he associates with the emergence among nomads of movable property, would also have to be re-examined. The advent of 'private property'[9] certainly brings significant changes in the position of women (Goody and Buckley, 1973), as Engels discerned, but we have seen that the causes for their submission are more intimate and have more distant origins.

Finally, and this is perhaps the ultimate alienation, it is through women that the elders maintain authority over the juniors, it is also through women that the latter emancipate themselves from the elders. In addition to the dependence of the collectivity upon women to reproduce itself, men depend on their wives to feed them. In all agricultural societies wives are answerable for the cooking, i.e. for turning the agricultural produce into an edible form: agricultural produce remains *sterile* unless it can be placed in the hands of a wife.[10] While the male hunter can exist on his own, for meat only requires cursory preparation, the agriculturalist is condemned to marry. Because of this dependence, which arises from the *cultural* division of labour, young men cannot fulfil themselves socially unless they have a wife. But this cultural choice is to the the elders' benefit: here again women are instruments of the latter's authority: the actual dependency of the young men is on their elders, not on their wives.

(ii) Juniors

Unlike the band which only *maintains* life, the domestic community is constituted to reproduce it. The dual end of this mode of production is the survival of the members beyond the productive age and the increase in the number of producers. If this end fosters the exploitation of women, it prevents an organised mutual

78

exploitation of males. Male producers, within their average life expectancy, recover the product of their productive agriculutral labour. In communities where production is decentralised, polygyny tends to be limited (often the headman is polygynous because he has inherited wives from his seniors, and is responsible for looking after them in their old age). Its effects in any case are alleviated by the circulation of children and of subsistence goods.

There would be exploitation between males if the redistribution of subsistence and/or of human energy was organically achieved at the expense of a defined category of them. Should this become *institutionalised*, and should it operate in favour of the emergence and reproduction of one specific *class* at the expense of another, we would be dealing with a different social system from the one we have described (even if it were to conceal its nature behind ideological representations borrowed from the domestic community).

In spite of this, the relations between seniors and juniors have been interpreted by several writers, in particular by Rey (1971, 1975) as class relations. Rightly, Rey says that the function of the elder is 'to redistribute producers between different production units' (1975, 519). But the exercise of the managerial function does not necessarily operate to the detriment of the juniors (the decisions of the elder are often discussed and shared with the oldest among them); on the contrary, the opposite is true, since this control offers the juniors access to the means of social reproduction. To support his claim that lineage elders as a whole constitute a social class, Rey relies upon the historical example of populations that had been brutally subjected to the effects of the European slave trade for which they were suppliers. Under such conditions juniors were not only producers, but ultimately commodities as well. The elders' severity towards them was exaggerated by greed. Banished for real or imagined crimes, the juniors were transformed into goods for the slave trade. Alliances were fixed between elders to allow them to sell their respective juniors to each other under the guise of pawning them or settling fines. That it became possible to alienate members of the community by selling them, radically altered the nature of the social system. In fact its end was transformed. Given this, it is possible to note indeed, through the transformation involved, the existence of inequalities between categories of people. But contrary to what Rey suggests, classes do not constitute themselves between the two categories he singles out, namely the group of *all* elders and the group of *all* juniors in the associated communities. Age, even understood in its social sense, is only a transitional moment in the life of an individual. If the elders do constitute an exploiting class, each of the members which compose it could only reach his position having previously been a member of the inferior, exploited class – that is, after having been exploited himself. If, on the other hand, the elder has always enjoyed a status of exploiter, it is not the category of 'elders' which is concerned but a far more complex social group, either able to produce and reproduce privileged individuals living off the labour of others, whatever their age or sex, or able to recruit its members before they themselves had been exploited. In the domestic community elders are such because they themselves have invested their own labour-energy in breeding juniors intended to reproduce the same cycle of advances and returns. They maintain themselves beyond their productive age only because they give these juniors access to the means of reproduction, i.e. wives. In so doing, they also weaken the juniors' dependence on them since the former thus acquire the possibility of becoming 'fathers' in their turn, and, in time, gaining increasing authority.[11] But by taking advantage first of the work done by their mothers[12] and then by their wives, junior men act like the partners of their elders in relation to women. In relation to their elders, the juniors' situation is comparable to that of clients rather than to that of the exploited group. Conflicts between elders and juniors reflect an opposition which remains within the system, that the junior members strive to reproduce to their advantage as early as possible by having a wife. But such an opposition is not radical and does not aim at questioning the institution but at benefiting from it, and so always, by alienating a woman.[13]

It is certainly true that access to the status of adult, of 'father', presupposes the obedience of juniors to the restrictive rules of the social order, of which the elders are the severe and vigilant guardians – rules which subject the juniors' individuality and their powers of decision to the collectivity. Juniors do not directly possess the immediate product of their labour, they cannot accumulate on their own account, cannot freely choose their wives, and are often subject to harsh sexual abstinence. When they are in conflict with the elders, the latter's council do not generally arbitrate in their favour. Segmentation is one way of resolving the tensions implicit in this form of discipline when it becomes too acute. We also know that, under the impact of colonisation and the money economy, village youths try to escape these constraints by emigration.[14] Younger brothers are disadvantaged in the process of attaining the rank of 'family head' and some are left out and remain unmarried. If they do not have the intellectual, physical or social means of leaving their communities, these men constitute a small exploited group. However, there are never many of them, and never enough to justify saying they constitute an exploited *class*, in other words one which is *maintained and reproduced as such*.

The mere exercise of authority by the elders over the juniors does not in itself create a class relationship. For this to occur, it must go along with an organisation of the relation of exploitation. Now no dominant class willingly gives up the means of power to the class it dominates. Capitalists do not give the capital to the worker; the feudal lord does not give land to the serf: such are the conditions for the reproduction of the dominant class. In contrast to this, to ensure domestic reproduction, the elder must and does give wives to his dependants. This does not happen any more when class relations develop: the male slave is not the *husband* of the woman he lives with, nor the father of their offspring; aristocratic classes do not offer their daughters to bondsmen from the exploited classes. Endogamy and hypergamy in fact indicate the consitution of social classes. Class relations are created, not out of *categories* like 'elders' and 'juniors', but through the dominance of entire, organically constituted communities which endow *all their members*, irrespective of age or sex, with prerogatives and privileges, over *all* the members of the dominated communities (Meillassoux, 1960). In fact, classes cannot be reduced to categories of age and sex. They are organic social groups, operating in functional relations, dependent one upon the other, and each possessing their own mode of reproduction. Among the Kukuya (Bonnafé, 1975, 350) social divisions split seigneural *lineages* from subordinate *lineages*, not elders from juniors. To see social classes (which are moreover exclusively male) as classes seems to me to derive from the same sort of confusion that is often made between castes and classes, that is between client groups and exploited classes (Meillassoux, 1973). Nor, let us add, does P. P. Rey accord women any particular position in his analysis of classes. In reality, what he analyses is a present society in which communal relations (originally matrilineal) have been profoundly altered under the impact of the slave trade and colonisation. Since the differences between the pre-slavery system and the subsequent system are not clearly presented, it is difficult to characterise the social relations which dominated either one or the other.

6. Contradictions and contacts: the premises of inequality

Is domestic society likely to be transformed as a result of the inner contradictions that we have detected in its mode of production and of reproduction?

At the political level the deepest contradiction arises from the necessary reinforcement of the elders' authority, as the objective basis for their power is progressively undermined by the very extension of the domestic community. We have seen how, as the power of the elders is displaced from material to matrimonial management, and as, consequently, the number of possible sexual partners within a growing community increases, exogamy must be reinforced. In addition, from a purely demographic point of view, the enlargement of exogamous units tends to disqualify a larger number of marriage partners. So young people belonging to junior branches of the largest exogamous units will have less chance of obtaining a wife and some will be at a disadvantage. The extension of the community exacerbates the risk of social tension while the conditions for the reproduction of the community itself are also threatened. Apart from his managerial functions and the authority which the elder draws from them, ideology is his main resource for maintaining the group's cohesion, e.g. morality, superstitious terror, sexual prohibitions, the sublimation of the father and of the ancestors that he represents, etc. This apparatus, sometimes backed by sanctions, tends to compensate for the weakening of the objective power base. However, such means cannot be employed beyond the point where social reproduction is threatened. Segmentation, even if delayed, remains the mode of resolving the contradiction between the enlargement of domestic community (made possible through the reinforcement of power) by matrimonial management, and the decline of that same power, due to this increase in size. Segmentation extends and repeats the structures of the domestic society but to the detriment of the strength of each community. The vigour and unity of the social

82

whole are maintained thanks to the multiplication and the weakening of each member community.

In order that a radical transformation of the domestic society can take place, social reproduction should operate for the benefit of one organic group at another's expense. *The productive and reproductive cycles* which, in the domestic community, merge both institutionally and organically, *must be dissociated.* We have seen that in the domestic community the two cycles are adjusted through a series of operations which subordinate paternity to productive capacity by moving people, particularly children. *The two cycles are dissociated in contrast, when the movement of people is replaced by the movement of products* (or of mediating goods which represent them) and when individuals remain attached by status to their family of origin. While the movement of children does not allow one household or descent group within the community to increase in size at the expense of others, moving subsistence goods makes accumulation possible either by the most prolific families, if transfers are in kind, or by the most productive if the transfers are made in terms of mediating goods.

For this dissociation to occur and become institutionalised, the reproduction of the domestic society as a whole must also be controlled by one social fraction and oriented to its own advantage. The control is achieved either by making all (or a decisive number of) pubescent women subject to this class or by monopolising marriage goods – provided these goods do not lose their representative value in the process. The use of bridewealth and its latent value creates, as we have seen, conditions which, though numerous problems remain to be surmounted, encourage confiscation. Such a situation is institutionally and structurally assisted when segmentation is not accompanied by the decentralisation of matrimonial control. The elder's prerogatives are then preserved and passed on to all the members of his lineage who thus acquire the prerogatives of seniority with respect to members of junior lineages. The senior lineage which, as a result of this 'elderly' privilege, controls matrimonial politics and ultimately the bridewealth goods of junior lineages, is thus in a good position to organise and manage the *social* reproduction of the collectivity to its own advantage (Meillassoux, 1960, in Seddon, 1978, 127ff.). As we have already said, this tendency, latent in domestic society, is only revealed when specific historical circumstances allow one section of the collectivity to take advantage of this tendency by organising it into a recurrent and institutionalised process. There do not seem to be many accounts of such a long process of change in the anthropological literature. The aristocratic society of the Bamileke described by Tardits (1960) could have originated out of such a transformation. The *fo*, the elder of the *senior lineage*, through the practice of *nkap* marriage, gathers control over the social reproduction of juniors or of subordinate lineages. The practices of the Kukuya 'lords of the sky', who demand women from subordinate lineages without counterpart (Bonnafé, 1975), and the *napogsyure* marriage of the Mossi (Izard, 1975; Capron and Kohler, 1975) are also comparable. Such societies, in which the social components are endowed through such practice with *distinct modes of reproduction* (some components being subordinate to the others) should be seen as class societies.[1] If the analysis of historical conditions showed that this process began and developed within the domestic community under the influence of its inner contradictions alone, we would have evidence of dialectical change.

However, changes are more often observed as a result of peaceful or brutal confrontation with foreign populations, rather than of internal transformation. If the structure and organisation of domestic communities lend themselves to an internal polarisation of authority, inter-community relations are not likely to seem to give rise to a co-ordinated power structure. The domestic community does not constitute a society by itself, but only in its association, for reproductive purposes, with other similar communities. Whether achieved through violence or law, this necessary association creates a delimited social entity, a collectivity which corresponds to a matrimonial area covering the space occupied by all the communities involved with each other in matrimonial exchanges. This collectivity (if isolated from the market economy)[2] may be considered as a *society* based on combined relations of production and reproduction which, at the level of the productive forces to which they correspond, constitute what may be named *the domestic mode of production*. Nevertheless, the contradictions we have located, which prevent marriage-exchange from proceeding smoothly and which give ambiguity to the bridewealth system, the attempts to exploit these contradictions to the benefit of one fraction, plus the ever-present possibility for each community to fall back upon its self-sustaining positions, all this keeps these societies in a permanent state of open or incipient conflict, in spite of alliances and arbitration, and the fact that they rest on an orderly system of marriage regulation. But the regulation of mar-

riages between the different and sometimes numerous communities
is left to the unco-ordinated decisions of the leaders of each community, which ceaselessly modify the matrimonial network, move
the boundaries of the matrimonial zone, and increase causes for
conflict. In many cases marriage comes to be considered as a *casus
belli* rather than an assurance of peace.[3] In addition, a historical
conjuncture often influences the establishment of matrimonial
groupings; the communities which compose them are frequently
descended from parties which settled *successively*, and in almost
all cases the group claiming to have been the first settled adopts
a position of anteriority in relation to those which came after (like
elder to junior). Did it now distribute to newcomers the seed and
food needed to start the agricultural cycle, and advance a few
wives as well? Thus, newly-arrived communities are placed permanently in a position of obligation according to the same process
which we have seen operating between elders and juniors of the
same community. There is, however, one very significant difference: the relationship is established not between individuals but
between social units organised for production and reproduction.
Ceding land is only the corollary of setting up these organic relations which must precede any agricultural undertaking. Thus, relations of inequality, more or less accepted, sometimes rejected or
reversed, tend to be established, and add to the tensions inherent
in matrimonial exchanges. The requirements of marriage arrangements do not always counterbalance the political effect of self-
sustenance nor hinder the existence of economically-independent
communities devoid of common *material* interests and always
anxious to guard or reassert their freedom of alliance.

Communities are vulnerable for other reasons: fixed domicile,
which makes their settlements easy to find; the storage of agricultural produce, which makes a much-coveted spoil; the scattering of
the adults in the fields during the productive period, etc. As a result,
such communities are easy prey for pillaging bands. This certainly
does not deprive them of the capacity to resist, as is shown by the
wooden or earthwork fortifications they built. It is not easy to
establish domination over such communities by force (colonial
troops more often encountered resistance from domestic societies
than from kingdoms or empires with a reputation for being powerful), but they are vulnerable to pillage, to razzias on their women,
slaves or cattle, and to sieges, etc. They need to protect themselves
against those who covet their products or their human producers
and this need imposes new requirements.

Several exogamous communities may unite and live together as one village, which fulfils several functions – communal protection, collective hunting, agricultural assistance, etc. Communal problems are then debated and solved by the representatives of lineages; though it is an observed fact that a centralised *power* does not usually emerge from the function of arbitrating conflicts. Sometimes military protection is sought by allying with neighbouring villages or collectivities, but since ties of neighbourhood and marriage are more often cause for dispute than alliance, such coalitions may prove unstable. Real protection will less often come from agreement between groups belonging to the same matrimonial area than from the domination of one lineage – sometimes foreign[4] – over the others.

Paradoxically, kinship reappears at this point, to support the ideology of power. When class domination is established over such communities it is expressed in the language of kinship even when it originates from outsiders. The ruling class, or the sovereign who represents it is identified with the elder (senior or 'Seigneur'), or with the father. He is authorised to 'eat' his subjects as the father is authorised to receive the products and labour of his children. In return he is expected to protect them. Seemingly redistributive mechanisms are set in motion between the sovereign and his subjects, as between the elders and his dependants. Sometimes the king even gives wives to some of them according to a complex process of matrimonial devolution. In other words, the sovereign claims to fulfil for the kingdom the outward and symbolic functions of the 'father' in his community. He 'feeds' and he 'marries'. These relations sometimes go along with an ideology which brings together the whole people in a common mythical kinship group, of which the sovereign is the successor of the ancestor. These relations are not in essence, of course, the same as domestic relations. They only preserve the same forms in order to mask relations of exploitation (Meillassoux, 1968a), for as soon as such relations are no longer between persons, but between constituted groups, as soon as they depend on the *status* of the parties concerned – that is to say on belonging by birth to aristocratic or commoner groups – then kinship no longer expresses relationships deriving from the growth and organisation of a society as it does in the case of the domestic community; instead it serves to give ideological support for the exploitation of one class by another.

This ideology produces the conditions for the simultaneous transformation of kinship relations at three different levels: within

86

aristocratic lineages in which, for example, vertical succession may predominate as a result of the practice imposed by political domination; within dominated classes to which will have been imposed an idea of kinship appropriate to their subordinate position and productive function and which this allows the relations of exploitation to be maintained; and, finally, between the dominant and dominated classes to safeguard the conditions necessary for the reproduction of each.[5] Thus, while ideology affirms the kinship of all classes, it is denied in practice through a reinforcement of endogamy and hypergamy. When kinship takes on a quality of religiosity, and the lord or king becomes the representative of 'God the Father' on Earth, it may become sufficiently binding to be understood and accepted as the divine justification for exploitation and domination. Society is being organised according to a dominant ideology, an ideology with juridical overtones which is 'given' as a charter for the social system, and which bears what cultural anthropologists call 'values'. At this juridico-ideological stage of social organisation, 'values' may in fact seem to provide explanations with which the ideologues of anthropology often content themselves – overlooking, as they do so, the economic and historical conditions from which originated the ideology and law whose manifestations they observe.

As we have described it here, *the domestic mode of production*, constituted of homologous communities which maintain organic ties only with communities of the same kind, no longer exists. Its ability to produce and reproduce itself in a coherent and orderly fashion, and above all to survive without preying on subordinate forms of social organisation, have rendered it subject to every form of exploitation. Indeed all other economies have been built upon the domestic community – from the aristocratic economy to capitalism, and including even slavery which, despite being its negation, could not exist without it. But crushed, oppressed, divided, counted, taxed, recruited, the *domestic community* totters but still resists, for *domestic relations of production* have not disappeared completely. They still support millions of productive units integrated to a greater or lesser degree in the capitalist economy, disgorging goods and energy under the crushing weight of imperialism. In the most advanced societies, domestic relations still structure the family, that narrow but vital foundation for the production of life and labour-power. The analysis of one superseded but tenacious form of production is not irrelevant for the understanding of the present, for we must be able to recognise its specificity to understand the vital role it has continued to play in social history, as well as the far-reaching implications of its disappearance.

The exploitation of the domestic community: imperialism as a mode of reproduction of cheap labour power

This second part is an elaboration of an unpublished paper delivered at the Colloque de Bielefeld on 'Application of the theory of pre-capitalist formations to so-called peripheral "capitalism"' in December 1972; its title was 'Imperialism as a mode of reproduction of cheap labour-power'.

1. The paradoxes of colonial exploitation

Many recent studies devoted to underdevelopment, by reputedly Marxist writers, concentrate on unequal exchange rather than the exploitation of labour. Unless, however, like classical economists, these authors wish to claim that exchange creates value, the wealth of imperialist countries can only derive from exploitation of workers in these countries and not from international trade.

These writers do indeed admit that unequal exchange is attended by low remuneration for labour, but they do not tell us which is cause and which effect. For Samir Amin (1970) the explanation is simple enough: if, 'given equal productivity', labour is paid at a lower level in countries on the 'periphery',[1] this is due to an increasing surplus of labour-power, itself organised by 'political means' (pp. 139, 145). The relative over-population (that is, at any given time, the excess population relative to the conjunctural capacity for employment in the capitalist system) would sometimes also be due to structural circumstances, such as the predominance of latifundia agriculture in Latin America, which invests very little but imports a great deal, or the disappearance of craft production, which is not then replaced by industry (pp. 103, 104). These circumstances together would lead to 'a growing imbalance between the supply of and demand for labour' (p. 183).

This argument comes straight from the arsenal of liberal economists. Extra-economic 'political' factors reaffirm stochastic contingencies that economists, enclosed within the narrow specialisation of their discipline, have to introduce when they reach the conventional and ever-mysterious point at which 'politics' begin. The managerial methods set up by the capitalist State, however – including the apparatus of coercion, repression and corruption – are part of the economic armoury of capitalism. They count as overheads. It is true that during the colonial period the labour force was driven from the countryside by force rather than expropriation: but is one method any more 'economic' than the other?

91

For colonial entrepreneurs coercive methods of recruitment had the advantage of placing the cost of labour almost entirely upon the administration, which meant they received a disguised subsidy in line with the overall orientation of contemporary imperial policy. When forced labour disappeared in the colonies, a minimum wage, sufficient to attract people into the capitalist sector, had to be offered, to obtain the same labour force. The cost of recruiting the labour force fell on the companies. Instead of being spent on administration and police, this cost was spent in the form of slightly higher wages. But the development of wage-earning does not eliminate completely the costs of law and order necessary for the exploitation of labour, which are always, both at home and in the colonies, supported by the capitalist State. In no case can the resort to such political means be treated as extra-economic. They reveal a given distribution of costs and labour, relative to each conjuncture, between private entrepreneurs and the capitalist State, to set up the structures which most effectively exploit labour and realise profit.

Explaining low wages in terms of supply and demand (another argument of classical economics) is also based on a series of errors. It has been clear since Marx that supply and demand, when they do operate, do not explain the level at which wages are fixed in the long term, once equilibrium has been reached. This level is established by the cost of the reproduction of labour power. Applied to underdeveloped countries, the law of supply and demand becomes almost completely irrelevant. In contradiction to what Amin thinks, it cannot explain low wages. As far as West Africa is concerned, A. G. Hopkins (1973, 229) reports a chronic shortage of labour which the wage level does not reflect. On the other hand, Hymer (1970) notes that when Ghana was first colonised 'wages were high, since much of the population had access to land to grow food or export crops, without paying high rent. [. . .] Europeans (including the United Africa Company, a Lever subsidiary) were able to obtain land; what they were not able to do was to earn a profit at the going wage-rate or to compete with Ghanean farmers. Similarly, the mines found it difficult to pay the going wages.' The problem was solved by the migration of the Northerners and people from the underdeveloped French territories who were not yet involved in export crops.

Development theorists also discovered, during these pioneer years of colonisation, that wages had to be lowered to increase the supply of labour, since workers from the rural sector would return home as soon as they had earned the sum they had set out to earn. If all these contradictory examples do not fit the law of supply and demand it is because, as Marx wrote (1867, Vol. I, p. 769), when the land is still largely owned by the people (allowing each one to settle as independent agriculturalist or craftsman) 'the law of "the supply and demand of labour" falls to pieces'.

In Africa, where this situation still prevails, another explanation for low wages must therefore be found. In addition, Amin's arguments only apply to the industrial sectors where the productivity is the same as that of the developed countries (at 'equal productivity'), in which case they are reduced to a banal statement of the fact that, since workers are paid lower wages on the 'periphery', then foreign companies, provided they do not employ expatriate labour, are obviously able to repatriate larger profits. What Amin does not explain, and it is the key to the problem, are the particular conditions under which the elements for reproducing labour power are produced, conditions that make payment of low salaries possible while productivity in the agricultural sector of subsistence production is lower than in developed countries – a fact which contradicts his hypothesis. Or, to put this another way, what are the conditions for the over-exploitation of labour in the colonised countries?[2]

There are inevitably ideological implications in choosing to exclude from discussion the problem of the exploitation of labour, and therefore the class struggle, and seeing underdevelopment only in terms of exchange. If the causes of and explanation for underdevelopment were to be found in the mechanisms of international trade, the problem could be resolved between States, as international institutions claim to do (G.A.T.T., F.A.O., the international conference on raw materials, etc.). The struggle of exploited peoples against domination and poverty would be channelled through the indisputable mediation of their governments. They would rightly reflect the terms of reformism and nationalism. 'Revolutionaries have nothing else to do but to 'advise' their governments – *whatever the regime;* the 'expert' and the economist, who is often foreign, would be vested with the complete armoury of political struggle. But if, on the other hand, underdevelopment results from the over-exploitation of labour, political action falls into the hands of the exploited classes of these countries once they are liberated from the 'protection' of charitable co-operation. Amin, by setting the discussion at the level of *international* exchange, places states and not classes in opposition to each other. The economic divide for Amin falls nicely along national frontiers. In reality, such theories are readily acceptable to, and accepted by the bureaucracies in power, still more by the local comprador bourgeoisies who claim to be nationalists and who, if they do not profit as they might wish from colonial exploitation, are nevertheless its accomplices (Amin, 1969). These theories allow them both to demand a larger share of the profit from their wealthy allies and at the same time appear as the defenders of the people.

Palloix (1970) poses the problem in a far more satisfactory manner. 'What has to be investigated', he writes, 'are the mechanisms that bring about an undervaluation of the value of labour-power in the unindustrialised countries, the undervaluation upon which, in the field of circulation, the effective realisation of unequal exchange depends.[3] (p. 27).

Palloix discusses the solution in a re-evaluation of the exchange-value of labour-power, which is assumed to be 'nonexistent' by the exporting capitalist sector in the underdeveloped countries, 'since it is possible for it to divert the cost of the reproduction and upbringing, as well as that of maintenance, onto the traditional sector from which it draws the workforce it needs' (p. 30).

This is indeed the crux of the matter. For all that, however, one cannot explain the low cost of this labour by the 'low productivity of the subsistence sector' (p. 33) – on the contrary. But Palloix's analysis stops on the threshold of the traditional sector, which he has not analysed.

As a result, and in spite of his correct premises, Palloix finally sees unequal exchange as occurring between *branches* of capital in which the organic composition of capital is different.[4] Thus he considers it to be only *the effect of transferring surplus-value from one branch* – in which the organic composition is weaker (i.e. which employs a proportionately larger labour force) – *towards the others*. Neither Palloix nor Amin considers that underdevelopment results first and foremost from a transfer between economic sectors operating on the basis of different relations of production. Their argument explains the transfer of profit, not the way in which that profit is realised.[5] In addition, these theories are unable to explain the double paradox of the agricultural economy in countries exploited by colonialism.

If the value of labour-power was derived from the labour-time socially necessary to produce the goods, in particular the subsistence goods required to reproduce the workers both physically and intellectually, and to reproduce future workers, then, *in the capitalist sphere*, subsistence agriculture with low productivity, such as exists in underdeveloped countries, would raise the cost of labour-power, since more hours are needed to produce the subsistence goods necessary to maintain the workers than in an agriculture with high productivity (Marx 1867, I, 4, p. 53, Ch. XII, p. 315 and III, Ch. XIII, p. 214). It so happens, however, that in these countries, labour power in the domestic sector as well as the goods produced by family exploitation, is cheap. This paradox cannot be theoretically resolved by resorting to arguments about the different organic compositions of capital nor to the laws of supply and demand, nor can it even be resolved by analysis strictly in terms of surplus-value. This paradox parallels another, for, according to the logic of capitalism, capital ought to be invested in this sector of low productivity, where profits resulting from such investment would be highest. In fact, capitalism has, until now, virtually ignored the subsistence agriculture sector in underdeveloped countries.

These two paradoxes are more understandable if we reconsider the theories of wages and primitive accumulation.[6] We know that in underdeveloped countries subsistence agriculture remains almost entirely outside the sphere of capitalist production while being totally involved with the market economy either because it supplies workers fed and bred in the domestic sector, or exports commodities produced by peasants also fed on their own harvests. The subsistence economy belongs therefore to capitalism's *sphere of circulation* to the extent that it provides it with labour-power and commodities, but remains outside the capitalist *sphere of production*, since capital is not invested in it and the relations of production are domestic and not capitalist. It cannot be held that relations between the two economies, the capitalist and the domestic, are relations between two branches of capitalism, as would suffice to explain unequal exchange: the relation is between sectors in which different relations of production predominate. It is by establishing organic relations between capitalist and domestic economies that imperialism set up the mechanism of reproducing cheap labour-power to its profit – a reproductive process which, at present, is the fundamental cause of underdevelopment at one end and of the wealth of the capitalist sector at the other. Socially and politically, it is also the root cause of the division in the international working class. Up to the present, wherever capitalism has developed, this process has continued at an ever-increasing rate and on an ever-growing scale, to such an extent that *it must be considered*, like other mechanisms of capitalist reproduction, *to be inherent in capitalism itself.*

Before going any further, the use of the notion of 'modes of production' within this argument should be discussed briefly. In Marx's works, this notion does not have a truly scientific status. It contrasts, *through time, successive* forms of economic and social organisations based on distinct relations of production, so as to illustrate the advance of history. This is qualitatively different from what we are doing here, namely contrasting *contemporary* modes of production as they meet, articulate and ultimately dominate or become dominated. If labour-power is reproduced, even in the capitalist system, within the framework of domestic social relations, this means that heterogeneity is organically involved in the capitalist mode of production (while the domestic mode, it will be remembered, operates on the basis of homogeneous relationships). If this is so, it follows that insofar as some modes – organically and not residually – contain the elements of others within their structure they cannot be considered as homogeneous and they could not fall within the same category as the domestic economy (i.e. the category 'modes of production'). Neither capitalism nor feudalism is exclusive of the domestic economy, for they rely on domestic relations to reproduce themselves.[7] A historical confrontation between them cannot be considered as entailing the substitution of one for the other, but rather their mutual transformation or the dependency of one on the other. This raises the question of to what extent they will remain in their original state of 'modes of production'.

Dialectical materialism grants that it is possible for value to be transferred from one mode of production to another through the mechanism of simple primitive accumulation, that is, when the transfer is achieved through the destruction of one mode of production by another.[8] But there is no theory dealing with the way in which value can be extracted continuously through preserving the relations of the dominated mode of production. In such a case, does the organic whole represent a new mode of production, or must we admit that the previous modes of production survive – and if so, to what extent? The great merit of Rey (1971) is that he posed the problem for the colonial period. According to him, it is correct (because effective) to contrast 'modes of production' in this context, even though one, being subject to the other, is degraded by the exploitation of which it is the object. 'Restricted'

96

reproduction is as conceivable as 'enlarged' reproduction, without affecting the essence of the social and economic organisation.[9] All the same, in his 1971 work, Rey can picture the articulation between capitalism and 'lineage modes of production' only as if mediated politically. In its relations with the capitalist mode of production, the 'lineage mode' – reduced to being a supplier of labour – would, according to Rey, carry out its functions with the political assistance of the colonial power which reinforces the position of the traditional chiefs whose job it is to drive the youths into the capitalist sector (Rey, 1971, 46). In the absence of the massive expropriation which forced European peasants into the factories, the historic task of the 'class' of elders would thus be to provide capitalism with 'free' labourers, by forcibly separating the direct producers from their means of production (*id.*). But Rey's view amounts to an extrapolation of some local effects of colonialism, which does not take account of an important present phase of imperialism. As I shall show, it is not in the immediate interests of capitalism, in given historical conditions and at a certain stage in its penetration, to encourage in all cases this separation. On the contrary, it is by *preserving* the domestic sector which is producing subsistence goods, that imperialism realises and, further, perpetuates primitive accumulation. 'Modes of production' are not only 'articulated' at the level of 'class alliances' between capitalists and corrupt lineage leaders, but also, organically within the economic sphere itself.

Initially, contact is obviously between two modes of production, and one of them dominates and begins to change the other. As long as the domestic *relations* of production and reproduction persist, rural communities, although in a process of change, remain qualitatively different from the capitalist mode of production. However, in the long run the general conditions for reproducing the social whole resulting from this interpretation no longer depend on determinations inherent in the domestic mode of production, but on decisions taken in the capitalist sector. By this process, contradictory in essence, the domestic mode is simultaneously maintained and destroyed – maintained as a means of social organisation which produces value from which imperialism benefits, and destroyed because it is deprived in the end of its means of reproduction, under the impact of exploitation. Under the circumstances the domestic mode of production both exists and does not exist.[10]

If various writers (Stavenhagen, 1969, 1973, 16; Frank, 1969; Amin, 1970) have rightly repudiated the liberal thesis of a dual economy, according to which two unconnected sectors, one industrial and the other 'traditional', exist side by side in underdeveloped countries, one cannot assume that under the impact of imperialism the domestic economy is *ipso facto* transformed entirely into an impoverished form of capitalism. According to the circumstances and above all according to the requirements of imperialism, the domestic economy undergoes various changes (Laclau, 1971; Wolpe, n.d.). It is not enough simply to deny dualism by claiming that under the influence of colonisation all productive relations become capitalist; we must study how modern imperialism manipulates all these diverse forms for its own profit. We will therefore be exploring not the destruction of one mode of production by another, but the contradictory organisation of economic relations between these two sectors (the capitalist and domestic), one of which preserves the other to pump its substance and, in so doing, destroys it.

2. Direct and indirect wages

The problem of capitalist exploitation must be set in the more general terms of the conditions of production and reproduction of labour-power. The fact that these processes take place within the family, an institution with its own standing (distinct from that of the capitalist enterprise) in which domestic relations of production and personal, not contractual, dependence prevail, sets theoretical problems for dialectical materialism which do not seem to have received enough attention.[1] The particular circumstances which govern the production and reproduction of labour-power require a re-examination of its content, particularly when domestic relations persist, not only as relations of reproduction but as relations of production as well (for example in underdeveloped rural areas).

Labour, in fact, is exploited under different conditions according to whether, capitalism being the exclusive mode of production, the market economy controls all transactions (that is in the theoretical case of integral capitalism) or whether capitalism dominates non-capitalist modes of production, and thus exploits not only free labourers, but structured cells of production, and thus exploits not only free labourers, but structured cells of production (imperialist capitalism). I will try to show that, if the theory of surplus-value, as it was put forward by Marx in *Capital*, is applicable in the hypothetical situation of integral capitalism, it must be modified to take account of the exploitation of labour in the context of imperialism.

It is generally admitted that Marx's *Capital* offers a model of an integral capitalism operating according to the following hypotheses:

(1) All products, including subsistence goods, are commodities, i.e. goods that can only be obtained on the market.

99

(2) Capitalist development is endogenous and, after the initial period of primitive accumulation, no longer receives free inputs from outside.[2]

According to Volume I of *Capital* the reproduction of labour-power is achieved through the purchase of labour-power at its value. Now the *purchase* of labour-power, is, in Marx's argument, linked to the analysis of surplus-value which is realised over a specific period of time – the duration of *the hourly sale of the immediately available labour-power of the worker.* In other words, surplus-value is linked to the time during which the worker's labour-power is employed, counted in hours of work; it is not realised either before or after this period. Marx explains that 'The value of labour-power is determined, as in the case of every other commodity, by the labour-time necessary for the production, and consequently also, the reproduction, of this special article[3] [. . .] the value of the labour-power is the value of the means of subsistence necessary for the maintenance of the labourer' – including, he adds, the means necessary for the substitutes for the worker, namely his children (Marx, 1867, I, pp. 170–1). He further makes it clear that [the workers'] 'wages suffice not only for [their] maintenance, but also for [their] increase'. (*id.*, p. 581).

These means of subsistence must also be sufficient to maintain the labourer 'in his normal state as a labouring individual', in other words, even through periods of unemployment, as a member of the industrial reserve army of labour.[4]

We can therefore isolate three elements of the value of labour-power: sustenance of the workers during periods of employment (i.e. *reconstitution* of immediate labour-power); *maintenance* during periods of unemployment (due to stoppages, ill-health, etc.); *replacement* by the breeding of offspring. Of these three elements which should make up the theoretical wage, only one, the first, contributes to the reconstitution of labour-power as a commodity immediately saleable on the market (i.e. the labour-power that the worker sells to the capitalist who realises its value during the period of contract, by applying it for a limited period – measured in hours of work – to the means of production which he owns). The labour-power of the worker's replacements, as well as the worker's own labour-power, maintained over future periods of unemployment, are actualised as commodities only at some unspecified future time, while the worker's labour-power supported through a previous period of unemployment is only realised *pro rata* from hours he works subsequently./ The worker's present employer (in the framework of contractual relations which connect them, i.e. the wage relationship) cannot buy a future commodity which he has no assurance of getting – and in fact does not do so. In practice the direct hourly wage paid to the worker only pays for the labour-power expended during the period of work. It is calculated over this period exactly, and does not take account of the worker's expenses on his family, his past or future periods of unemployment and illness, or of whether he has been brought up, physically or intellectually, inside or outside the capitalist sphere of production. Whether the worker is a father or a bachelor, sick or well, fortunate or not, immigrant or local, from town or country – none of these factors is taken into account when the wage paid to each worker is calculated, and is fixed according to the worker's professional category.[5] In other words, the *hourly* rate of pay, the price paid to each worker for the purchase of his labour-power, is based on the cost of supporting the worker during, and only during, his period of work, and does not cover his maintenance and reproduction. We know that in France, for example, the minimum wage (S.M.I.C.)[6] is calculated to cover the needs of a bachelor (one who is therefore not reproducing), on the implicit assumption that he is employed uninterruptedly for the total number of legally workable hours in the year, thus presupposing that he is never ill or unemployed and that he dies at the age of retirement.

The provision for the maintenance and reproduction of labour-power therefore involves capitalism in contradictions which cannot be resolved through the hourly wage system. /To realise surplus-value, wages have to be based on the precise length of time during which the worker really worked. On the other hand, if workers are to be reproduced, their incomes should also cover their individual needs *throughout their lives* (from birth until death) irrespective of the amount of labour-power they actually supply. ↘

↙ In other words, one equalisation is needed to ensure that, whatever the length of a worker's active life, the price of his labour-power is the same at all times and for all employers, and another so that the running costs of the worker's family do not alter the present price of his labour-power. Solving this problem raises another: making provision for the reproduction of labour-power, as a future *commodity* (raising the children) ought logically to be an *investment*, and therefore part of capital, but under capitalism the wage-earner's income which comes to him in return for work cannot be composed of capital without the worker becoming, *ipso facto*, a capitalist. Reproduction of labour-power (this follows from above) therefore must take place outside the norms of capitalist production, in the context of such institutions as the family, where members maintain non-capitalist social relations and whose economic position, in legal terms, is not that of a capitalist enterprise. This means that *labour-power*, an essential commodity without which the capitalist economy cannot function, and *free labourers*, social agents crucial in the formation of capitalist relations of production, both escape from the norms of capitalist production though they are produced in the capitalist sphere and are dominated by it.

The bourgeoisie overcomes these contradictions and turns them to its advantage by distinguishing between two kinds of payment, the direct and the indirect wage (or fringe-benefits). The first is paid directly by the employer to the wage-earner and is based on the number of hours of work he has supplied; it provides at least as much, though not necessarily more than, the worker's subsistence and ensures the immediate reconstitution of labour-power. The indirect wage, by contrast, is not paid in the context of the contractual relationship that ties the worker to his employer, but is redistributed through a socialised institution. It represents the share of the social product necessary to maintain and reproduce the labour-power at the level of the nation as a whole. This part is not paid by reference to the time worked, *but strictly according to the cost of the maintenance and reproduction of each worker considered individually* – to his family situation, to number of children, to the number of days of illness or unemployment – all being taken precisely into account for the computation of the indirect wage. As a result the proportion of the social product devoted to reproduction is converted, not into a means of investment, but into a means of consumption. In addition, the law defining the age of majority prevents parents (unless they own means of production) from taking advantage of the income thus invested in the upbringing and maintenance of their children, who can only be put to work by the holders of capital. Capitalists alone are in a position to employ them and legally exploit their labour-power. Thus the portion of the social product devoted to reproducing labour-power is equalised at the level of the process of capitalist reproduction as a whole and in the form of income, not investment. So the benefits derived from producing labour-power as a commodity are taken from the worker to the profit of the capitalist. (This process as a whole takes place in practice at the level of the state when the latter represents national capitalism's historical development). The development of social security systems in countries where the proletariat is integrated – where the worker's only revenue is his wages and where he has no family farm or allotment – illustrates this process.[7] It is therefore due to the payment of an indirect wage or to fringe benefits, and not simply to the purchase of immediate labour-power through wages, that labour-power is paid at its cost and reproduced.[8] This is also the means by which the wage earner is reintegrated into the capitalist economy on a lifelong – and not just hourly – basis.[9]

If the above argument is accepted, then, when the proletariat is paid only direct hourly wages (which was the case for a long time in Europe and still holds for most underdeveloped countries) it can be considered that the reproduction and maintenance of labour-power are not taken care of within the sphere of capitalist production but are necessarily born by another mode of production. Here we find ourselves in a situation that does not conform to Marx's model, for he makes it clear that 'if production be capitalistic in form, so too will be reproduction' (1867, I, Pt. VIII, Ch. XXIII, p. 566).

The examination of this particular issue leads to a reassertion of the concept of primitive accumulation, as a corollary of the foregoing arguments.

3. Primitive accumulation

Marx's concept of primitive accumulation corresponds to a precise historical period and context: the emergence of capitalism from the ruins of feudalism, which he situates in the fourteenth century (1867 I, Pt. VIII, Ch. 28). 'In this respect their [the industrial capitalists'] conquest of social power appears as the fruit of a victorious struggle both against feudal lordship and its revolting prerogatives, and against the guilds and the fetters they laid on the free development of production and the free exploitation of man by man.' (1867, I, Pt. VIII, Ch. 26, p. 715.)

He attaches considerable importance to landed property, by which the peasantry was dispossessed of its means of labour. Landed property, resulting here from the transforming impact of merchant capital on the feudal domains and common land, represents the first step towards agrarian capitalism. It is landed property which dissolves the ancient ties of personal dependence and delivers the 'submissive hands' of a proletariat 'without hearth or home [. . .] definitively deprived of their land to capitalist employers' (1867, I, Ch. 28).

Marx looks at two simultaneous transfers which occurred at this period: the transfer of land (which is integrated into capital through appropriation) and the transfer of labour-power, as peasants migrate to the towns. As far as the latter is concerned he particularly stresses the 'historical process of divorcing the producer from the means of production' (1867, I, Ch. 26, p. 714), the social transformation of the dependent worker (and independent producer) into a 'free labourer', who is freed from his ties of personal dependence (kinship, bondage, etc.) and 'free' to sell his labour power to whoever will buy it, a revolution which will provide the capitalist entrepreneur with a variable capital whose supply will for a long time, surpass that of constant capital (1867, I, Ch. 28, p. 738). On the other hand he does not stress the effects of this input of labour-power produced outside the capitalist sphere, though he is not unaware of it. (1867, III, 238, and above, pp. 99–103.)

Primitive accumulation is therefore, for Marx, an initial historical phenomenon, the point at which, through the dissolution of feudalism, capitalism takes off. Once this event has occurred it is no longer taken into consideration. Once built on this basis, the capitalist economy, according to the theoretical model in *Capital*, is supposed to grow and operate in terms of strictly capitalist norms of production and reproduction, without relying further upon other modes of production. Historically, however, this hypothesis does not take account of the real process of capitalist growth and expansion which is achieved through the continuous incorporation of new lands and, still more, of new peoples under the influence of colonialism and imperialism. History shows that the free transfer of values of pre-capitalist societies to imperialist powers is a permanent, and until now an accelerating phenomenon, which has continued to feed the capitalist economy from its outset. It is thus not enough to assert that primitive accumulation is a transitory and initiatory phenomenon; it is *inherent* in the process of the development of the capitalist mode of production. Lenin and Rosa Luxemburg have shown that expanding capitalism does not correspond to the working hypotheses advanced in *Capital*, but they explained imperialism more in terms of the search for outlets than in terms of surplus-value. Underdeveloped countries – usually pictured as settler colonies of the American and British type – are shown more as outlets for the products of a capitalist economy which is caught in the contradictions of unequal growth, than as a source of labour-power. In fact, Rosa Luxemburg (1913–15, 224/1972, 142) argues that the colonial countries are able to provide only an 'almost useless' proletariat to the industrialised nations. Lenin does not provide either an economic analysis of rural migration and its effects on the capitalist sector, although he often touches on the problem. This is what Balibar's article on Lenin and immigration reveals (1973): Lenin (1913, 1916) did note the historical reversal of a migratory trend in favour of increasing emigration of foreign workers towards the most industrialised nations but he dwelt mainly on the political effects of colonial exploitation on the working class (the formation of 'higher' and 'lower' strata and the development of working-class opportunism). It must also be said that the Second Congress of the Communist International in 1920 (1934. 54ff.) took up these issues again, and this time emphasised that the colonial exploitation of labour and of raw material was of such crucial importance for capitalism to prevent bankruptcy that 'surplus-value was sacrificed at home' in order to protect the profits arriving from the colonies, thereby gaining the complicity of the labour aristocracy. It also noted that foreign imperialism stood in the way of development, preventing, in the colonies, the formation of 'a proletarian class in the proper sense of the term [. . .] the vast majority of people being forced back into the countryside, thus compelled to devote themselves to agricultural work and to the production of raw materials for export'. At this period, the Congress only perceived 'a concentration of agricultural property creating a powerful mass of landless peasants', in other words *definitively* expropriated peasants; it remained unaware of what was to become the extended phenomenon of the rotating migration of labour.

4. *Without hearth or home: the rural exodus*

permanent migration

Labour-power is transferred from the non-capitalist to the capitalist economy in two ways: firstly by what is known as the rural exodus, and secondly, and more recently, by the organisation of rotating migration.

The rural exodus has affected and still affects millions of human beings in all areas of capitalist expansion. It emptied the English countryside, and throughout Europe it has turned peasants into a minority of the population. Until very recently in our history much of the labour force was reproduced in this way through the irreversible migration of peasants towards towns.

When primitive accumulation is achieved by expropriating peasants, the expansion of capitalism's sphere of influence is enough to produce and to renew part of its labour-power by bringing into its orbit an ever-increasing flood of 'labourers [who] enter the world as ready-made adults' (Marx 1867, I, p. 769). But if permanent migration is a way of reproducing freely part of the labour force available on the capitalist market, it does not contribute to its maintainance. The size of the labour force that entered the labour market in the above way was determined, not by demand from the industrial sector but by the pace of expropriation, bankruptcies or rural famines, and its arrival on the labour markets of Europe resulted in relative over-population which was worsened by increasing productivity of labour in the factories. Malthusianism, as we know, was born of this situation, of the fear of the bourgeoisie that they would be overwhelmed by the proletariat and the unemployed they had created (Mattelart, 1969). The excess workforce was left to poverty and death (Thompson, 1963), to charity, or forced to emigrate all over again into even more distant countries where these uprooted people – without hearth or home – expected to re-establish the conditions of country life. The history of the United Kingdom in the nineteenth century is a classic example of this kind of mechanism, by which the need for an industrial labour force was met by a flood of migrants from

107

the English and Irish countryside, which constantly brought fresh workers to the factory gates while the worn out and redundant migrated to the new lands of America or the dominions. Thus come what may, an even level of labour-power was maintained.[1] In Europe rural migration and the relative overpopulation that it caused were enough to exempt capital from having to create the institutions necessary to organise and manage the reproduction of the labour-power (and allowed economists to avoid examining the problems of this reproduction). This situation persisted until it became clear that the controlled supply of labour required some attention and that long-term emigration of workers into and outside the system, was lacking in flexibility and was likely to exacerbate, rather than alleviate, crises.

The cost of maintaining and reproducing this labour-power had to be resolved by setting up equalisation mechanisms, more and more sophisticated as the proletariat became more fully integrated into capitalist relations of production. Charity gave way to public assistance and finally – while the workers tried different forms of mutual aid – to social security. The latter was first set up at the level of groups of private firms (e.g. Krupp in the nineteenth century), then for all branches of industry and finally at the national level. Sometimes, until speculation on land developed, 'workers' gardens' were also supplied, returning workers to a semi-self-sustaining economy in which their free time was spent on producing some of their own food. This lowered the cost of labour-power for 'competition permits the capitalist to deduct from the price of the labour-power that which the family earns from its own little garden or field' (Engels [1872], p. 14).[2] Before they were completely urbanised, workers out of necessity continued, as far as they were able, to maintain ties with the land, via members of the family who remained in the country. The progressive destruction of the peasantry, the decline in rural emigration and the gradual weakening of the urban workers' ties with the countryside, correspond to the formation, within the industrial sector, of an increasingly stable proletariat, the counterpart of an integral capitalism, in which labour-power is produced, maintained and reproduced exclusively in the framework of capitalism. In which, in other words, labour is a commodity in every sense, according to Marx's schema.

These vast population-movements that marked the rise of industrial capitalism, these transfers of millions of man-hours to the

capitalist sector, have been and remain the driving-force of its
growth. Marx (1867, I, VIII) described its genesis in what he called
primitive accumulation; but the movement never stopped. Between
1800 and 1930 it has been estimated that 40 million people were
affected by migrations. The displacement of refugees after the
Second World War was responsible for a number of economic
'miracles', like the one in West Germany where population rose by
13 million (an increase of 25% in its active population). The return
of thousands of Japanese to their country after its defeat, along
with an unprecedented level of rural emigration[3] are two key
factors explaining the dynamism of the Japanese economy. All
these migratory movements coincided with a new wave of capitalist
expansion caused by the free input of labour-power that these
transfers to areas of employment represent. The other side to
these advantages (which lasts only as long as the immigrants' working lives) is a sharp increase in the cost of replacing this labour
force in the second generation, which has to be borne entirely by
the capitalist sector (Dupriez, 1973). The high price of stabilising
labour is very probably as much a part of the explanation for the
recession of the 1970s as is the so-called oil crisis.

5. Periodic migration:
the eternal return to the native land

In addition to this process which supplies the labour market by irreversible migration, through the destruction of the peasantry and of the domestic relations of production, an improved form of primitive accumulation has continued to increase in importance since the Second World War, to the particular benefit of European capitalism. This is temporary and rotating labour migration, which preserves and exploits the domestic agricultural economy.

During the early period of imperialist expansion the domestic mode of production suffered the same fate as feudalism and slavery. Whole populations were hunted down, and sometimes partly or entirely wiped out, to make room for colonial farms or business concessions; but this did not occur universally, nor was it immediate. For various historical reasons, particularly in colonies of exploitation, the land was safeguarded from private appropriation and numerous peoples remained in, and were sometimes returned to, their self-sustaining domestic mode of production. Certain groups even found themselves being freed from the exploitation of aristocratic classes which had been preying upon them. This was particularly true in Africa where as late as 1950 only 5% of the total surface area was exploited by colonialism. Even in the settler colonies of eastern and southern Africa the expansion of private property for the benefit of colonialists was limited by the creation of 'reserves'.

After trying various methods of exploitation – forced labour, business concessions, compulsory crop production – the returns from which were as mediocre as their application was brutal, one colonial strategy came into fairly widespread use all over Africa, which took advantage of the structured productive capacities of the domestic economy. The domestic economy, in fact, differs from other modes of production that are based on class and exploitative relations in that over the middle term it can be better exploited if it is preserved rather than destroyed. Exploitation of the domestic economy relied on two of its characteristics: on the one hand it is a collective, organised cell of production whose exploitation is more efficient than that of an individual; on the other hand, it produces surplus-labour.

The first point emerges relatively clearly from the analysis developed in the first part of this book. Since labour-power is the community's social product, then as long as one of its members is exploited (he or she continuing to belong to it) so are all the others. Exploitation does not operate only at the expense of an individual worker but, into the bargain, at the expense of the entire group to which he belongs.

As we have also seen, the domestic community produces an amount of surplus labour equivalent to the length of its 'free time' or to the difference between the work time it needs to produce its subsistence goods and means of production, and the time it takes to consume its produce; barring accident, this period is equivalent to the solar year. Surplus labour corresponds to the sum of energy E_r or $E_d + E_r$ in the argument presented above. The feudal lord or aristocrat who exploits the domestic community receives surplus labour in the form of labour rent, that is in terms of a supply of free labour time. According to Marx, labour rent exists when the worker divides his productive time between the self-sustaining activities necessary to support himself and his replacements, on the one hand, and the work carried out without return for a third party on the other. In cereal agriculture economies the division between labour time and free time is clearly delineated by the succession of one productive season and one dead season.[1]

The continuity and relatively long duration of the dead season make it easier for an exploiting class to mobilise peasants, but given the low level of the productive forces, limited use can be made of labour-power mobilised in this way, for it can be directed only into non-agricultural and off-season activities, like craft work, and building projects which are sometimes productive (dams, irrigation canals, granaries, etc.) and sometimes non-productive (fortresses, pyramids, etc.). Furthermore, to extract a maximum rent, the worker must remain close to his granaries and to his wives who prepare his daily food.

With technological progress the opportunities for extracting the labour-rent diversify and improve. In this respect, capitalism is in a better position to extract the rent than the feudal lord because it can use a more advanced agricultural technology, a wider range of industrial means and more efficient transportation which, taken together, allow it to spread its use of labour-power over the year.

Since aristocratic or feudal exploitation is partial and yields low returns, it eventually gives way to the more efficient forms of exploitation that colonial capitalism can introduce. Capitalists and aristocrats may temporarily ally to share the rent, each exploiting different parts of the population, or the whole population in turn. This alliance may be political when the aristocratic class are preserved by the colonial power on condition of their keeping order for it. In some cases, the aristocracy's income continues to be derived from its own modes of exploitation, but more frequently the coloniser maintains aristocrats by paying them a salary taken from the income gained from colonial exploitation. Even though there may be a tactical alliance there is never 'articulation' between aristocratic and capitalist modes of production which are, essentially, in competition.[2]

For capitalism to benefit from labour-rent, a way must be found of extracting it without simultaneously destroying the self-sustaining economy and the domestic relations of production which produce the rent. This involves drawing off labour-power in such a way that domestic reproduction of the labour force is not, by its partial absorption into the capitalist sector, put at risk.[3] There are therefore limitations to this kind of exploitation.

Labour-power thus extracted can be used in various ways: to grow export goods if this can be done mainly or wholly outside the periods of subsistence production (or by moving the workers to areas with a different climate during the dead season); or to the production of non-agricultural goods, which do not depend on the seasons. One corresponds to the development of cash cropping, the other, which I am about to examine, to the organisation of rotating labour migration.[4]

Before looking at the practical conditions under which this particular form of the exploitation of labour can function and its limitations, we ought to try to characterise it by means of a few hypothetical cases.

Suppose that an entrepreneur, owning capitalist means of production, buying the component parts of his fixed capital and selling his products on the capitalist market, makes peasants work in his firm or on his lands during the dead season of their agricultural cycle; suppose also that these peasants live close enough to their own houses to feed themselves daily from their reserves. This peculiar capitalist would not need to pay wages or invest in the agricultural sector to sustain, maintain and reproduce the labour-power he employed: this would be done entirely by the work of the peasants themselves. He would use fixed capital but no variable capital; he would enjoy a labour-rent, but no surplus-value. This apparently aberrant hypothetical case is nevertheless almost exactly the model for the forced labour by which, on colonial farms for instance, unpaid workers and their families till their plots, close to the farm, in order to feed themselves. In practice, however, peasants are compelled, by means of constraint, to give their labour free, and the cost of these operations, generally borne by the colonial authorities who controlled the forces of repression, is necessarily deducted from profits derived from exploiting them (Meillassoux 1964, Chapter XII).

More often the worker is taken to work in places far from his home. If (still with reference to the dead season) the worker is away from home for more than a day (i.e. for longer than permits him to reconstitute his energy from access to food produced by his community), the employer must provide him with food or with the means to buy it; he must be paid in proportion to the time he works. In this case labour rent cannot be realised in its entirety for the (very small) sum given to the worker for food must be deducted from it.

In a third case, when the worker migrates for longer than the dead season, his community's subsistence production falls by an amount corresponding to what he would have produced during the agricultural season. Such a worker costs his employer more, for, to maintain the conditions for reproducing labour-power in the domestic sector, the latter has to pay wages which, in addition to the cost of reconstituting immediate labour power, should also cover the loss to the domestic food-producing sector of the worker's labour while he is employed in the capitalist sector. Finally, there is the worker who no longer returns to his original community but settles definitively in the capitalist sector – this is the case of permanent migration.

To summarise, we can therefore distinguish three variants by which labour rent is extracted by the capitalist.

(1) The worker is employed in the capitalist sector only during the dead season and lives upon food from his domestic stores throughout this period. The employer is in a position to extract from him labour rent equivalent to E_r, if not $E_d + E_r$. This form of

113

labour exploitation is analogous to corvée labour, the capitalist replacing the feudal lord.

(2) The worker is employed in the capitalist sector only during the dead season but he works relatively far from his home and cannot feed himself from domestic supplies. The value of the subsistence goods with which the worker is provided by his employer during his period of employment (to reconstitute his immediate labour-power) must therefore be subtracted from the rent. For the worker the situation is slightly better, to the extent that he can save some of the supplies of the domestic community.

(3) The worker is employed in the capitalist sector for a period longer than the dead season. Thus, over and above the subsistence needed to reconsistute his immediate labour-power during his period of employment, he should be paid an amount equivalent to what he did not produce because he was absent during the productive period. The exploitation of labour in such conditions means that, on a *pro rata* basis relative to *the migrant's age and the time he is employed in the capitalist sector*, there is a transfer from the domestic to the capitalist sector of: (a) A proportional fraction of αA_0 equivalent to the market value of the subsistence goods and care invested by his kin in breeding him as a producer of labour-power; (b) A proportional fraction of αB_1 which is the market value of the subsistence goods consumed by the worker during his periods of unemployment spent in the domestic sector (including stoppages, illness, incapacity); (c) All of αC_1, for his 'retirement', which will be taken care of by his own work or by that of his kin.[5]

There is clearly a major difference between the first and second variants. In the first case, the corvée worker is not paid; in the second he receives a wage. In the first case, the employer clearly enjoys only a labour rent; in the second, his profit does not show as a free rent but as a surplus-value made up of the difference between the price of the subsistence goods consumed by the worker during his working period and the price of the goods produced by the worker in the same period. What has happened to the rent?

The rent still exists because the wages paid by the employer only cover the immediate reconstitution of labour-power.[6] The employer's profit would, if it was limited to surplus-value, be reduced by the totals enumerated in (a), (b) and (c). The colonial employer enjoys another indirect source of profit (not possessed

114

by his metropolitan counterpart who employs migrants from the same colony) deriving from the fact that the subsistence goods bought on the local market, if they are produced in the domestic sector, will be sold below their value because of the labour rent they also contain.[7]

On a theoretical level, the fact that labour-power of the producer is used for his immediate sustenance through his production of use values, means that we cannot assimilate this labour-power with an abstract labour subjected to the general equalisation of prices in the capitalist sphere. The use of time as a measure of labour is not directly relevant. This is what allows the domestic sector to survive, despite its low productivity, even embedded within the capitalist system. Furthermore this situation maintains the distinctive features of the self-sustaining food sector, as a producer of use values.[8]

In a general way, it can therefore be stated that when a worker is employed simultaneously in self-sustaining agriculture and in paid employment in the capitalist sector, he produces both labour-rent and surplus-value. The first derives from the free transfer of labour-power produced in the domestic economy to the capitalist sector of production; the second from exploiting the producer's labour-power bought by the capitalist. The labour-rent does not show itself as such because the worker does not supply in succession his employer with one period of free labour and one period of paid labour: he only supplies one period of cheap labour time. Furthermore rent is realised simultaneously with the surplus-value and at the *pro rata* of the hours of work for which he is paid. Finally, in the hands of the capitalist, rent and surplus-value combine in a single profit. We know, however, that despite this method of extracting rent, indistinguishable in appearance from extraction of surplus-value, the labour rent is still there, since, over a longer period than that of his current employment, the worker divides his labour-power between self-production at home and the production of commodities for his employer in the workshop.

This distinction has considerable social and political implications, for *rent is not realised in the same way as surplus-value* and does not require the same institutions. To extract labour rent the complex and particular mechanics of *rotating migration* must be set in motion, a *double labour market* established and an efficient *discriminatory ideology* maintained.

115

The book on immigrants edited by Centre Socialiste de Documentation et d'Etudes sur le Problèmes du Tiers Monde (1975) contains the basis for an economic analysis of migration, but the first part concludes in classical fashion by explaining differences in wages in terms of differences in standards of living (pp. 33, 34). It is not Marx but the bourgeoisie who use the kind of argument which says that: 'These people don't have the same needs as we do.' It is also tautological, since needs are not expressed at the level of the individual nor of the particular milieu in which he lives, but in relation to the social needs of social reproduction in general, in this case those of the capitalist mode of production. Marx in fact explains that the conditions under which labour-power is reproduced, are located, *for any one society*, in a given historical context which changes over time and which justifies the demands of the integrated proletariat for higher wages as conditions improve, not simply because this is fair, but because the general progress of production must depend on a concomitant development of the productive forces of which the proletariat is itself a part. One cannot therefore explain, let alone justify, the low wages paid to some groups, when they are employed in the capitalist economic sphere, by reference to the poverty existing in their countries of birth – poverty of which the low wages are the cause, not the consequence.

Further on, the authors add: 'by fixing lower wages . . . the employers pay immigrant workers' labour below their value in France, that is in terms of an amount of goods which would not generally be considered as able to reconstitute their labour-power – but which are acceptable in their own countries'.[9] This analysis therefore excludes the possibility that a worker may be overexploited through this same method in 'his own country'. The reference to 'unequal exchange' shows that, as far as the writers are concerned, economic relations are between nation states and not between 'modes of production'. Finally, the first part fails to distinguish between permanent and rotating migration. However, in the analysis dealing with African workers (CEDETIM, 1975, 205ff.). one finds a correct understanding of the problem which avoids the pitfalls of economism.

6. The maintenance of labour-reserves

Several conditions must simultaneously be satisfied in both the area of emigration and the capitalist labour market in order that *systematic*, and not occasional over-exploitation of labour takes place through the double extraction of a labour-rent and surplus-value.

In the area of emigration such conditions are connected to the whole or partial preservation of self-sustaining agriculture and domestic relations of production. For this to happen, capitalists must, paradoxically, block the extension of capitalism into the rural areas which supply labour. How much importance capitalism attaches to this method of exploitation can be judged by the preparations made in this context by the racist states of east and southern Africa, where prosperity over the last three-quarters of a century had been based on exploiting these 'reserves of black labour' (Murcier, 1973) – reserves which are even more rewarding than diamond and gold mines.[1]

In settler colonies portions of the colonised territory, protected against private ownership by settlers, are turned into 'reserves' within which the African population is confined. Called land reserves, they are really reserves of labour, until now pillars of the racist states' political economy.[2] Under the pretence of preserving the conditions of 'tribal' life the authorities try, by suitable laws, to block the growth of private landed property and the formation of capitalist relations of production. According to its size, each family receives, in principle, a plot of land to live on – *one man one plot*. These plots are subject to rigorous restrictions; they cannot be sold, which prevents their concentration in the hands of a local class of landowners, and it is forbidden to employ paid labour on them or to undertake cash cropping. Furthermore, the circulation of money in the reserves is reduced to a minimum, thus preventing any concentration of capital which might lead to changes in the relations of production or a shift of labour-power toward lucrative activities within the reserves.[3] The theorists of British colonialism formulated the philosophy behind these policies: 'It is clearly to the advantage of the mines that native labourers should be encouraged to return to their homes after the completion of the ordinary period of service. The maintenance of the system under which the mines are able to obtain unskilled labour at a rate less than ordinarily paid in industry depends upon this, for otherwise the subsidiary means of subsistence would disappear and the labourer would tend to become a permanent resident upon the Witwatersrand, with increased requirements . . .' (From a report of the *Mine Native Wages Commission*, quoted by Shapera, 1947, 204). Another official report from Uganda (1954) explains that: 'It is policy whenever practicable to leave the care of the destitutes and the disabled in the hands of the tribal clan and family organisation which have traditionally accepted this responsibility.' (Quoted by Mukherjee, 1956, 198) The principle is obvious; legal and repressive means must be used to preserve an area in which labour-power can reproduce itself, but strictly at subsistence level. Drawn out of the reserves to obtain cash in exchange for their labour-power the workers are only accepted for short periods in the sector of capitalist employment, so that they do not become a charge for the employer. In this way, a situation is created whereby thousands of workers move permanently between the reserves and the mining and industrial areas. This economic policy can be established without an institutionalised reserve system. 'Natural' reserves form by themselves in colonised regions where they are not threatened directly by capitalist appropriation and still untouched by the development of cash-cropping. Such is the case in colonies of exploitation, in areas which are too far from transport lines and unsuitable for export agriculture, and where there are few colonists. In addition to its reserves, South Africa also used the labour of people from Mozambique and Angola whose cyclical migration was organised by the Portuguese colonial administration. In present-day French neo-colonies similar natural reserves have formed, as in Haute-Volta which supplies the Ivory coast and Ghana with seasonal agriculture labour,[4] and particularly in the Senegal and Faleme valleys which export tens of thousands of Malians, Senegalese and Mauritanians to France (CEDETIM, 1975, 205ff.). In these reserves, which are growing larger all the time and now extend to Niger and Tchad, the inhabitants have nothing else to sell but their labour-power. Their cash needs (to pay taxes, to buy local goods which used to be bartered, to replace craft by industrial products, etc.) force them to enter the capitalist market. Since land remains available and conditions of subsistence production change little, domestic relations of production persist because they are the only ones able to support the survival and perpetuation of their communities. What the racist legislature in South Africa attempts to maintain by force is achieved here by relative neglect which, condemning the peasants to creeping poverty, drives them out of their villages.

7. The double labour market and segregation

Drawn now into the capitalist sector by necessity, then driven back into the domestic sector by powerful economic drives, these peasant-proletarians form a distinctive labour force, in relation to which an equally distinctive mode of exploitation has evolved.

Both in overtly racist regimes, such as South Africa or Rhodesia, and in European countries, we meet the same conditions of employment of migrants. To extract labour-rent requires precise, and therefore identical mechanisms, institutions and ideologies. These are the double labour market on the one hand, the rotation of the rural labour force on the other, achieved through periodic discharge back to the domestic sector, and the racist ideology necessary to support these policies.

The *double labour market* sets out to divide the proletariat into two categories corresponding to the forms of exploitation which are experienced: that of the workers who are *integrated* (or stabilised) and who reproduce wholly within the capitalist sector; that of the migrants who only partly reproduce themselves within it. This double market takes shape around various forms of discrimination.

The first major discrimination relies on the distinction between direct and indirect wages. Family allowances, unemployment benefits, costs resulting from illness or accidents at work, pensions, are allocated in a discriminatory way; various pretexts are given to refuse all or some of them to those workers expected to maintain and reproduce themselves wholly or in part outside the capitalist sector.

This policy is actually practised in the racist states of Africa, and to varying degrees by European governments which employ an immigrant workforce. Thus, the French government pays its immigrant workers three or four times less in indirect wages than French workmen would receive in similar conditions.

The second major sort of discrimination springs from the fact

120

The double labour market

that employers maintain an unstable labour policy in some branches and sectors of industry where they pay low wages so as to deter integrated workers – who, since they are completely dependent upon the market, could not in any case survive on such incomes. These industries therefore attract only those workers who reckon themselves well off to have a job and can rely on the support of their rural kinfolk.[1] French employers recognise this double labour market explicitly: 'foreign labour is often employed in temporary jobs [. . .] *it does not have job-security* [. . .] It thus constitutes a kind of *second labour market* which is flexible and very busy' (*Entreprise*, no. 948, 9 November 1973). As another consequence of this, immigrants' wages are 20–30% lower than those of integrated workers (*id.*).

Various procedures are employed to reinforce, guide and facilitate the operation of the double labour market. In particular there is the cultivation of racist and xenophobic prejudices among the population of the host countries. These prejudices class foreign workers as being *a priori* unskilled and result in their being arbitrarily directed into the most badly paid and *least stable* employment. Racism, xenophobia and other ideologies of discrimination, are indeed vital to the operation of the double labour market (Wolpe, 1972). In particular it is the function of fascistic political parties and papers to carry out this vile job for capitalism by maintaining in host countries the atmosphere of racism that is essential for the over-exploitation of the so-called underdeveloped peoples.[2] In this way employers and governments take advantage of the contradiction which is forced upon them by this type of over-exploitation (whereby they simultaneously have to attract and expel foreign rural-born workers): they claim to arbitrate between racists and immigrants, sometimes being hard on, more often tolerating or leaving alone the groups which specialise in racist murders, but never taking measures which could crush this unacknowledged repression which is indispensable for the realisation of surplus-profit.[3]

The second function of racism, quite as important, is to keep this over-exploited section of the proletariat, who would have every reason to rebel and turn to violence, in a state of fear. Surrounded by a hostile population and targets of their workmates' prejudices, immigrant workers find themselves in a social environment which makes it difficult for them to put forward their demands and to demonstrate publicly.

Finally, racism helps to delay class consciousness by opposing

121

immigrants against the indigenous workers or against other immigrants on the basis of their ethnic differences or national identity to which they are referred for self-recognition, identity, and organisation.

The rotation of the migrant labour force is thus achieved by these forms of discrimination which, through depriving the immigrant worker of both social- and job-security, force him to return home. Administrative measures and certain illegal practices used by employers reinforce this constraint. Work-permits are granted only for limited periods and renewed only on specific conditions. The 'pass' system operating in South Africa by which African workers are moved about as it suits their racist employers, is matched in France by the various permits (residence-permit, work-permit) which leave the immigrant worker vulnerable to the hazards of police, administrative and employers' control and make it easier to fix their length of stay in accordance with the needs of economy.

These are efficient methods since it is estimated that immigrant workers stay an average of three years in France. In conjunction with other forms of manipulation (the blind eye turned to illegal immigration, the police and employer intimidation from which workers suffer as a result, and arbitrary expulsions which deprive them of the benefits of long service, etc.), they make immigrant workers strangers, not only in relation to the host population but in relation to the working class to which they belong.

Finally, numerous clauses in the legislation of labour-importing countries restrict the entry of wives and children and discourage immigrant workers (from certain countries) from settling in the land in which they are employed.[4]

The same mechanism of rotating migration operates either within a single country, between rural and urban areas, or at the international level between predominantly rural and industrialised countries. It lies behind the massive and continually increasing movements of population between Africa and Europe since the Second World War. These are the migrations that certain backward, blind or collaborationist sociologists continue to attribute to 'native mentality' or to 'tradition'. These 'hindrances on economic progress' which experts so freely attribute to 'mentality' or 'custom' and which serve as blanket explanations for the repeated checks to their so-called development projects, are in fact the products of a situation which is imposed on dependent peasantries and to which they try to adapt as best they can.[5]

Another effect of the double labour market is 'flexibility' which is the result of instability and which has become a feature of the cheap labour market. The numbers of active immigrant workers vary with the economic conjuncture of the countries which employ them. They can be reduced during troughs by banning or restricting immigration and by refusing to renew the contracts of those workers who are already employed. In this way the host countries are in a position to export their unemployment to the poorer countries which bear its costs for them.[6] When the economic situation is favourable, in contrast, immigration is encouraged, restrictions are lifted and controls relaxed.

It is an integral part of the French government's employment policies to use immigrant workers as an industrial reserve army of labour, as 'free-floating labour', as a mass of employees acting as a buffer. In 1972, when he was President of the French Republic, G. Pompidou stated this clearly: 'Immigration allows us to reduce some of the pressure on the labour market and alleviate social tension.'[7]

8. The profits from immigration

Table I gives some of the figures for immigration in Europe, and concerns immigrants of all nationalities. No distinction is made between permanent and rotating migration.

Table I. *Foreign population in seven European countries*

	Total foreign population (number)	Per cent of total population	Active foreign population (number)	Per cent of total population
	A	B	C	D
France, 1973	3,775,000	7	1,800,000	8
Germany, 1973	3,600,000	5.9	2,345,000	10.9
Belgium, 1971	720,000	7	220,000	7.2
Netherlands	204,000	1.6	125,000	3.2
United Kingdom	2,580,000	4.7	1,782,000	7.3
Sweden, 1972	417,000	5.1	220,000	5.6
Switzerland, 1971	1,000,000	16.1	865,000	28.8

Source: *Entreprise*, no. 948, 9 November 1973.

The number of single immigrants is considerable. According to the 1968 census of the immigrant population in France there were 720,740 unmarried men plus 53,960 widowers and divorcees, in other words, out of 1,618,340 individuals, 774,700 were single men. Out of 1,405,720 female immigrants, 581,880 were single (Morokvasic, 1974). The importance of this non-integrated group can be seen by comparing column D and Column B in Table I: the number of *active* immigrants as compared to the number of *active* individuals in the total population is always greater than the entire immigrant population in relation to the total population. A relatively simple computation gives us the theoretically minimum number of single immigrants. If the active foreign population was involved in minimum family relations (a spouse and two children) which would ensure simple reproduction, then if we take 20% of

124

female immigrants as being active (this is the average percentage of active female immigrants in France; Morovasic, 1974), the active members would be A/3.8. The difference between C (the real active population) and A/3.8 thus represents the estimated minimum number of workers who are unable to obtain the conditions for their own reproduction in the country where they work.

If we apply these ratios to the figures in Table I we get the results shown in Table II.

Table II

	A/3.8	(C-A/3.8) Single people	Per cent of single people
France	992,000	808,000	44
Germany	925,000	1,420,000	61
Belgium	211,000	9,000	4.3
Netherlands	50,100	75,000	60
United Kingdom	985,000	797,000	45
Sweden	150,000	70,000	32
Switzerland	320,000	545,000	63

Some of these computations seem to be supported by other evidence: 60% of immigrants in West Germany in fact stay for only two years at a time and in Switzerland only 20% of immigrants remain more than four consecutive years.

Huge profits are made by international capitalism through these movements of population. According to Luas (1970) world capitalism draws 40 million dollars worth of profits from labour immigration.

The magazine *Entreprise* (no. 948, November 1973) claims that since 'the host country does not have to pay for the upbringing and the education of the immigrants', and given that the cost of breeding each French worker to the age of 18 is approximately 150,000 francs, during the period of the VIth Plan (1971–5) the French economy would appear to have benefitted from a free input of 90 billion Francs, corresponding to 600,000 immigrants.

This latter calculation, like that of Luas, is not altogether accurate since it assumes that the immigrant workers settle and spend their entire active lives in the host country. The contribution should however be calculated according to the immigrants age *pro rata* and the length of his period of employment. But as we have seen, sending him back to the domestic community from time to time saves capitalism part of the cost of maintenance, reproduction

and retirement that is paid to permanent workers.[1] According to
Entreprise family allowances awarded to immigrants are three to
four times lower than those which are given to French people,
which represents a saving of more than two billion Francs in social
security, an amount that gives only a slight indication of the real
profits made on migrant labour.[2]

The profits resulting from rotating migration can be estimated
more accurately in two ways; they are equivalent to the cost of
the labour time socially necessary for the reproduction and maintenance of an equivalent labour-power *within the capitalist sphere
of production.* Alternatively they represent the total indirect wage
which would be paid to integrated workers who would have to do
the same work as rotating migrants, in addition to the difference in
wages between the two categories of workers (the loss which
results from the lower productivity of this workforce is due to
savings made in the cost of their training and may not therefore
be taken into account).

Since the beginning of the colonial period this surplus product
has been appropriated by the capitalist class and colonialist countries. As the continuous process of primitive accumulation extends
to an ever increasing number of peoples, it deprives them of the
means to achieve industrial take off. Colonialism and neo-colonialism continue to allow the capitalist powers to benefit from this
continuously regenerated mechanism. Today, thanks to the rotating system of migration, the colonial and European bourgeoisie
have succeeded in controlling and managing a situation which,
barely a century ago was explosive. Beneath their apparent anarchy,
migrations are organised to coincide with the needs of international capitalism and operate for its profits.

9. The limits of the over-exploitation of labour

Clearly a more or less artificially maintained zone of self-sustenance can only be preserved within an expanding capitalist economy and only for a critical transitory period. The limits of such a
situation can be observed in the emigration areas under varying
circumstances, according to whether they are closed zones, where
access to land is limited by the narrowness of the territory, or if
they remain open. In any case, due to the very fact of emigration,
the domestic sector slowly degenerates and its capacity to reproduce itself and to provide a continuous supply of labour power to
the market are eventually compromised.

It is not our intention here to write a history of the way in
which colonised peoples were drawn into capitalist exploitation.[1]
We should remember however that in contrast to the European
experience the expropriation of land was not everywhere the
cause of exploitation. Other methods of coercion were employed
to drive labour out of the villages: taxes which forced people to
look for cash only available in the colonial sector; forced labour,
whose importance is still underestimated (Hopkins, 1973), recruitment, debt, etc., all these methods served to establish an irreversible rural dependence. Craft work (weaving or smithing for instance) and subsidiary activities (building, hunting, gathering) were
gradually abandoned in favour of paid (or wage-earning) activities,
making the domestic sector dependent for the supply of essential
goods on the colonial sector. The growth of the cash economy
exacerbated the situation as one item, currency, which originated
in the colonial sector, pervaded every transaction even within the
domestic community. At the same time none of the productive
efforts exacted from the peasants were ever accompanied by measures likely to increase the productivity either of subsistence agriculture or of land or labour. In such circumstances the peasant
does not migrate under administrative compulsion. He enters the
colonial sector because of the economic conditions which prevail

127

in his home area and, in particular, because there is no other way to increase production but through an increase in labour. In other words, *because of the impossibility of introducing progress within the domestic sector.*

On the other hand, because its means of production are much more efficient, the capitalist industrial sector is able to offer a wage whose purchasing power is superior to the market value of goods produced in the domestic sector in the same length of time. To attract the rural labourer it is enough to offer a wage which *partially* reflects the difference in productivity between the two sectors. Provided the wage is less than the average price of labour-power in the capitalist market, then both labour-rent and surplus-value will be realised.

In this way, once the rural economy begins to be dependent on the industrial sector, this clamp-down on the domestic sector of production, whether it is intentional or not, will, in combination with the increasing productivity of the capitalist sector, and independent of any coercion, set the migratory process going. For the worker from a rural background, the wages available in the capitalist sector have at least two advantages: (1) he has access to cash which is scarce and 'dear' in the domestic sector, and through which he can gain access to goods which replace craft products; (2) the prospect of a relatively higher income compared to that which is possible for him using the same labour-power within the domestic mode of production. Certainly, when making such a calculation, the rural labourer omits to count the labour-rent which he gives to the capitalist, just as the latter omits to pay it to him. Through this exploitation, his immediate income is nonetheless raised because, on average, the productivity of his labour has been increased.[2] In short, and even in the medium term, employment in the capitalist sector can deceive the rural worker. He is over-exploited but the difference in productivity between the sector from which he originates and the sector in which he works is great enough for his immediate gains to encourage him to endure the sacrifices required by his life of semi-exile, the hard and dangerous work imposed on him and the housing and health conditions of which he is a victim. His real misery is less obvious. It comes from the insecurity of his employment, from the fact that he cannot settle and live with his family, from uncertainty regarding his old age. Because of his position in the labour market, in fact, the advantage he derives from working in the capitalist sector can only be precarious and temporary because, *and this is the condition which enables the realisation of the rent, he cannot enjoy job security.*

This fact, the job insecurity of the migrant proletariat in the capitalist sector, eventually also destroys the conditions for reproduction of the rent within the domestic sector.

(i) The poverty datum-line

Unable to integrate organically within the capitalist sector, the immigrant worker must preserve his home community, so as to be able to benefit from its produce during his visits and to maintain the economic structures which allow him to offer his labour-power cheaply to the capitalist sector. It is therefore important that the domestic community does not cease production while he is away. The population must retain sufficient balance and capacity to divide its forces between the domestic and capitalist sectors of production, and to compensate for the loss of production from one sector to the other, and vice versa according to the situation.[3] When periods of migration last for more than a year, the domestic community, almost permanently deprived of part of its working population, does not find that its subsistence needs diminish in proportion to the reduction in consumption which results from these absences. For the production βB of an active producer during the productive months not only covers his own annual consumption but all or part of that of his dependents and elders as well. The working population which is left behind has to make up this deficit in production in various ways – people previously idle help with agricultural labour, periods of activity are extended, and fallow periods on land close to the village are shortened to make more intensive use of the time available. Since, because of the dual impoverishment of both people and land, these methods prove increasingly unable to ensure the community's subsistence, a growing proportion of the money provided by migrant workers is spent on buying subsistence goods on the market or, in other cases, on employing seasonal workers to bring fallow land under cultivation.[4] The monetarisation of the economy which thus establishes itself further increases the need for cash by transforming goods, formerly bartered, into merchandise, thus inducing an irreversible process.

It is at this point that the overall prices policy for subsistence goods in the areas of emigration comes in. In open land reserves, where there is no strict limit on access to land, it is necessary, in order to encourage the peasant to seek paid employment, to ensure that the price of the foodstuffs on the market does not rise so high that he is led to concentrate exclusively on strictly subsistence agriculture which can cover both food and cash requirements. Besides, a rise in the price of subsistence goods also raises the price of the labour of those workers who purchase food in the local or national market. Maintaining subsistence foods at a low price is particularly necessary when the country of emigration produces export crops, so that the production of marketable foodstuffs is not discouraged.[5] This policy is only possible through importing subsidised food or grains produced in conditions of high productivity. It is today thus the only means by which an increasing number of underdeveloped countries can feed their urban populations. Numerous consequences follow from such a situation. Apart from the fact that it makes the importing countries totally dependent on the food-exporting countries (and notably on the United States),[6] an imbalance between local subsistence resources and demographic growth is created which can only be corrected by a continuous and adapted supply of food which depends entirely on the goodwill of the great powers. Food aid leads in this way to a sort of stock breeding of labour reserves, whose size and survival depend on the capitalist countries which only invest for economic or strategic reasons.

'Food aid' and the insecurity induced by the inherent instability of the immigrant workers' situation are the basic reasons for the high rate of natality observed among these populations. Demographic growth, a symptom of the crisis in the domestic economy, is one way of holding at bay an uncertain future.[7] We have seen how in the domestic society, this future was provided for by reinvesting the product of labour in future agricultural producers. Workers of rural origin long retain this same hope of seeing their children provide for their old age according to the values of kinship ideology.[8]

In this insecure situation the use of money is equally uncertain. The preservation of the community as a unit of production and reproduction entails that money is used for what Balandier (1959, 38) has called 'sociological investment' intended 'to gain or to reinforce the dominance of traditional forms' (bridewealth payments, generous contributions to the Islamic faith, pilgrimages to Mecca, gifts, matrimonial assistance, etc.) and through which domestic and village relations are best maintained. However, since the objective conditions of migrant labour adversely affect the conditions for social reproduction and the security associated with

130

it, money comes to be seen as a means of speculation likely to p.
vide an income and insure against the future. Buying taxis, o.
urban shanties, and taking up small-scale retailing are increasingly
seen as possible alternatives, sometimes by people who have no
idea of how such investments need to be managed. This quest for
profit is usually an individual project undertaken without the
knowledge of other kinsmen and affines, which 'isolate the "entrepreneur" from his home milieu' (Balandier, 1959, 38) while it sur-
renders those who opt for it to people (businessmen, shopkeepers,
usurers) alien to them, operating within a system which they do
not understand and over which they have no hold. Once resort to
money from the capitalist sector is accepted as a means of long-
term saving, the degeneration of the domestic economy accelerates.
Each individual saving for himself so as to supply his future needs
as a retired worker, does so to the detriment of the present maintenance of his community. The portion of the product intended to
feed future producers in the community cycle is made, through
individual monetary saving, into an amount which is consecrated
to an uncertain future without being reinvested meanwhile in the
domestic productive cycle. A proportion of the domestic social
product is thus diverted: from a domestic investment it is transformed into a capitalistic 'savings' of which the management and
interest are transferred to the business sector, and to the manipula-
tors of money. Extended diversion of funds in this way helps to
aggravate the crisis which domestic communities suffer under the
impact of colonial capitalism.

The combination of all these factors drive these populations out
of the domestic economy. When the process by which the conditions of production degenerate is accelerated, the turnover of
workers also tends to be faster. An increasing proportion of food
is bought on the market. If wages in the capitalist sector do not
rise - and there is no reason for them to adapt to such a far-off
and localised situation - real wages decline, irrespective of any
price increase. These workers' wages are determined not so much
by the amount of labour-power they supply, as by changes in
prices, in wages and in exchange rates. A point will be reached
when the return on domestic agriculture is too low, the cost of
transport to centres of employment too high and the composition
of the family unit too disproportionate in age and sex for it to
remain the support for the reproduction of labour-power. An ever-
widening fringe of the domestic economy, doomed to bankruptcy,
survives only because of the effort and costly sacrifices of its men

and women who have no other place in which to take refuge or live, while an ever-increasing proportion of workers drift out of reach of the domestic economy and lose the benefit of the resources which it could offer them.[9] If these workers gain access only to the bottom end of the labour market, to the most unstable and lowest paid jobs, they no longer find in any sector, domestic or capitalist, the means of their reproduction. They become what certain sociologists have termed 'marginal'. They are in truth, authentic proletarians, they make up the greater part of the industrial reserve army of labour, sentenced, by reason of their position on the labour market, to a regressive situation of non-reproduction, in other words, in some circumstances to absolute poverty.[10]

When we are dealing with territorially limited 'reserves' subject to *ad hoc* legislation, like those in South Africa for example, the relatively small size of these areas makes it impossible to bring new land into cultivation. It also gradually makes the domestic economy's cultural techniques for restoring the soil (by shifting cultivation, long fallow periods, mixed cattle–cultivation, etc.) impractical. The preconditions for domestic agricultural production decline with increasing rapidity. When the migrant workers' wages no longer cover the loss of agricultural production, poverty sets in and increases to the point at which the physical reproduction of workers is put at risk (Meillassoux, 1980).

The great cyclical migrations in southern Africa started in the 1930s. By the 1940s the Rand mines were already concerned about 'increasing poverty in the Transkei reserves which was undermining health in one of their principal labour reserves' (Gluckman, 1940).[11] To 'remedy' this situation it was decided to extend recruitment to the Portuguese colonies which had not until then been prospected. As a result, the wages of South African workers in some sectors, such as mining, which employs the largest proportion of men, have in some cases not been raised for more than 20 years, because these workers are paid at the same rates as workers recruited more recently in Angola or Mozambique (Wilson, 1972). In other words no account was taken of the fact that economic conditions in the reserves, which originally justified the low wages, have since declined below the level which prevails in more recently prospected rural areas.

On 12 March 1973, the *Guardian* revealed that: 'The majority of British companies in South Africa are paying substantial numbers of their African workers below officially recognised subsistence levels.' In other words below the rate at which malnutrition is unavoidable. Indeed an enquiry revealed that the children of these employees did show symptoms of advanced malnutrition. An official inquiry was set up in Great Britain and the companies involved were instructed to raise their wages. Of the hundred companies investigated only three paid wages over the minimum level that provides against malnutrition: 60% of the money invested in South Africa is British.

This situation seldom emerges into public view because of the blackout imposed on information about the reserves, but it is in fact widespread in South Africa, to the extent that the South African government and economists occasionally voice concern (cf. Van der Horst, 1942; South Africa, 1944). But their concern has not helped to improve things, however, as attempts were made since then to define a 'poverty datum line' below which labour-power ceases to reproduce itself (B.I.A.A., 1975).

Capitalism faces a difficult contradiction here. Improving lands in the reserves by supplying fertiliser bought on the capitalist market involves capital and creates the risk of changing social relations in areas which are supposed to be left out of capitalist development. If it makes these economies dependent on the capitalist market, it could destroy their capacity to produce labour rent. But if, on the other hand, this agriculture is left alone it will decline and this also means giving up the cheap labour-power it produces. This situation has become critical in South Africa's reserves and it is what pushes the racist government to look for other solutions. Hence the 'Homelands', territories which are constitutionally distinct from the Republic. In this way, the white Republic will be able to transfer the economic cost and political responsibility for the areas which produce labour onto the black workers themselves. It will also provide a dumping ground, to which the unemployed or the recalcitrant can be driven back. Thus the regime will create a 'neo-colonial' situation, closer to that which exists between European states and the former colonies. This is the meaning of the shift from 'segregation' to 'apartheid', (Wolpe, *op. cit.* and 1972) or to 'separate development'.

(ii) The objective criterion for the division of the proletariat

In all cases, whether we are talking of open or closed reserves, the over-exploitation of labour, and the exhaustion of both men and land that this involves, supports a process of differentiation within

133

the international working class. Continuously supplied with cheap labour through the 'development' of new rural areas and populations, the capitalist system induces a continuous flood of workers deprived of their economic and social means of production, but not yet incorporated into the capitalist labour market. Thus we can distinguish three major groups of the proletariat according to their ability to reproduce within the capitalist sector.

The first is the integrated or stabilised proletariat, which receives both direct and indirect wages, that is, the proletariat whose labour-power is in theory bought at its price of production.

The second is formed by the proletarian-peasant who receives from capitalism only the means for the daily reconstitution of his immediate labour-power, but not for his maintenance and reproduction; these he obtains for himself within the framework of the domestic economy.

The third is composed of the proletariat which has no means of reproducing itself in any sector.

The level of class consciousness, the behaviour, the demands and union tactics of these three groups will be different. The first will insist on preservation of its standard of living, of the advantages it has acquired in relation to the other two categories of workers; it will demand a larger share of capitalist profit and, sometimes, in the most advanced sectors, control over production and working conditions. The second will demand above all better working conditions and lodging during periods of employment, but to the extent that it plans to fall back upon the rural community at home it will develop relatively little class consciousness. In a social and political crisis the third group may become pugnacious if it becomes aware that its own survival depends upon obtaining wages from capitalist employers which will permit it to reach the position of integrated labour.

The battle for economic integration and the acquisition of the means of reproduction from within the capitalist system, the battle for work and wages and for security, has been the major theme of the history of the labour movement. It confirms that one important section of the working class has long been composed of a non-stable proletariat, and that it is still so composed wherever claims of these kinds are being put forward. This makes sense of Lenin's analysis of the political content of union struggles; the demand to be integrated into the capitalist system, the insistence that the latter should bear the full costs of the proletariat, is not in itself

134

revolutionary because it <u>does not challenge the system itself</u>; it only claims for the working class the place to which it is logically assigned by capitalist relations of production.

(iii) Competition

The use of a non-stable and non-integrated proletariat is not without problems for the capitalist sector of employment.[12] The employers' problem is to calculate the nature and amount of investment that should be made in branches that employ an immigrant work force which is barely trained and semi-educated, not only because the latter comes from a foreign country but above all because it is too mobile for even limited professional training.[13] The means of production must therefore be adapted to this relatively low level of qualification. At the same time, however, the lower cost of this work force does not encourage entrepreneurs to put in highly productive means of production. 'Our industrialists prefer investments in men, cheaper than investments in equipment. . . . Multinational corporations postponed plans to modernise their capital stock to take advantage of the lower cost of this labour' (*Entreprise*, no. 948). Cheap labour thus enables some backward sectors to remain in the market, creating meanwhile the opportunity of even greater super profits to the most mechanised sectors which also employ it.

As Marx observed, the <u>over-exploitation of labour</u> counteracts the tendency for the rate of profit to fall. To the extent that it favours some branches of industry more than others, it <u>also sharpens capitalist competition</u> and arouses the hostility of some so-called liberal sections of the bourgeoisie against those who are branded as backward because they employ this labour force.

In a country like South Africa this competition is exacerbated because, since 70% of the population are underpaid Africans, this policy limits the development of the domestic market and national consumer industries, which need an internal outlet to help them place their products competitively on the international market.

In South Africa it is the semi-public Afrikaner sector which maintains segregation against the soft opposition of the Anglo-Saxon 'liberals', whose industries are seeking a labour force which is more specialised and cheaper than white labour (Oppenheimer, 1954–5). However, their antagonism and apparently anti-racist

attitude last only as long as the employment of this kind of under-
qualified labour force is made difficult by the nature of the investment structure. In fact, under the influence of international competition, increasing numbers of industries are turning, in various
ways, to this kind of over-exploitation of labour or organising
themselves to do so, either by employing immigrant labour or,
increasingly, by establishing factories in underdeveloped countries.

These options coincide with those of governments perturbed at
the spectre of a large force of restless foreign labour. If it is easy
to subject the first waves of migrant workers to miserable living
conditions, putting them in slums and keeping medical services out
of their reach, this is no longer true when the migrant workers
have gathered some political experience. In France less than ten
years ago these workers agreed to live in basements and hovels, but
now they even refuse to accept the housing conditions imposed on
them in hostels. Governments are also finding the hospital bills for
immigrants are rising, not only because they have no families to
take care of them at home, or because their health deteriorates
after several stays, nor because industrial accidents are increasing,
but because, thanks to their own organisations, they have managed
to obtain better health-care. The presence of several million of
foreigners in the country, inevitably concentrated in the most
industrial areas and grouped in hostels and slums, represents a possible trouble-centre all the more dangerous as the immigrants gain
practical experience of struggle and the support of local humani-
tarian or political organisations. This is why governments are trying to keep immigration within limits, subject it to police controls
so as to change its structure and eliminate the illicit entries (which
are so profitable to some firms) (CEDETIM, 1975, Annexe 2).

Such are the considerations which encourage the capitalist states
to make arrangements for exploiting these cheap workers in their
own countries, according to a new and improved method of colonialism, one that has been delayed until now by the inadequate
industrial and commercial infrastructure of underdeveloped countries. Employed in local firms the cost of this local labour-power
will be relieved of the cost of transportation[14] and the costs of
accommodation, and a proportion of subsistence costs as well,
since the worker will be fed on local produce which is paid for at
less than its value. Certainly most labour-maintenance costs will
fall on the country which will receive the foreign capital, but the
local bourgeoisies, which see that in the short-term they can bene-

136

fit from this over-exploitation, are ready to guarantee the social order – that is, to maintain the conditions for this exploitation – for as long as possible.

We are therefore witnessing a general redeployment of the resources of European capitalism in this direction, following the example of American businesses which, having imported men, opted, with the McCarran Act, to export capital and set up firms in those areas propitious to local over-exploitation of cheap labour.[15] The French bourgeoisie is preparing to implant in some of its neo-colonies – in Senegal for example – where a relevant infrastructure is being undertaken on the Cap Vert peninsula, while the hinterland will act as a reserve of cheap labour. In South Africa too French businessmen – who are not of course racists! – do not want to be the last to squeeze the last drops of blood from the victims of South African racism.

These solutions will not immediately halt immigration into Europe, or into France. In 1973, the National Council of French Employers estimated that countries now employing immigrants would have a deficit of 11 million workers by 1982, whereas countries of emigration would have a surplus of no more than 7.8 to 10.4 million active workers (*Entreprise*, 948).[16] The present 'crisis' and international capitalism's plans may perhaps change these figures. In any case they confirm that labour exploitation does not take place strictly within the limits of relations between states nor between a 'centre' and a 'periphery' but between social classes; a split which is moving into the arena of the dominated countries; the same factors will also make it clear that returning workers from the domestic sector to the countries from which they came, or maintaining them there, will not put an end to their over-exploitation.

Conclusion

Resorting to domestic production as a way of reproducing labour-power means that capitalism is faced with a double contradiction. For, this use of domestic production operates at two different levels: on one, capitalism supplies itself with free labour-power, by a process we have examined in Part II, and on the other, it procures for itself the one ingredient which remains necessary for the operation of the system – the free labourer.

Can capitalism continue without this double social and economic input from the domestic sector?

All arguments about wages start from the hypothesis that capitalism can reproduce its basic labour-power from a population formed within its own confines, and that in the long term, wages cannot be lower than the cost of social reproduction of labour-power without putting capitalist reproduction at risk.

All the same, it is clear from the above that the historical development of capitalism up till now has contravened this law by a continuous and sustained absorption of populations deriving from the domestic sector of production.

For capitalism to reproduce itself, that is for it to grow according to the logic of its development, its growth must correspond to that of the productive forces upon which it depends, and in particular upon labour-power, which must increase in proportion, both in quality and quantity. European imperialism provides an original solution to this problem by dividing the international proletariat: the stabilised, urban section of the national working class are ensured a training and selective education in order to raise their productivity, while all that is expected from people in the colonial zones is a continuous increase in numbers.

Now, as we have seen, the latter are relatively unqualified, but they are cheap because they can, partly or wholly, reproduce themselves through the unpaid labour they apply to the agricultural means of production which have been left to them. When, through imperialist expansion, capitalism acquires a continuous flow of fresh workers from abroad who are set in competition with one another as they reach the labour market, it ensures its reproduction at the expense of these populations, for, rather than integrating them and thus enabling them to reproduce themselves, it exploits them in this destructive way. Because of the inherent contradiction of this kind of over-exploitation (developing a labour-rent within the capitalist mode of production), these peoples undergo social, political and often physical decline, which is linked to the decline of the domestic mode of production, back into which they are nevertheless ceaselessly being thrust.

In the cases we have referred to (Europe and southern Africa) over-exploitation of labour is based on models of organisation, control and management which reveal its organic and regular character. The policy of 'exporting capital' into predominantly rural nations, which is rapidly being extended at present, is another attempt to profit from the over-exploitation of labour; but the wide dispersal of companies in areas that are under-administered, and the competition between the various national and trans-national industrial sectors, make it more difficult to exercise the same degree of control over the turnover of the rural labour force.

The accelerated introduction of industry also speeds up the destructive exploitation of labour-power at the expense of conservation policies – the limits of which we have already seen.

Wherever capitalism is introduced its immediate effect is to produce a rural exodus which tends to prevail over rotating migration, re-creating in an ever larger measure the disruption and misery of Europe's 'industrial revolution', and rapidly exhausting the resources of the domestic economy.

The rural exodus – instigated by the expansion of capitalism – which today operates on a world scale as it did 150 years ago in Europe – is not always everywhere kept in check by the international bourgeoisie. On the contrary it has become so vast that, as a result of expropriations by imperialist agricultural policies and colonial wars, the slightest climatic or political accident exposes the economies of nations or whole sub-continents to terrible famines which expropriate *de facto* entire rural populations whose numbers bear no relation to the employment capacities of local industrial sectors. Neither the disasters nor the mass exodus, nor, above all, the starvation and death of the millions of people involved, can be checked by the agencies set up by international capitalism (FAO, AID, etc.), while they are the effects of policies instigated by other, similar agencies (BIRD, FMI).

American imperialism's solution to this problem, which also tends to operate in other dependent imperialisms, is repression in all its forms: neo-colonial war, establishment of repressive and dictatorial regimes, 'taming' the people through the institutionalisation of torture and murder.[1]

So it is right to remember that a similar model for the lethal exploitation of labour, pushed to extremes by circumstances, is provided by Nazi Germany. Driven back inside its national boundaries by the Treaty of Versailles, German imperialism attempted to colonise Europe and apply to it imperialist methods of over-exploiting labour, with even greater effect where the exploited populations were already industrialised and were more readily organised; it was in the specific, historical condition of total war that the essential nature of this exploitation was revealed. Part of Nazi Germany's labour-power was reproduced under the system of rotating migration, administered by the Forced-Labour Office, and part by final and fatal emigration. Concentration camps, which one forgets were *labour camps*, were places in which capitalist exploitation was pushed to a logical extreme. They provided virtually free labour for Thyssen, I. G. Farben, Krupp and other large and still respectable industrial corporations. They were supplied with men, women and children rounded up throughout colonised Europe, exploited to the point of physical exhaustion, then physically liquidated as soon as they could no longer work. German capitalism was thus spared the cost of maintaining and taking care of its ill, weak or aged workers.[2]

In the end, imperialism – as a means of reproducing cheap labour-power – is leading capitalism to a major crisis, for even if there are still millions of people in the world, not directly involved in capitalist employment, how many are still capable owing to the social disruption, famine and wars it brings about, of producing their own subsistence and feeding their children? When the labour force supplied by the domestic sector is physically and socially exhausted, when, worn-out and starving, these people disappear or are all caged in overcrowded cities on a 'food aid' system, then the shock absorbers of the racist theoreticians of overexploitation and Pompidou's 'alleviation of social tensions' will disappear. In the same way that the stabilisation of migrant workers entails a rise in the cost of labour-power, so world labour's increasing integration into the capitalist sector – even on the threshold of physiological poverty – causes profit margins to decline sharply. Deprived of

the historical intake of labour-value produced outside its sphere
and of the principal brake on falling rates of profit, capitalism
may well show itself to be too costly a mode of production to
successfully mobilise, as it did at the outset, the productive forces,
and therefore to guarantee progress. The coming 'final' crisis
would then be foreshadowed by the present situation, which corresponds to the stabilisation, at different stages of integration, of
this input of labour – unless it solves itself through war or coups,
as the means of punishing non-cooperative peoples, and through
famines as a solution of the problem of overpopulation.

By this policy of the squandering and destruction of man's productive forces capitalism condemns itself, but, pushed to its limits,
the totalitarian exploitation of man by man also condemns humanity along with it. The final and fatal crisis of capitalism, which is
awaited by some as a deliverance, may drag us into the barbarism
that Marx predicted as an alternative to socialism if the international proletariat does not organise to resist it. This barbarism was
foreshadowed by the Nazi world and is being re-created by the
international bourgeoisie – led by the USA – wherever dictators
are thrust upon peoples to guard the imperialist order.

The second contradiction which faces the capitalist development
comes from the persistent use, even within the most developed
countries, of the family to reproduce the social ingredient which
up until now has fed capitalism: the 'free labourer'.

Having been formed as the institutional framework of the
agricultural productive unit, the family has survived, in modified
forms, as the social structure supporting the wealth of the mer-
chants, landlords, and, finally, the industrial bourgeoisies. It has
lent itself to the transmission of inherited wealth, patrimony and
capital – the long-lasting confusion between which has asked for
its protection.

Today, however, certain bourgeois milieux excepted, the family
has no economic infrastructure. It has little or nothing to transfer,
neither property nor, therefore, the patriarchal ideology by which
it justified their possession and control. Among the working class,
the family lives according to an ethical pattern imposed by the
ruling class, for it remains the institution within which birth,
nurture and education of children take place thanks to the largely
unpaid labour of parents, particularly of the mother. It remains
the locus of the production and reproduction of labour-power.
Though it lacks any other productive role, we find in the conjugal

141

family the same paradox whereby domestic relations of reproduction are organically combined with capitalist relations of production.

Contractual relations between partners in the conjugal reproduction of labour-power – that is the production of a merchandise – do not however correspond to the contractual norms which characterise business. Marriage relations are personal and no clause binds the parties in respect to hours of work, distribution of household tasks or payment for them. The legal marriage contract merely settles the distribution of inheritance and does not take into consideration the work carried out within the household, which in legal terms has no existence. Management of the family budget is a private matter, still largely dependent on the husband's will. The work which the wife puts into producing the child – a future producer – is never paid for in wage terms, that is, in terms of the time effectively spent on production (in 1973 it was estimated that 3000 Francs was the average monthly cost of this labour-power while the minimum wage was 939.99 for 173 hours of monthly work).

Above all, the labour-power produced in this way, for all that it is a commodity on the labour market, cannot be sold by those who produce it. In fact, legally, the age of consent releases the child from all obligations to his parents practically as soon as he reaches productive age. Legally, therefore, his labour power can only be exploited by those who own the capitalist means of production and are in a position to offer him a job. The cost of 'manufacturing' a producer is never accounted for in capitalist terms, neither as a private investment, nor as a product which brings the producer of the producer a profit in interest or by sale. Since the family is not a business concern, it does not enjoy either of the legal advantages accorded to corporations. Except in the case of the bourgeois family which owns a business and is therefore in a position to employ its offspring, the investment devoted by parents to the reproduction of labour-power is made without security.

Thus, to reproduce itself, the capitalist mode of production depends upon an institution which is alien to it, but which it has until now maintained as that most adapted to this function, and also the most economical, on account of its capacity for utilising unpaid – particularly female – labour, and by exploiting the emotional attachment which still dominates parent–child relations.

Since the age of legal majority releases children from all obligations to repay their parents, it is in the interests of capital to make this age equivalent to the earliest point at which an adolescent is physically able to produce, thus lengthening his active life to the maximum while withdrawing as soon as possible from his parents the benefit which might eventually have accrued to them from his wages. (His subsequent intellectual development may also be directed more easily from outside the family.) The notion of an age of consent – non-existent in domestic society – legally fixes the moment at which there appears on the labour market what Marx called the 'free labourer'.

The 'liberation' of the female labour force offers similar advantages, but its effects are more radical. Employing women allows the advanced capitalist countries to recover the cost of all the education which women received at school or university, and which, at home, they put more to personal and cultural than productive use. In fact, at a certain point, family policies make it less advantageous for capitalism to employ the mother at home – where she has use of less productive means of production – than in the capitalist employment sectors, where her abilities can better be exploited and where it is easier to absorb the cost of her public training.[3]

Child-benefit allowances to women, certain labour-saving household devices, and collective child-care, all help to dissolve the family. Both economically and culturally it is becoming increasingly unnecessary, and sometimes even disadvantageous, for the husband to live with his wife.[4] More and more, the State is replacing the isolated mother, entrusting the education and upbringing of her children to specialists, who work more cheaply with a larger number of children.

Objectively, therefore, the struggle of young people and women to free themselves (however progressive it may be when it is subordinated to, and reinforces class struggle) falls into line with the social development of capitalism. It recruits (and produces) 'free labourers' by depriving the domestic community – now the elder, now the father (and now, today, the mother) – by emancipating dependents earlier and earlier so as to deliver them the more quickly to employers. The emancipation of the minors favoured today by the bourgeoisie in the advanced countries, is in accordance with the logic of capitalism's historical development and, far from impeding it, is to its immediate advantage. If, until recently, the patriarchal family was the single locus of the reproduction of labour-power, perpetuating a repressive, authoritarian ideology

143

suitable for the Napoleonic and militaro-taylorist capitalist order (Reich, 1933), it is today becoming increasingly dispensable.[5]

Nazi Germany - again - pioneered this field. The *Lebensborn* system, under cover of its racist ideology, was also a ruthless experiment in the capitalist production of labour-power through the gradual elimination of the family. But capitalism's logical advance here contains its own contradiction, for, by removing all vestiges of freedom, it modifies the very nature of productive relations. Ties of personal subjugation may disappear with the family, but so will the 'free labourer' who is freed from one set of bonds (the family) only to be reduced to a condition of *total* alienation *vis à vis* his employer. The prospect is of a resurgence of slavery in sophisticated form, where the production of the producer is taken completely in hand by the ruling class. In this way employers or the state will be able to satisfy their production needs, moving labour where they wish, training it as they wish, and suppressing it when it suits them - legally. In this perspective, in which labour-power becomes a true commodity, produced under truly capitalist conditions of production, the state and the capitalist employers already pervade the most intimate corners of private life.[6] They oversee birth, illness, death, and the affections. Thus threatened, the family is coming to be regarded, by reason of the few affectionate relationships it preserves, as one of the last bastions of individual liberty. It is, however, a very fragile bastion, for nothing any longer predestines it to withstand the corrosive influence of money-relations; and in this we have the measure of the totalitarian menace with which capitalism is heavy. Totalitarianism, which the bourgeoisie holds up as a bogy before the masses, invoking the example of the bureaucratic forms of socialism, is flourishing (and in a still more inhumane fashion) in the foreseeable changes in capitalism, in the necessary destruction of all ties of affection. All it can put in the place of these ties is the barbarism of absolute 'profitability' - the last stage of the metamorphosis of human beings into capital, their strength and intelligence into commodities, and 'the wild fruit of women' into investments.

Notes

Introduction

This work is part of a study programme concerning African economic systems which began in 1964 with the aid of the Wenner Gren Foundation and in which Eric Pollet, Grace Winter and J.-L. Amselle have also participated. During this time we have collaborated a great deal, and I have been greatly assisted by their contribution to our collective work and to our common discussions.

Part I. The domestic community

1. The title usually given to the passage in the *Grundrisse* (p. 471ff.) devoted to precapitalist societies (*Grundrisse. Introduction to the Critique of Political Economy*, Penguin Marx Library, Penguin Books, Harmondsworth, 1973).

2. 'In the most primitive communities work is carried out in common, and the common product, apart from that portion set aside for reproduction, is shared out according to current need.' (Engels 1884, French edition, p. 196, quoting a letter of Marx to Vera Zasulich, dated 8 March 1881; the whole letter is reprinted in Marx-Engels, *Archiv*, I, pp. 335–8)

'The more deeply we go back into history, the more does the individual, and hence also the producing individual, appear as a dependent, as belonging to a greater whole: in a still quite natural way in the family and in the family expanded into the clan [*Stamm*]; then later in the various forms of communal society arising out of the antitheses and fusions of the clans' (Marx, 1857–8, p. 84).

'In the most ancient, primitive communities, equality of rights could apply at most to members of the community; women, slaves and foreigners were excluded from this equality as a matter of course.' (Engels, 1877–8, p. 144)

'[The most archaic communities] are based upon relations of kinship between their members. There is no membership of them, save by way of natural or adoptive kinship. Their structure is that of a genealogical tree.' (Engels 1884, French edition, p. 295, quoting Marx's letters to V. Zasulich of 8 March 1881, reprinted in Marx-Engels, *Archiv*, I, pp. 335–8)

'These small and extremely ancient Indian communities, some of which have continued down to this day, are based on possession in common of the land, on the blending of agriculture and handicrafts, and on an unalterable division of labour which serves, whenever a new community is started, as a plan and scheme ready cut and dried [. . .] The chief part of the products is

145

destined for direct use by the community itself and does not take the form of a commodity. Hence, production here is independent of that division of labour brought about, in Indian society as a whole, by means of the exchange of commodities [. . .] The simplicity of the organisation for production in these self-sufficing communities, which constantly reproduce themselves in the same form, and when accidentally destroyed, spring up again on the spot and with the same name [. . .] remains untouched by the storm-clouds of the political sky,' (Marx, 1867, I, 357–8)

3. According to this 'law', peasant families adapt their efforts to their needs; there is a marginal equilibrium between the discomfort occasioned by extra effort and the satisfaction resulting from the product out of this effort. Chayanov, who bases his hypothesis on the Russian peasantry at the beginning of the twentieth century, is cautious about the applicability of this law to the model of the ancient *oikos*. (1925, 22)

4. No contemporary 'primitive' society, however, has a lithic industry comparable to those of prehistoric societies – and there is nothing to lead us to suppose that they operate according to the same economic categories.

1. Locating the domestic economy

1. Labour processes are not to be confused with 'modes of production' however, as Terray tended to do in this book. It should be noted that Terrary has since corrected himself on this point.

2. Exogamy: marriage outside the group to which one belongs.

3. 'The exchange of women' is only part of a more general phenomenon, the mobility of adults of both sexes. Female rather than male mobility is neither necessary nor universal.

4. F. Korn (1973, 15) demonstrates that Lévi-Strauss' arguments are tautological, when he makes incest the basis of the principle of reciprocity and of prescriptive systems.

5. Middleton (1962) makes a serious contribution to the subject, and recalls that Firth had already claimed incest was relative as early as 1936. So, indeed did Engels in *The Origins of the Family*.

6. R. Needham (1974, 67, 68) considers that prohibitions relating to incest are too varied in character to be considered *a priori* as universal or subsumable to a general theory (pp. 62–3). Moral prescriptions regarding certain women are, according to him, the negative aspect of the regulation of access to women.

7. My emphasis. C.M.

8. Here, Leroi-Gourhan clearly points to a line of research which remains neglected for reasons which he indicates himself when he observes that in the social sciences 'the technical-economic infrastructure is usually brought in only when in a very obvious way it influences the superstructure of matrimonial practices and rites [. . .] so that we know more about the exchange of prestige than everyday exchange, more about ritual prestations than ordernary services, more about the circulation of marriage values than of vegetables and much more about how societies think than about their structures'. (1964, 210)

9. Hunters' economies have already been the subject of earlier work, about

which I only wish to make certain additional remarks (Meillassoux, 1967, 1973).

10. The word 'land' should be understood in terms of the natural context which surrounds the producer; in the English edition of *Capital* the term 'soil' is used. Marx expressly includes water in the term.

11. Fishing is apparently also included. But fishing seems to be associated with more compact and sedentary forms of social organisation than are hunting societies, so that it is not possible to reduce them *a priori* to the same categories (Cf.Sauer, 1969, who argues, very convincingly, that fishing rather than hunting led to agricultural activities; see also Rivière, 1974).

12. Turnbull introduces the notion of 'flux' to characterise the mobility of individuals between bands (in Lee and Devore, 1968, 132f.).

13. The *elima* and *molimo* religious rites described by Turnbull (1965) are borrowed, as their name and the author clearly indicate, from Bantu. Turnbull shows how they reveal a process of identification with the Bantu who dominate them. Godelier, however, analyses them as if these ceremonies belonged to the original hunting culture of the Mbuti (1973a).

14. Reacting to a theory which was favoured at the time, Malinowski stressed that 'sociability develops from the extension of family ties (inherited from animals), not from the gregarious instinct' (1927, p. 184). In contrast, see Reich (1932, p. 21): 'The family is not [. . .] the fountain of civilisation.'

15. Williams (in Lee and Devore 1968: 130) explicitly remarks this shift of meaning.

16. The term 'kin' is borrowed from the British aristocracy (Gould and Kolb, 1964).

17. Thus the term 'brother' would, in the band, designate membership of a functional age-group, while in the lineage, it means membership of a generation which derives from a common lineage ancestor. The works of E. Benveniste are particularly helpful regarding these problems: see in particular on the subject his work on the development of the notion of 'brother' and of 'sister' (Benveniste, 1969, 213f. and 220f.; also Jaulin, 1974, II, 142).

18. 'Elementary structures of kinship are those systems . . . which prescribe marriage with a certain type of relative or, alternatively, those which while defining all members of the society as relatives, divide them into two categories, viz., possible spouses and prohibited spouses. (Lévi-Strauss, 1967, 1969, p. xxiii)

19. A society is divided into *moieties* when it recognises two main 'classes' within it – themselves sometimes further divided into subsections – to which all who belong to the society are attached according to their parents' membership, and between which mating is either disapproved or banned. The distinction is entirely taxonomical because individuals who belong to the same moiety do not necessarily live in the same band, or in separate bands. Out of this system, anthropologists have constructed combinations going back several generations which are so complex that a degree in higher mathematics is required to solve them. In practice it appears that these prescriptions are often transgressed, that people change sides when it suits them and that individuals only define themselves in these terms only from one generation to the next.

20. This should not be taken to imply that I make a comparison between men and primates. The idea of a social or cultural continuum between men and animals is a dominant idea in present-day *ethology*, according to which it

147

is possible to find in animals the origin of certain of our social institutions and behaviours; it is based upon an implicit anthropocentrism, supported by examples which are taken at will from numerous different species. This apparently naïve anthropocentrism, more pronounced even than the ethnocentrism of anthropologists, leads straight to a blind naturalistic determinism and to totalitarian theories of power.

21. For a comparison of the functioning of the two systems, and the consequent contradictions, see the excellent study by A. Marie (1972).

22. The practice of wet-nursing, which allows for an increase in reproduction by entrusting children, born to one mother while she is still suckling a previous child, to a lactating but childless woman, seems possible to regulate only within a polygynous extended family, i.e. the domestic community.

23. Referred to below as 'planting agriculture'.

24. See Part I, Chapters 2,2 and 3 for the development of arguments about the conditions for the formation of the domestic relations of production.

25. The 'physical weakness' of women, often suggested to the the *cause* of their inferior condition, is more likely to be the present-day consequence of their social weakness and the product of a long-term evolution rather than from natural inferiority.

26. Exclusion from war in particular is crucial, once war has become the institutionalised way of social reproduction.

27. Jaulin (1970, II, 287) relies upon Clastre and Lizot, both inspired by the Rousseauist notion of the 'noble savage', to deny, against all the evidence, that war is important among Amerindian societies, hoping thus to keep untarnished their image as 'societies of compatibility'.

28. Civil power (which I contrast here to warrior power) develops from the collective recognition of political problems which need to be resolved through an equally collective decision-taking process, either at the level of society as a whole or at the level of a ruling class of its own. Warrior power, by contrast, as distinct from military or aristocratic power, is that which is seized by the individual who is most capable of heroic deeds, bravery, or intimidation; it is arbitrary and personal.

29. This development would appear to be visible in, for example, the Motilone *boyo*, described by S. Pinton (Jaulin, 1973): when the interpersonal relations between inhabitants are examined, it is seen that four out of eight households are related to the same man, which amounts to a total of four married men out of ten and eight out of sixteen married women. However, the data provided by the authors, who know nothing whatever of the social relations between *boyo*s or their evolution, and limit themselves to a single example, are such that we can only speculate about the significance of the observation.

30. We are not talking here about the ritual or conventionalised abductions, regulated by *a posteriori* or *a priori* agreement, which are practised by certain peoples.

31. The most promising studies and analyses seem to me to be by Augé (1969, 1975), Bonnafé (1975) and Etienne who has developed the idea of the cognatic society applied to the Bawle (1968, 1971a, 1971b) but who, unlike A. Marie (1972), does not consider that the problem of 'reciprocity' is different in matri- and patrilineal societies.

2 Domestic reproduction

1. Fire should also be mentioned as it is used in craft and agricultural operations (shifting cultivation).

2. *Collective means of production*: those which develop from the collective work of several production units, but which subsequently are used to satisfy the needs of each of them. (Thus, for example, irrigation works require an investment of labour from several communities, but the water from them is then used to produce subsistence goods for each community on its own.) *Social means of production*: means of production which incorporate social labour and are used to manufacture a product for the market or the collectivity as a whole, in the context of a social division of labour.

3. Unlike French anthropologists, I use the term 'affinity' (not 'alliance') to designate the relations one individual has with his or her spouse, and 'affine' (not 'allié') to designate the individuals who are in such relations. I reserve the term 'alliance' for relations sanctioned by 'acts' (oaths, pacts, treaties, etc.) which are binding outside kinship and affinity relations.

4. The sale of patrimonial goods, that is their conversion into commodities, is an uncommon act which, even in our capitalist merchant societies, requires legal guarantees and precautions.

5. *There is a social division of labour* when production units are only able to satisfy their needs via equivalent exchange of their products. In domestic society, we must speak rather of the *distribution of tasks*.

6. Moreover, the concept of self-sustenance is necessary to understand over-exploitation, to which this mode of production is exposed in the colonial period (see Part II of the present work and Dupriez, 1973).

7. Godelier (1973a) has still not grasped this phenomenon completely; he distinguishes only between 'commodities' and 'goods to give'! ('biens à donner').

8. Is it still necessary to point out that this situation does not contradict historical materialism but the technological determinism which is too often confused with it?

9. J.-P. Olivier de Sardan, studying the Wogo (1969), puts marriage at the centre of social relations.

10. Not many works yet describe the social organisation of production with precision, so the remarkable study by E. Pollet and G. Winter (1971) should be mentioned here. Beginning from a meticulous in-depth study of the Soninke of Diahunu, the authors develop a theoretical discussion which is a most important contribution to dialectical materialism applied to anthropology. Although the society they describe practised slavery and therefore has a different historical context, their analyses and descriptions of how the community relations work in it consistently touch upon the theories proposed here.

The research which Jean Schmitz is currently doing should also be mentioned; though arrived at independently, his ideas are along the lines of those presented here.

11. 'Human energy' is used in preference to 'labour-power' for reasons explained in I, 3.

12. Since the active life of the woman is entirely dominated by her condition as a wife, and since her conjugal relations take precedence over all others,

in the analyses which follow, as in life, the woman remains hidden behind her husband, who mediates all social relations. The produce of her work is assimilated to his. The term 'producer', therefore, should be understood economically to mean the mono- or polygynous household and, politically, to mean the husband.

13. Details about access to seeds are rarely found in anthropological literature.

14. Hence the plethora of laws supporting paternal filiation, which would not otherwise rest on any evidence.

15. The practical difficulty of enforcing these agreements testifies to the fact that kinship is subordinated to constraints more demanding than purely constitutional rules.

16. Mary Douglas' observations (1963) among the Lele illustrate this development.

17. J.-Y. Martin (1970) demonstrates the existence of these matrimonial areas very clearly among the Matakam; 80% to 90% of marriages take place within them.

18. In Part I, Ch. 3, § iv, I come back to the conditions under which multilateral exchanges take place.

19. See the Soninke case described by Pollet and Winter (1971, 387), or that of the Guro (Meillassoux, 1964, 123f.).

20. Marriages between cousins, customarily considered to be preferable in certain societies.

21. Patriarchal ideology or religion then take over the managerial authority, to support and strengthen the elders' power.

22. P. Bonte (1973, 93) wrongly objects to P.-P. Rey's view that the lineage society is unable to compensate for demographic accidents.

23. See E. Benveniste's remarks on the theme of 'the feeding sovereign' (1969, II, 85).

24. The father's curse, often institutional in this kind of society, is one way of breaking parental ties.

25. See Nadel's reflections (1942, 3f.) regarding the determinant influence of the economy on kinship among the Nupe. Also, Glickman (1971).

26. It will be noted that in the kinship terminology of agricultural communities, the notion of 'brother' tends to be defined more precisely to distinguish between 'older' and 'younger' brothers. This sort of collateral filiation never occurs between women, whose productive functions are not institutionally recognised.

27. The emergence of filial succession by primogeniture is always very slow and often realised through bloody dynastic squabbles. History is full of these fratricidal wars between pretenders to the throne of dead kings, transforming collateral into lineal filiation. How, otherwise, to decide between the first-born of classificatory brothers, the oldest son of the oldest brother, the oldest son of the first wife, etc.? (Bruyas, 1966.)

28. This conclusion emerges from a fairly common bias among proto-Marxists. Starting from the idea that a mode of production necessarily depends upon control of the material means of production – according to the capitalist model – land is given a central position. Rightly stating that the distribution of the land is controlled by the social organisation, not the other way round, the proponents of this view accord the social structures the quality of 'infrastructure'.

3. The alimentary structures of kinship

1. The portion used for sowing does not circulate among producers and is normally renewed between cycles. It need not enter into the formula. I also make the hypothesis that social activities in which part of subsistence production is offered to people outside the community are matched by reciprocal gifts so that no overall loss is incurred (cf. Jaulin, 1966). This amount likewise does not figure in the formula below.

2. We should also add the amounts stored to insure against deficit years, which, over the longer period, have a regulatory function. But this storage, being constant, does not alter the fundamentals of the basic problem dealt with here. For the share devoted to feeding the post-productive members of the community, see below p. 57.

3. It is clear that the amount consumed varies according to age and sex. To apply this formula to actual figures, simply multiply α by the appropriate coefficient.

4. In actual life this division between producers and non-producers is not abrupt: children take part in certain agricultural activities very early on (bird scaring, household tasks, etc.) before becoming fully-fledged producers. Old people also often continue to work until of advanced age, as far as their health allows. The progressive spread of activity is here clustered together in conventional time-periods in our formulae.

5. The respective amounts E_b, E_i, E_d, depend on the level of production the community has reached. Improvement in tools raises E_i at the expense of E_b, so does improvement in agricultural techniques.

6. For $E_d + E_r$ to appear, it is necessary to abide by our initial hypothesis, namely that agriculture must be sufficiently productive to satisfy the necessary food requirements, to maintain and reproduce its members and also to repeat the agricultural cycle (cf. I, 2, I).

7. This surplus-labour is, in essence, the labour-rent of the feudal economy and the surplus-value of the capitalist economy. In both cases it is through the dispossession of this free time that man falls into a condition of alienation.

4. The dialectic of equality

1. By bridewealth portion I understand the specific amount of material goods and/or the prestations conventionally required from the bride-taking community by the bride-giving one. Bridewealth is different from the dowry – which is composed of the personal objects the wife takes to her husband's house and which stay in her possession – and from personal gifts offered to certain relatives.

2. Thinking of bridewealth portions as IOUs helps in understanding how the system works.

3. Free choice of a partner is of course restricted in such a conjuncture.

4. The problems relating to the use of cattle as matrimonial goods belong to a study of pastoral societies, although many settled agricultural societies have adopted the practice. Because cattle production is slower and less controllable than the production of material objects, beasts are more often accumulated by raiding than by labour. Cattle production usually supports

warlike activity. On the other hand, stocks of cattle continue to exist only through natural reproduction, which may be seen as 'parallel' to the reproduction of the group, and therefore less subject to destruction. Finally, the conventions governing the representative uses of cattle in matrimonial dealings may spread among more numerous populations (although the colour of cloth often establishes the limits of matrimonial exchange between neighbouring cattle breeders).

5. The elements which make up the bridewealth payment cannot therefore be asimilated to money, since the payment of bridewealth does not operate an exchange between different values. For values to be exchanged, the objects exchanged must be different, the function of money being to reduce this difference to an equivalence (Brunhoff, 1967). Bridewealth does not fulfil this function, since it merely transfers over time a value which remains identical to itself, though it may not itself be constant or identical.

6. Gifts made to certain non-amalgamated social groups (such as castes) of outsiders (i.e. groups with whom it is forbidden to marry), are equivalent to a destruction. In royal societies, the destruction of *productive* goods has another function (Meillassoux, 1968).

7. This seems to be the process observed and analysed by Terray among the Dida (1969b): 'The bridewealth mechanism makes available to the communities a means of regulation and control which enables them to avoid both a dearth of women in one place and too many of them in another [. . .] In the traditional society, the nature of these means of exchange [which go to make up the bridewealth payment, C.M.] and the fact that it is impossible to produce or acquire them at will prevents inflation and no one benefits from hoarding them since they cannot circulate outside the sphere of matrimonial exchange' (p. 237). Now initially, first under the influence of trade, and now under the present cash-crop economy, means of payment are continuously introduced into bridewealth circuits while women from the north are introduced into Dida society. Terray also notes the first signs of hierarchisation of lineages via matrimonial procedures (213-14) which seems logically related to the fact that 'marriages conforming to the procedure which was supposely "normal" - where the bridewealth given comes from bridewealth received for a girl - are today a minority of cases (37.8%)' (p. 223). See also Augé, 1969.

5. Who are the exploited?

1. The study by G. Althabe (1965) may be borne in mind here: he shows how institutions borrowed from the Bantu developed among the Mbaka pygmies as they adopted agriculture.

2. By cultivated land (*terroir*) we are referring to worked land in which a significant portion of the energy of the past and present community has been incorporated.

3. In cereal-producing agricultural societies, it is more rare for women to work in the fields (Goody 1863, 108).

4. W. Reich (1932, transl. 1972) observes that practices like excision or infibulation demonstrate 'the patriarchy's efforts' to suppress women's sexuality with the unique aim of turning them into specially docile child producers.

5. 'By final paradox, the African woman must, to be truly adopted by her

husband's family, cease to be capable of motherhood [. . .] beyond a certain age, women are barely distinguishable from men' (D. Paulme 1960, 21).

6. Women may only acquire economic status by disposing of what they produce in the form of commodities, outside the domestic circuit. Hence women's active role in commerce as soon as historical circumstances are favourable.

7. *Sororate*: institution by which an unsatisfactory wife is replaced by one of her classificatory sisters; *levirate*: institution by which a widow is given in marriage to a classificatory brother (older or younger, according to the situation) of her dead husband; *classificatory kinship*: extension of the lineal (or vertical) kinship link to all collateral kin (for example, where all my father's brothers are called my 'father', and all my father's brothers' children are called my 'brothers'; 'brother' and 'father' are classificatory terms).

8. In aristocratic society, replacement of vertical by collateral filiation creates contradictions in kinship ideology. From the juridicial point of view it is wholly arbitrary to affirm vertical male filiation while denying the same, more obvious, filiation between a mother and her children.

9. It should rather be said that it is the emergence of *patrimony* than that of private property (cf. Pt. I, Ch. 2, § 5).

10. By preparing food, women also assert themselves as procreators (Weil 1970).

11. P.-P. Rey (1973, 115) denies all exchanges between elders and juniors; according to him, exchange only occurs between elders, and there are only prestations without redistribution between juniors and elders. What Rey does not see is the metamorphosis from juniorship to eldership. He argues as if the junior remains in the same situation for ever, belonging *a priori* to a distinct social category.

12. Sahlins points out that in numerous domestic societies the young men work little until puberty (1972, 53–4).

13. Women's opposition to the patrimonial system can be radical, and might even reverse the relations of domination between the sexes, as can be seen, in the colonial context, in the remarkable analysis of one such instance by R. Waast (1974).

14. One knows of recent cases, too, where the break was suggested by the family head. On the contradictions caused in domestic relations by colonisation see Pollet and Winter (1971, 377f., 513f.), M. Samuel (1978) and Part II below.

6. Contradictions and contacts: the premises of inequality

1. Pollet and Winter (1971, 524) make the same point regarding slavery.

2. That is from an influence strong enough to allow goods to acquire a market value in an external market and allow matrimonial transactions to be extended to peoples in contact with this market.

3. In several societies in Mali and Senegal which I have studied, political alliances contain a clause prohibiting marriage between the parties concerned.

4. This was true of the Mandinke dynasties of the Senegambia (communications of Innes, Sidibe, Cissoko at the Conference of Manding Studies, S.O.A.S. and International African Institute, London, 1972), and of the Alur, for example (Southall, 1956).

5. J.-P. Olivier de Sardan (1975) introduces elements for analysis of this

type in his studies of slavery. See also the differences in organisation of kinship relations between the peasantry and 'gentry' in Imperial China (Feuchtwang, 1974) – studies which open the way to a deeper understanding of this subject.

PART II. THE EXPLOITATION OF THE DOMESTIC COMMUNITY: imperialism as a mode of reproduction of cheap labour-power

1. The paradoxes of colonial exploitation

1. S. Amin distinguishes countries in the 'centre', that is, industrialised countries, from those on the 'periphery', or underdeveloped countries.

2. In a later work, Amin (1973) modifies the opposition between centre and periphery when he admits that relations between different 'modes of production' are established; this completely destroys his arguments for 'world accumulation'. Alongside some valuable analyses, Amin continues to find 'unequal exchange' wherever over-exploitation of labour occurs (p. 63) – on this occasion introducing differences in productivity – and still seems to accept implicitly the theory of 'immobile labour'.

3. We should really speak of under- rather than non-evaluation: cf. below and Comité Information Sahel, 1974, Ch. 3.

4. According to Marx, the organic composition of capital is the relation between fixed capital (machinery, buildings, materials, etc.) and variable capital (wages and salaries).

5. As applied to the French historical situation, the analyses of Servolin (1972) offer one of the best foundations for discussion, in showing that the commercialised produce of small-scale market production is 'necessarily sold below its value' and that as a result 'prices are lower *than they would be if production took place under capitalist conditions*'.

6. Primitive accumulation takes place when the accumulation results from the transfer of value from one mode of production to another.

7. This is enough to deprive the expression 'mode of production' of any rigorous scientific content and to limit its use to that of a first approximation, identifying the body of productive and reproductive relations organically linked to a given level of development of productive forces.

8. See also the discussion in P.-P. Rey (1973, 139f.) on the notions of Marx, Lenin, Rosa Luxemburg and Otto Bauer concerning imperialism; also Laclau, 1971, and Nettl, 1966.

9. P.-P. Rey (1973) also proposes the notion of a 'transitional mode of production' corresponding to neo-colonialism.

10. This is no longer the case as soon as domestic relations of production are predominantly replaced by wage relations, when land, an inalienable patrimony, becomes a commodity and when the means of labour are bought on the capitalist market and not produced and transferred in the context of domestic relations.

2. Direct and indirect wages

1. Barel (1973), in a learned work devoted to social reproduction, leaves little room for the institution of the family. Nicolaï (1974), by contrast, poses the issue in correct terms.

2. 'In order to examine the object of our investigation in its integrity', Marx writes, 'free from all disturbing subsidiary circumstances, we must treat the whole world as one nation, and assume that capitalist production is everywhere established and has possessed itself of every branch of industry' (1867, I, p. 581, n. 1).

Naturally, Marx was not unaware of the problems raised by capitalist expansion, and re-integrates them in his discussion on the general rate of profit to explain its stability. He observes that capital invested in the colonies returns a higher rate of profit for two reasons. The first, which we try to explain here, is a greater exploitation of labour (Marx mentions the cases of coolies and slaves); the second is due to the weaker organic composition of capital in colonial industries (*id.* III, 237ff.).

3. The French translation published by Les Editions Sociales (1950) does not include the phrase 'and consequently also the reproduction of this special article'.

4. 'Subsistence' is all that which permits human energy to be reproduced physically and intellectually. In its strict sense, the sense in which I prefer to use it here, it refers to the food deriving from crop-producing agriculture. I am therefore leaving to one side as elements of labour-power, both education and apprenticeship, although if they were included in the argument my thesis would be even further strengthened. Education raises even more radically than does the supply of food, the problem of the enlarged reproduction of capitalism, i.e. the concomitant growth of the skills of the labour force and of the productivity of the means of production put at its disposition.

5. We shall see why nevertheless discrimination does play off workers of different ethnic, national or sexual origins against one another, although it does not change the argument in the case of an integrated capitalism.

6. *Salaire minimum interprofessional de croissance* (minimum wage).

7. The United States, where social scurity at a national level is not very advanced, seems to be an example which contradicts this argument. However, while taking account of the fact that this institution is being expanded, several points should be made. For a long time a large proportion of labour power has been renewed by immigration. The first immigrants may have found unlimited land by expropriating or massacring the Indians, but following this 'frontier' era of 'heroism', most were expropriated in their turn, thrown onto the labour market and abandoned to destitution. At the same time, the emancipation of black slaves brought a relatively abundant labour force onto the industrial market. During the 1960s, Harrington (1962) estimated that between 40 and 50 million people – most of them peasants or blacks – lived in poverty in the United States, hungry, lacking adequate housing, education and medical services. This enormous mass of internal underdevelopment still helps even today to supply the market with cheap labour. This is one condition of American prosperity. Since then, the MacCarran act has slowed immigration in favour of a massive foreign investment policy which allows American capitalism, outside of its national frontiers, protected by the armed forces and the CIA, to exploit cheap foreign labour, without having to import it and therefore to meet its costs. (However, even the most recent available statistics indicate no decline in social inequality in the United States, Herman, 1975.) Finally, we should add that, in addition to federal insurance and assistance programmes, a significant proportion of indirect wages is – more often than in Europe – supplied by employers

155

or unions, organisations created by collective labour agreements. Private insurance, more widespread than in France, covers only a minority of wage earners whose labour-power and services are bought above their real cost.

8. In fact, because this reproduction takes place within the family, where the wife's domestic labour is generally not paid for at its value, it is still paid, in particular among the working class, at lower than its cost.

9. The equalisation realised among all enterprises at a national level by social security institutions, by which a proportion of the social product is redistributed so as to ensure reproduction of labour power, may be compared to the equalisation of profit (Marx 1867, Section II, Ch. 9). In a similar way the value of the abstract labour-power is transformed into a '*price of production*'. Generalised social security 'strips both wages and surplus value of their specifically capitalist character' (*id.* III, p. 876).

4. Without hearth or home: the rural exodus

1. The employment of children born or bred in the capitalist sector not only had the effect of increasing the active population and pressure on wages, it also shortened these workers' pre-productive period and lowered the cost of reproducing them. At the other extremity, the low life-expectancy of the working class – which characterises it even now – reduces the cost of maintaining the old.

2. In relation to this one should mention the pioneer study of the C.E.R.A.T. (1971) which explains the history of the appropriation of space in Roanne (Loire), beginning with analysis of the confrontation of different modes of production and including women's domestic labour as an element in the reproduction of labour-power.

3. The farming population after the war represented 70% of the total population; by 1970 this figure had fallen to 19%. Between 1960 and 1970 the Japanese labour force rose by 8 million (*Le Monde, Dossiers et Documents*, No. 7: 1, 3).

5. Periodic migration: the eternal return to the native land.

1. This is not the case for other activities, such as gathering or hunting, or even for planting-agriculture, where productive and non-productive periods are closer together, making it more difficult and sometimes impracticable to extract a labour rent.

2. This is shown very clearly by R. Waast's work (n.d.) on the relations between the French colonial administration and the Malagasy aristocracy; these relations were largely political, but this did not eliminate the economic competition between them.

3. It is through the idea of self-sustenance that G. Dupriez (1973) discovered the 'industrial subsistence wage' and the mechanisms of over-exploitation of workers linked to the sector of agricultural production. To my knowledge this is the only study by a classical economist which has managed to integrate such factors, which are generally neglected by his peers, and as a result to provide an important and original contribution to the problem of employment in underdeveloped countries.

4. Of course, these two forms of exploitation are not independent, particularly when they occur in the same country; but they are not inevitably linked.

In fact one often finds that areas producing export goods and areas exporting labour are geographically distinct. For an analysis of the means by which domestic communities are exploited through cash-crop agriculture, see: C. Reboul, one of the first to show how commercial agriculture lives off the food-producing sector (1972) and the Comité Information Sahel (1974); Bukh (1974); Kahn (1974); for peasant agriculture in the Senegal basin see Copans *et al.* (1972) and Copans (1973); D. Cruise O'Brien (1971); and for the effects of this agriculture Copans (1975), Raynaud (1975), Reboul (1975) and D. Cruise O'Brien (1974).

5. In the case of those who migrate definitively, the rent equals αA_0 (minus the difference between the age at which the producer was trained and the age at which he enters the labour market). In the case of the rotating migrant αA_0 is not realised so completely since his period of activity is interrupted by returns home. However, the rent contains in addition a proportionate fraction of αB_1 and all of αC_1.

6. This short-cut wage is called in French 'salaire d'appoint', similar to that which women are paid, for analogous reasons (CERAT 1972, 77f.).

7. As soon as the worker is a wage-earner, paid partly or wholly in cash, capitalism must set up a subsistence market in order to realise surplus-value. For Laclau (1971, 25), the existence of such a market marks the difference between capitalism and feudalism (which is, for him, a closed self-sustenance economy).

8. Marx clearly saw the possibility of the small peasant, not subject to rent or profit limitations, exploiting himself – for he is bound to sell his produce below its value, even below its price of production (1857, III, p. 876).

9. As I have tried to show, it is not the immediate reconstitution of the workers but the maintainance and reproduction of labour-power which are partially taken over by the domestic sector while the worker remains in it.

6. The maintenance of labour-reserves

1. Regarding South Africa, the works of H. Wolpe (1972, 1973) are essential reading: he demonstrates that this system, geared to the production of cheap labour was deliberately engineered, and shows how the racist ideology of segregation and apartheid are articulated with this economic policy. It was following a discussion I had with H. Wolpe regarding our closely-related researches that I elaborated the present considerations.

2. J. Woddis (1960) rightly observed that 'one of the chief aims of white land policy in Africa is to provide the mines and European farms with cheap labour'. But he does not analyse the difference between the permanent migration caused by the expropriation or the impoverishment of the peasantry and the rotating migration organised from the reserves or neighbouring colonial territories.

3. This policy is modified in the plans for the 'independence of the homelands' to favour the emergence of such a small black capitalist class – expected, of course, to ally itself to the racist government in Pretoria.

4. The works of Deniel (1972), Ancey (1974), Kohler (1972) and Capron & Kohler (1975) should be consulted here. 'It is widely agreed that in Mossi country, agriculture can do no more than supply subsistence needs.' (Kohler, 1972, 49).

7. The double labour market and segregation

1. When the wages of the scavengers were raised in Grenoble, French workers took the jobs held by immigrants.

2. Cf. in France the campaigns of the weekly paper *Minute* and the attacks of the extreme right against 'wild immigration', which are likely to arouse feelings of fear, hostility and contempt for immigrant workers.

3. In general one can say that racism increases in virulence as the gap between the two labour markets widens: its most extreme form was in the labour and extermination camps of Nazi Germany where races and groups thought to be inferior were exploited to death.

4. For practices leading to development of the double labour market and rotation of migrants, see: Union Générale des Travailleurs Immigrants en France (1970), particularly Chapters 1–5; N'Dongo (1972), especially Chapter 3; CEDETIM (1975) and Minces (1973).

5. 'Africans realise that, at the present, there is no final security for them in employment. In the event of unemployment, failure, accident or ill health, real security lies only with the tribe' (Watson, 1959, 40). In this article the author perceives the key problems of emigration very clearly and insists that security is the main reason why Africans are attached to the land. Gluckman (1960, 68) writes similarly: 'The tie to tribal land is of utmost importance to a man. Dependence on land and on the social relations arising from this dependence give modern Africans . . . security against the vicissitudes of industrial employment.'

6. It should be noted that from this point of view European countries, whose national frontiers separate them from countries which supply them with labour, are in an even better position than South Africa for example, whose 'reserves' are incorporated inside the country, which therefore is 'responsible' for them. This is another reason why the South African government is changing the status of these reserves and turning them into 'autonomous' territories or 'homelands' – a poisoned gift which is intended to widen the gap between the cost of maintaining the labour force and the profits which derive from it.

7. Quoted in *Cahiers de Mai*, February 1972, no. 35, p. 10.

8. The profits from immigration

1. See above p. 000.

2. In France this sum is paid to the Fonds d'Action Sociale [FAS: a department of the French equivalent of the British DHSS] which is supposed to use it specifically to finance housing for immigrants (and various cultural activities). The terms of this financial support, however, are such that the workers do not benefit, for the FAS loans the money to associations which rent rooms whose construction has been paid for by these loans; but not only do the rents take no account of the fact that these buildings have been subsidised by those who live in them, they are often higher than the legal rates allow. Moreover, these associations are frequently governed by the law of 1901 (on non-profit-making associations) and are therefore subject, in practice, to no control in matters of book-keeping and taxation.

9. The limits of the over-exploitation of labour

1. A still neglected area of history as Hopkins (1973) has observed, but basic material may be found in Coquery-Vidrovitch et Moniot (1974, Chapter 8), J. Woddis (1960, Chapters 4 and 6; 1961, Chapter 2), and Suret-Canale (1964: Part II). There is also of course the classic account given by Rosa Luxemburg (1913, II: Chapters 27, 29).

2. Do we need reminding that, when the productivity of the means of production made available to the workers is increasing, the degree of exploitation can rise, and can be accompanied by a growth in real wages? This is why, as Bettelheim reminds us, the rate of exploitation is highest in sectors where capital's organic composition is strongest (*contra* Amin, 1973, 70).

3. A study of a few families in Tiyabu in Senegal reveals the structural forms of reestablishing equilibrium by which they manage to maintain reasonably strong economic and social cohesion, in contrast to peoples who engage in commercial agriculture and suffer complete disintegation.

4. Kane and Lericollais (1975).

5. The situation is to be seen, for example, in Senegal, from where both groundnuts and labour are exported. The policy of revalorising subsistence goods (1974–5), and the situation of the world market in grains (whose prices tend to rise), may compel Senghor's type of 'socialism' to encourage large private estates and the capitalist appropriation of virgin land. If not the peasantry may return to self-sustenance lands they continue to think are theirs, a really serious threat which will always weigh upon the economic policy of neo-colonial Senegal. In regard to the way that 'food aid' is used in imperialism's economic strategy see: Comité Information Sahel, 1974, II, 3; Reboul, 1975.

6. In 1985, the surplus in rich nations will exceed 50 million tons, more than enough to fill the deficit in poor countries (Beckerman, 1975), and these will then be utterly dependent on the big powers' economic policies.

7. A. Retel-Laurentin (1974, 135f.) has shown that most African peoples are familiar with voluntary abortion and practise birth control (which varies in extent according to the situation). They are not therefore defenceless victims of some disorderly population explosion. All the methods of contraception or sterilisation which Malthusians might recommend will have not the least effect while workers and peasants, subject to capitalist exploitation, do not benefit from adequate social security, which would alleviate their fears for the future.

8. Most African workers in France expect that their retirement will be assured by the emigration of their children (Camara, *et al.*, 1975). The first generation of migrant workers is now in the process of being replaced.

9. P. Gutkind (1975) gives information about the 'progressive isolation' of part of the urban population of Ibadan (Nigeria). Like others who claim to be Marxists, however, this author uses the term *lumpen-proletariat* to name the poorest section of the proletariat. Must it be repeated that for Marx (1895) the notion of *lumpen proletariat* is dialectical and not taxonomic: it designates the misled, dissolute section of the proletariat from which capitalism recruits the stooges it turns against their own class. In France, for example, certain racist bands which kill Arabs and Africans are recruited among the *lumpen* element – it is the *lumpen proletariat* that is the base of fascist

recruitment. The term derives from the German word *Lump* (rascal, villain, blackguard), and not from *Lumpen* (rags) as is generally thought.

10. Statistics collected in Ghana between 1939 and 1959 show a constant decline in real wages paid to unqualified labour in Accra. 'Given that real salaries in 1939 were close to the level of subsistence for an unmarried man, for the next 20 years the worker has had to seek assistance from others or put up with a serious physical decline' (Birmingham, 1960: see also McLoughlin (1963)).

11. The same author describes how white farmers and industrialists were opposed to attempts to raise livestock in the reserves, for, by giving them an opportunity to live off agricultural activities, this would divert African workers from the labour camps.

12. 'The dilemma is clear: on one side migrant labour is grossly inefficient and, to improve its quality and efficiency, it is essential to stabilise it in the employment zone; on the other, maintenance of ties with the tribal system has great advantages for family cohesion and morality and therefore for social peace and political stability' (Report of the Fédération d'Afrique Centrale, referring to the situation in Ruanda-Burundi; it is quoted by J. Woddis (1960, 107)).

13. In addition the employer and political authorities concerned fear all teachings likely to arouse class consciousness and to increase the militancy of the worker.

14. The cost of transport from the country of origin to the place of work is generally met by the migrant workers, but indirectly or directly this cost adds to the cost price of labour.

15. Especially in Latin America and South East Asia, areas where U.S. violence and subversion are at their most virulent; in Europe too – increasingly, for it has the double advantage of having a very developed infrastructure and cheap immigrant labour.

16. The French government plans to slow emigration which had already declined by 41% in 1974. It considers maintaining an inflow of permanent skilled immigrants intended to supply industry with qualified labour and raise the birthrate which in 1975 hovered at break-even point.

Conclusion

1. 'It is one of the principal characteristics of Latin-American military regimes to compress wages and the peasants' standard of living, and this is simply a manifestation of polarised dependent development.' (Stavenhagen, 1971).

2. The Nazis' principal difficulty was how to dispose of the 'waste' created by this economy: how to get rid of the corpses? As Nicolaï observes (1974): 'No economist has written of the economy of concentration camps, of the misery or of the genocide of whole ethnic groups.'

3. Eicher (1973) expresses the shallow point of view of economists who want to make education profitable and who consider it an 'input' rather than a way of broadening the individual.

4. In the United States, the number of women household-heads increases rapidly in poor areas, partly because, unemployed and demoralised, the men leave home, and partly because family allowances are higher for single mothers.

Notes to pages 143–4

5. The experience of 'communes', which allow of the redistribution of income among a still larger number of people – who profess moreover to despise money – shows that they can guarantee reproduction of labour-power more cheaply: much too cheaply in fact to survive the claims and enmity of the petty-bourgeois family which, dimly but rightly, sees in them a dangerous competitor threatening to nullify all its social gains, founded as they are on its still barely acknowledged reproductive functions.

6. See the study by the CERAT (1973) and Hallam (1974).

References cited

Comments sometimes refer only to those passages which are relevant to the subjects examined in this book.

ADAMS, A. 1974, 'Prisoners in Exile: Senegalese Workers in France', *Race and Class* XVI, 2, 157-78.
  Immigration is more of a solution than a problem for the French and Senegalese governments. It is a problem only for migrants.
ALEXANDRE, P. (ed.), 1973, *French Perspectives in African Studies*, Oxford University Press for the International African Institute, 240p.
ALTHABE, G. 1962, 'Problèmes socio-économiques du Nord-Congo', Cahiers de l'ISEA, V, 5, November 1962.
  'In the world of the self-sustaining society, wealth has no existence apart from the individual, it is not dissociated from he who embodies the status of which it is the attribute.'
  1965, 'Changements sociaux chez les pygmées Baka de l'Est Cameroun', *Cahiers d'Etudes Africaines*, V, 4 (20, 561-92.)
  A remarkable case study of the three stage transformation in the economy and society of Baka hunters.
  1972, *Les Fleurs du Congo*, Maspero, Paris, 376 p.
  The ideological reproduction of labour-power.
ALTHUSSER, L. and BALIBAR, E. 1968, *Lire le Capital*, Maspero, Paris, 2 volumes. [*Reading Capital*, tr. B. Brewster (abridged ed.) London 1970.]
  (Can historical materialism be renewed by structuralist idealism and Maoist empiricism?) Does not deal with the reproduction of labour power. The schema 'The elements of all modes of production' (II, 209) leaves no place for human means of reproduction nor for societies where relations of 'appropriation' are mediated by personal relations. . .
AMES, D., 1955, 'Economic base of Wolof Polygyny', *South Western Journal of Anthropology*, II, 4, winter 1955, 391-403.
  'Children are wealth.'
AMIN, S., 1969, *Le Monde des affaires sénégalais*, Editions de Minuit, Paris 207p.
  [The necessary alliance between the Senegalese bourgeoisie and bureaucracy.]
  1970, *L'Accumulation à l'échelle mondiale*, IFAN, Dakar; Anthropos,

162

References cited

Paris, 591p. [*Accumulation of Capital on a World Scale: a Critique of the Theory of World Development*, tr. B. Pearce, Monthly Review Press, New York, 1974.]

[Economistic Marxism, stripped of its revolutionary content.] Inequality exists between countries (not classes) due to the worsening balance of payments and exchange rates.

1973, *L'Echange inégal et la loi de la valeur*, Anthropos, IDEP, Paris, 145p.

An attempt to correct *L'Accumulation à l'échelle mondiale*, this time taking into account the nature of relations of production and of differential productivity.

AMSELLE, J.-L., 1977, *Les Négociants de la Savane. Histoire et organisation sociale des Kooroko (Mali)*, Anthropos, Paris, 290p.

The institution of the family as a support for trading activities. Trade and ideology.

ANCEY, G., 1974, *La Monnaie mossi, un pouvoir non libératoire de règlement*, ORSTOM, Ouagadougou, 176p. roneo.

The domestic community's resistance to the monetary depreciation caused by migrants' incomes.

ANDRADE, M. de and OLLIVIER, M., 1971, *La Guerre en Angola*, Maspero, Paris, 161p.

AUGE, M., 1969, *Le Rivage alladian*, ORSTOM, Memoire No. 34, 264p.

The opening up of a matrimonial system to the effects of trade. Précis of the mechanisms of redistribution.

1969, 'Statut, Pouvoir et Richesse: relations lignagères, relations de dépendance et rapports de production dans la société alladian', *Cahiers d'Etudes Africaines* 9, 3 (35), 1969, 461–81.

1972, 'Sous-Développement et développement: terrain d'étude et objets d'action en Afrique francophone', *Africa*, 52, 3, July 1972, 205–16. Critique of the ideology of development.

1974, 'Sorciers noirs et Diables blancs', in *La Notion de personne en Afrique noire*, published by the CNRS, 519–27.

'Every accusation points to a shortcoming in the social personality of the accused (rich too young; old and poor; rich and sick etc.).'

1975, 'Les Faiseurs d'ombres', in Meillassoux (ed.), 1975, 455–76.

The manipulation of matrilineal kinship by the incorporation of slaves into the kinship system.

BAECK, L., 1957, 'Une société rurale en transition: étude socio-économique de la région de Thysville', *Zaire*, 11, 2, February 1957: 115–86.

(A conservative view of the effects of rural migration.)

BALANDIER, G., 1955, *Sociologie actuelle de l'Afrique noire*, PUF, Paris 510p. [*The Sociology of Black Africa*, tr. D. Garman, Deutsch, London 1970.]

(Rebirth of French anthropology via an original re-interpretation of British functionalism.)

1955a, 'Social Change and Social Problems in Negro-Africa', in C. Stillman (ed.), 1955, 55–69.

1955b, *Sociologie des Brazzavilles noires*, A. Colin, Paris, 274p.

Wage-labour and unpaid labour in a colonial town.

1959, 'Structures sociales traditionnelles et Changements économiques', *Revue de l'Institut de sociologie*, 1:27–40.

References cited

The adaptation of the old order to the advantage of chiefs. Economic investments, 'sociological' investments, 'sacred' investments: how to preserve social security under the influence of the colonial economy.

1960, 'Structures traditionnelles et Changements économiques', *Cahiers d'Etudes Africaines*, 1, 1-14.
Personal relations, official relations.

1965, 'Problématique des classes sociales', *Cahiers internationaux de sociologie*, XXXVIII, January–June 1965, 131-42.
Where should class lines be drawn – between town and country, or Europe and Africa, or the bureaucracy and the people?

1967, *Anthropologie Politique*, PUF, Paris, 240p. [*Political Anthropology*, tr. A. M. Smith, Alan Lane, London, 1970.]
Research into the paths of 'modernism' and change.

BALIBAR, E., 1973, 'Lénine, les Communistes et l'Immigration', *L'Humanité*, 8 June 1973.
Résumé of Lenin's analyses concerning the exploitation of workers from backward countries.

1974, *Cinq études du matérialisme historique*, Maspero, Paris, 295p.
'The process of the permanent reproduction of the working class tends in turn to become a world process.'
'Crises in the schools, crises of the family, crises of "youth", are so many symptoms of the overall crisis in the reproduction of labour-groups.'

BAUCIC, I., 1974, 'Temporary or Permanent – the Dilemma of Migrants and Migration policies', *Colloque européen sur les problèmes de la migration, Louvain, January 31st to February 2nd, 1974*, 18p. roneo.
[Promising but thin.]

BAREL, Y., 1973, *La Reproduction sociale*, Anthropos, Paris, 558p.
[Philosophical theory culminating in a mechanistic and unilluminating 'interlocking' of different 'levels of reproduction'.]

BARTH, F., 1973, 'Descent and Marriage Reconsidered', in GOODY (ed.) 1973a.
Choice and behaviour are not dictated exclusively by the structures of kinship; the latter is subject to constraints.

BAUER, P. T. and YAMEY, B. S., 1957, *The Economics of Underdeveloped Countries*, CUP, Cambridge, 270p.
(A plea for private enterprise and classical economic policies serving the great colonial powers.)

BECKERMAN, W., 1975, 'Réquisitoire contre le Club de Rome', *L'Expansion*, 83, March 1975.
'It is the surrender to market forces which would bring about widespread famine.'

BECKETT, J. 1956, *Akokoaso*, LSE Monograph No. 10, 95p.
Social and economic effects of the introduction of cocoa growing: 'permanent draining of income for the benefit of the towns [. . .] extremely unequal incomes'.

BEHAR, L., 1974, 'Surpopulation relative et Reproduction de la force travail', *La Pensée*, 176, August 1974, 9-92.
Marx did not advocate a demographic solution ('a strike of the wombs') but a political one (union of workers and unemployed).

164

References cited

BENNETT, H. H., 1945, *Soil Erosion and Land Use in the Union of South Africa*, Pretoria, Dept of agriculture and Forestry, 28p.

BENVENISTE, E., 1969, *Le Vocabulaire des institutions indo-européennes*, Editions de Minuit, Paris, 2 vols. [*Indo-European Language and Society*, tr. E. Palmer, Faber, London, 1973.]
[Masterly study of *semantics* which reveals the lost but still functional meaning of the social, economic and political vocabulary.]

BERG, E., 1965, 'The Development of a Labour-Force in Sub-Saharan Africa', *Economic Development and Cultural Change*, 13, 4, 1, July 1965, 396-412.
Inventory of the methods employed to 'dislodge' the peasant labourforce.

BESSAIGNET, P., 1966, *Principes de l'Ethnologie économique*, Pichon et Durand-Auzias, Paris, 190p.
[An unrecognised pioneer.]

BETTELHEIM, C., 1967, introduction to LAULAGNET A.-M., 1967.
'Reproduction models do not refer us to a process over time but to the same conditions infinitely repeated.'

BIOCCA, E., 1968, *Yanoáma*, Plon, Paris, 470p. [*Yanoáma – the Story of a Woman (Helena Valero) Abducted by Brazilian Indians, as Told to E. Biocca*, tr. D. Rhodes, Allen and Unwin, London, 1969.]
[Rare testimony on the intimate life of a population of primitive cultivators.]

BIRMINGHAM, W., 1960, 'An Index of Real Wages of the Unskilled Labour in Accra 1939-1959', *Economic Bulletin, Accra*, 4, 3, March 1960, 2-6.
The declining living standards of the originally rural proletariat in Accra.

BOHANNAN, P., 1954, *Tiv Farms and Settlements*, HMSO, Colonial Research Studies, No. 15.
Social organisation of the unit of production. Control over work, crops, land. [A fine, penetrating study.]

1959, 'The impact of Money on an African Subsistence Economy', *The Journal of Economic History*, 19, 491-503.
Spheres of circulation among the Tiv. Notions of 'transfer' (within spheres) and of 'conversion' (between one sphere and another). The different functions of money in this mode of circulation.

BOHANNAN, P. and DALTON, G. (eds), 1962, *Markets in Africa*, Northwestern University Press, Evanston, Il. 762p.

BONNAFE, P., 1975, 'Les Formes d'asservissement chez les Kukuya d'Afrique Centrale', in MEILLASSOUX (ed.), 1975, 529-56.
The contradictions and social politics of a matrilineal society under the effects of the slave-trade. How lineages come to be hierarchised.

BONTE, P., 1973, 'Quelques problèmes théoriques de la recherche marxiste en anthropologie', *La Pensée*, 171, Oct. 1973, 86-107.

BOUDON, P., 1967, 'Essai sur l'interpretation de la notion d'échange', *L'Homme*, VII, 2, April-June 1967, 64-84.
Categorisation of the modes of exchange in terms of Chomsky's linguistics, originating from Mauss and Polyani. [A method based on analogy and without scientific weight.]

BOUILLER, L., 1923, *De l'obligation au travail pour les indigènes des colonies d'exploitation*, La Vie Universitaire, Paris, 185p.

165

References cited

BRADBY, B., 1975, 'The Destruction of National Economy in Peru: a Problem of the Articulation of Modes of Production', *Economy and Society*, 4, 2, May 1975: 127–61.
> A critique of *Alliances de Classe* by P.-P. Rey. What is the driving force of imperialism? The production of raw materials or the extension of capitalist relations of production? Is it violence or the difference in productivity between capitalist and precapitalist modes which drains the labour-power towards the capitalist sector?

BRAZZA, S. de, 1886, 'L'Occupation du Congo', *Comptes Rendus des Séances de la Société de Géographie*, 2–3, 49–85.
> 'You must strive above all to prepare the change of the natives into agents of labour, of production and of consumption; later the European will come, in the simple role of intermediary.'

BREMOND, Claude, 1968, 'Spécificité du thème africain de "l'impossible restitution"', *Cahiers d'Etudes Africaines*, 8, 2(30), 201–5.
> The inverted ideology of exchange.

BRIZAY, B., 1973, 'Peut-on se passer des travailleurs immigrés?', *Entreprise*, No. 948, November 1973.
> [How the employers see the problem. Lucid and informative.]

BRUNHOFF, S. de, 1967, *La Monnaie chez Marx*, Editions Sociales, Paris, 191p.
> 'The mysterious power of making commodities commensurable among themselves.'

BRUYAS, J., 1966, 'La Royauté en Afrique noire', *Annales Africaines 1966*, 157–227.
> The change from collateral to lineal succession.

BUKH, J., 1974, *Attempt to Conceptual Structuring of Data from Field Survey (Ghana) and some Models for Discussion*, Institute for Development Research, Copenhagen, 19p. roneo.
> Domestic and capitalist relations of production in cocoa growing; transfers from one sector to another.

CAMARA, M., MARC, E., SAMUEL, M., n.d. (1975), *Les Travailleurs africains noirs en France*, UNESCO, Dp. Ref. 508191.
> [The basis for a good introduction to the problem, seen through the eyes of fieldworkers.]

CAPRON, J. and KOHLER, J.-M., 1975, *Migrations de Travail et Pratique Matrimoniale*, ORSTOM, Ouagadougou, Conv. FAC. No. 13/C/71/F, 63p. roneo.
> Class domination through control over marriage. *Pug-siure* marriage. How power politically corrupts the lineages.

CEDETIM, 1975, *Les Immigrés*, Stock, Paris, 384p.
> [A well documented work which raises the essential issues.]

CELIK, H. (ed.), 1969, 'Les Travailleurs immigrés parlent', *Cahiers du Centre d'Etudes Socialistes*, 94–8, September–December 1969, 175p.
> Statistics, living conditions, interviews, particularly of Algerians.

CERAT, 1972, *La Place de l'institution communale dans l'organisation de la domination politique de classe en milieu urbain. Le cas de Roanne*, Université des sciences sociales, Grenoble, 221p.
> Housing and space as elements in the reproduction of labour-power.
> [An exemplary piece of work.]

CHAGNON, N. A., 1968, *Yanomamo, the fierce people*, Holt, Rinehart and Winston, New York.

166

References cited

The importance of war and violence as means of settling the problems of reproduction among this Amazonian people. A well-documented work which contradicts the work of the French Americanists (Clastre, Lizot, Jaulin) whose theses, though written later, were developed in ignorance of it.

CHAYANOV, A. V. (1925), *The Theory of Peasant Economy*, R. D. Irwin, Homewood, Ill., 1966, 317p.

[The more, the merrier . . . and the less the peasant works. Soviet 'marginalism'!]

CLASTRE, P., 1974, *La Sociéte contre l'Etat*, Editions de Minuit, Paris.

[A critique of ethnocentrism based upon ethnocentric political concerns: savages (conceived in the way of eighteenth-century philosophers) invented ways of defending themselves against premonitions of the State – but only as long as conditions for its appearance did not occur. Power nevertheless imposed itself. Politics is the basis of economics.]

CLUER, S. W., NEAL, J. V., CHAGNON, N. A., 1971, 'Demography of a Primitive Population: a Simulation', *American Journal of Physical Anthropology* 2, 35, 2, September 1971.

Yanoama women have three to four children during their period of fertility.

COMITE INFORMATION SAHEL, 1974, *Qui se nourrit de la famine en Afrique?* Maspero, Paris, 278p.

An economic and political analysis of the food crisis in the Sahel – which goes beyond the documentary evidence. The dramatic effects of 'food aid'.

C.O.N.C.P., 1965, *La lutte de libération nationale dans les colonies portugaises*, Information C.O.N.C.P., Alger, 229p.

One fifth of Mozambique's foreign currency is provided by the 'return' from labour migrants abroad, that is from an annual movement of about 400,000 workers shipped to Rhodesia and South Africa.

COPANS, J., 1972, *L'Idéologie comme instance de reproduction sociale: l'exemple de la confrérie Mouride*, Centre d'Etudes Africaines, 11p. roneo.

'Colonial capitalism needs elements of pre-capitalist modes of production, whose formal subjection explains the colonial and neo-colonial superprofits [. . .] they help to reproduce the conditions of production (and therefore of their domination).' The role of ideology in this process.

1973, *Stratification sociale et Organisation agricole dans les villages wolof-mourides du Sénégal*, Thesis (3e cycle), Ecole pratique des hautes études, Paris, 2 vols. roneo.

The religious framework for the colonial exploitation of Senegalese groundnut farmers.

1974, *Critiques et politiques de l'anthropologie*. Maspero, Paris, 148p.

[The real problems of anthropology, posed uncompromisingly for anthropologists.]

COPANS, J. (ed.), 1975, *Sécheresses et Famines au Sahel*, Maspero 'Dossiers Africains', 2 vols.

Documents and analyses. Bibliography.

COPANS, J., COUTY, Ph., ROCH, J., Rocheteau, G., 1972, *Maintenance*

167

References cited

sociale et Changement économique au Sénégal. I: *Doctrine économique et Pratique du travail chez les Mourides*, ORSTOM 'Travaux et Documents' No. 15, 264p.
> Elements for defining the Mouride economy. Divergent points of view.

COQUERY-VIDROVITCH, C., 1969, 'Recherches sur un mode de production africain', *La Pensée*, 144, April 1969, 61–78.
> A combination of community agriculture and long distance trade seen as the basis of the African mode of production.

COQUERY-VIDROVITCH, C. and MONIOT, H., 1974, *L'Afrique noire de 1800 à nos jours*, PUF, Paris, 462p.
> [The best handbook on the history of Africa in French. Integrates theory with economic and social history. Deals with colonialism and imperialism.]

CRESSANT, P. 1970, *Lévi-Strauss*, Editions Universitaires, Paris, 155p.
> [Structuralism revealed through its contradictions.]

CRUISE O'BRIEN, D., 1971, *The Mourides of Senegal*, Clarendon Press, Oxford, 321p.
> Descriptive analysis of an Islamic brotherhood, through which the commercial production of groundnuts is being developed in Senegal.

1974, 'Don divin, Don terrestre: l'économie de la confrérie mouride', *Archiv. europ. sociol.*, XV, 82–100.
> The peasants benefited from the Mourides' social revolution which also protects them from the potentially destructive intrusion of the market economy.

CRUISE O'BRIEN, R., 1971, *Unemployment, the Family and Class Formation*, Conference on Urban Employment in Africa, University of Sussex, September 1971, 16 p. roneo.
> Preservation of family relationships among the least integrated, proletarianised sections of the population. Development of class consciousness among those who benefit from greater job-security.

DALTON, G., 1960, 'A note of Clarification on Economic Surplus', *American Anthropologist*, 3, 62, June 1960, 483–90.
> The role of a material surplus in bringing about socio-economic organisational change is not clear. The term 'surplus' does not have the same meaning in a market and in a non-market economy.

1961, 'Economic Theory and Primitive Society', *American Anthropologist*, 63, 1, February, 1961.
> Précis of Polyani's ideas.

DAMPIERRE, E. de, 1960, 'Coton noir, Café blanc', *Cahiers d'Etudes Africaines* (2), May 1960.
> The role of plantation foremen.

DENIEL, R., 1972, 'Mesures gouvernementales et/ou intérêts divergents des pays exportateurs de main-d'oeuvre et des pays hôtes; Haute-Volta et Côte d'Ivoire', *Notes et Documents Voltaïques*, 5 (3), April 1972, 5–13.
> Features of the dual labour market in the Ivory Coast.

DOUGLAS, M., 1958, 'Raffia-Cloth Distribution in the Lele Economy', *Africa*, 28, 2, April 1958, 109–22.
> 'Women are the ultimate reason for the possession of raffia.'

1963, *The Lele of the Kasai*, OUP, London, 286p.

References cited

From bilateral marriage-exchange to multilateral exchange.
1967, 'Primitive Rationing', in Firth (ed.), 1967, 119–47.
[Looks at the problem of matrimonial claims and the way in which, by manipulating goods, control is exercised over them – but does so through reference to the inadequate notions of liberal economics.]

DUPRIEZ, G., 1973, *La Formation du salaire en Afrique*, Drukkerij Frankie, Leuven (Belgium), 430p.
[An accurate view of the problem in terms of classical economics.]

EICHER, J.-C., 1973, Réflexions sur l'économie de l'éducation', *le Courrier du CNRS*, 10, October 1973, 15–18.
Human beings are considered as an economic 'product' by this new discipline. [The individual is no longer the aim of production and of education, he is 'human capital' put at the service of the profit oriented economy.] Favours a computation of the 'rate of return on education'. [The terrifying logic of capitalism exposed with the easy conscience of economic cretinism.]

ENGELS, F. (1845), *The Condition of the Working Class in England*, (Introduction by E. J. Hobsbawm, Panther, London, 1969, 336p.
(1872), *La Question du logement*, Editions Sociales, 1957, Paris, 111p. [*The Housing Question*, tr. C. P. Dutt, Lawrence and Wishart, London, n.d.]
It has not changed since the beginnings of capitalism: 'The housing crisis is not an accident, it is a necessary institution' for the making of profit.
(1877-8), *Anti-Dühring*, Editions Sociales, Paris, 1956, 511p. [*Anti-Dühring*, F.L.P.H., Moscow/Lawrence and Wishart, London, 1955.]
(1884), *L'Origine de la famille, de la propriété privée et de l'Etat*, Editions Sociales, Paris, 1954, 358p. [*The Origin of the Family, Private Property and the State*, Lawrence and Wishart, London, 1940.]
[Remains, despite its mistakes, a great classic.]

ETIENNE, P., 1968, 'Parenté et Alliance chez les Baoulé', *l'Homme*, VII, 4, 1968, 50–76.
1971a, 'Du mariage en Afrique occidentale' (Introduction), Cahiers de l'ORSTOM, *Sciences humaines*, VIII, 2, 131–42.

ETIENNE, P. and M., 1971b, '"A qui mieux mieux" ou le mariage chez les Baoulé, Cahiers de l'ORSTOM, *Sciences humaines*, VIII, 2, 165–86.

EVANS-PRITCHARD, E. E., 1940, *The Nuer*, Clarendon Press, Oxford, 271p.
Relations between like communities within a political system of 'organised anarchy'.

FALLERS, L. A., 1956, *Bantu Bureaucracy*, Heffer & Sons, Cambridge, 283p. (Reprinted 1965, Chicago University Press, Chicago, Ill.)

FEUCHTWANG, S., 1974, 'Some Notions about an Agricultural State', *The Journal of Peasant Studies*, I, 3, April 1974, 379–83.
Differences in the social organisation of the different social classes in imperial China.

FIRTH, R., 1936, *We, the Tikopia: a sociological study of kinship in primitive Polynesia*, Allen and Unwin, London, 605p.
1939, *Primitive Polynesian Economy*, Routledge, London, 387p.
The discovery of spheres of exchange.
1951, *Elements of Social Organization*, Watts & Co., London, 257p.

169

References cited

Introductory texts. Discussion of the economic organisation of the unit of production. Mutual aid. 'Incentives'.

1956, *Human Types; an introduction to Social Anthropology*, Th. Nelson, London.

[Accurate observation, but a tendency to define the traditional economy negatively by reference to the capitalist economy.]

FIRTH, R. (ed.), 1967, *Themes in Economic Anthropology*, Tavistock, London, ASA Monograph, 6, 292p.

[Functionalism with its limitations as applied to economics: borrowings from bourgeois liberal economics.]

FORDE, D. 1934, *Habitat, Economy and Society: a Geographical Introduction to Ethnology*, Methuen, London, 1963, 1971, 500p.

[Well summarised monograph treatments of sixteen peoples: hunters and gatherers, farmers, nomads.]

FORDE, D. (ed.), 1956, *Aspects sociaux de l'industrialisation et de l'urbanisation en Afrique au sud du Sahara*, IAI, UNESCO, 799p.

[Collections of articles and research projects of uneven interest, mostly descriptive.]

FORDE, D. and DOUGLAS, M., 1967, 'Primitive Economies', in DALTON, G. (ed.), 1967, 13–28.

FOUNOU-TCHUIGOUA, B., 1974, 'Marché réel et Marché formel de force de travail', *La Pensée*, No. 176, August 1974, 30–45.

Commodity producers, being connected by the market, are in fact sellers of their labour-power in a 'real' labour market. An attempt to establish a logical link between the situation of workers and of peasants. Open to criticism.

FOX, R., 1967, *Kinship and Marriage*, Harmondsworth, Penguin Books.

[A functionalist classic on kinship.]

FRANK, A. G., 1972, *Le Développement du sous-développement*, Maspero, Paris, 399p.

Dialectics or dualism?

FRANKENBERG, R., 1967, 'Economic Anthropology: one Anthropologist's View', in FIRTH (ed.), 1967, 47–89.

'Like Dalton, Bohannan and Sahlins, I believe Herskovits, Firth and others have wasted their time.'

G.A.I.D.E., 1956, 'Au Tchad, les transformations subies par l'agriculture traditionnelle sous l'influence de la culture cotonnière', *L'Agronomie Tropicale*, 5, 597–623; 6, 707–31.

Decline in millet yields. Sharp increase in work required by cotton. No increase in productivity. Warning against this cotton-growing policy.

GARLAN, Y., 1973, 'L'Oeuvre de Polyani. La place de l'économie dans les sociétés anciennes', *La Pensée*, No. 171, October 1973, 118–28.

[Official Marxism at last discovers Polyani.]

GIRARD, R., 1963, *Les Indiens de l'Amazone péruvienne*, Payot, 308p.

[Outdated and disorganised ethnography. Very little useable material.]

GLICKMAN, M., 1971, 'Kinship and Credit among the Nuer', *Africa*, XLI, 4, October 1971, 306–19.

The effects of traditional economic constraints on kinship relations.

170

References cited

GLUCKMAN, M., 1940, 'Analysis of a Social Situation in Modern Zululand', *Bantu Studies*, 14, 1, March 1940; 14, 2, June 1940.
> The development of the labour market and of segregation in Zululand. The destruction of men in the Transkei reserves.

1941, *Economy of the Central Barotse Plain*, Rhodes-Livingstone Papers No. 7, R.L. Institute, 130p.
> The social effects of an economy based on flooded agriculture. Effects of cash-earning on the economy. Migration.

1942, 'Some Processes of Social Change Illustrated from Zululand', *African Studies*, 1, 4, December 1942, 243-60.
> Two types of society: repetitive and changing. Process of change through confrontation of cultures.

1960, 'Tribalism in Modern British Central Africa', *Cahiers d'Etudes Africaines*, I, 1:55-72.
> Tribalism is maintained by the economic conditions established for Africans.

GODELIER, M. (ed.), 1970, *Sur les sociétés précapitalistes: textes choisis de Marx, Engels, Lénine; Preface de M.G.*, Editions Sociales, Paris, 414p.
> Collections of texts by Marx, Engels, Lenin. Preface by M. Godelier: 'kinship is both infrastructure and superstructure' (p. 139).

1973a, *Horizon, Trajets marxistes en anthropologie*, Maspero, Paris, 395p.
> Collection of articles.

1973b, 'Modes de production, Rapports de parenté et Structures demographiques', *La Penseé*, 172, December 1973, 7-31.
> Kinship is both infrastructure and superstructure. Brings in elements for a demographic and ecological causality.

GOODY, J., 1958, 'The Fission of Domestic Groups among the Lodagaba', in *The Developmental Cycle in Domestic Groups*, J. GOODY (ed.), CUP, Cambridge, 145p.
> Various processes of segmentation; the cyclical process of domestic fission over three generations, described through comparisons between groups of agricultural production, food consumption and residence.

GOODY, J. (ed.), 1973a, *The Character of Kinship*, CUP, Cambridge, 251p.

GOODY, J. 1973b, 'Polygyny, Economy and the Role of Women', in J. GOODY (ed.), 1973a.
> 'The greater economic role of women could theoretically lead to their retention as daughters rather than to their alienation as wives [. . .] The critical consideration would be the labour of her (male) children rather than of the woman herself [. . .] Plurality of wives may be desired for reproductive purposes.' (p. 188).

GOODY, J. and BUCKLEY, J. 1973, 'Inheritance and Women's Labour in Africa', *Africa*, XLVIII, 11, April 1973, 108-21.
> 'The contribution of women to agricultural production is greater where the basic means of production, land, is inherited matrilineally than it is in a patrilineal system' (p. 110).

GOSSELIN, G., 1970, *Développement et Tradition dans les sociétés africaines*, BIT, Geneva, 343p.
> Especially useful for the anthropology of labour among the Gbeya: the position of the young, of women, of the old in the domestic

171

References cited

economy, and as affected by the relations of production introduced with cash cropping. The enduring economic and social roles of food production.

1972, *Travail et Changement social en pays gbeya (RCA)*, Klincksieck, Paris, 356p.

The social organisation of production. Statistics about the makeup of production units. Ideological contexts.

1973, *Formations et Stratégies de transition en Afrique tropicale*, Doctorat d'Etat, Paris University V, 2 vols.

'In the context of policies which seek to bring about popular participation in the putting into practice [...], of a development that concerns the people but which is beyond their conception, traditional values, structures and fuctions raise more problems than they solve. This study is almost wholy a reworking of the material contained in GOSSELIN 1970.

GOULD, J. and KOLB, W. L., 1964, *A Dictionary of the Social Sciences*, Tavistock Publications, London, 1964, 761p.

GOUROU, P., 1954, 'Les Kikuyu et la crise Mau-Mau', *Cahiers d'Outre-Mer*, 28, 7, October–December 1954.

Denounces the deliberate low wages policy practised in Kenya, when it was a British colony, which was intended *to increase the supply of labour* (since workers left their jobs after earning the amount they had set themselves as a target).

GRAY, R. F., 1960, 'Sonjo Bride-Price and the Question of African Wife-Purchase', *American Anthropologist*, 62, 1, February 1960.

Marriage is a purchase of women! [The absurdity of classical liberal economics applied to domestic economics.]

GUNN, H. D., 1956, *Pagan Peoples of the Central Area of Northern Nigeria*, Ethnographic Survey, IAI, London, 146p.

Segmentary societies.

GURVITCH, G., 1955, *Déterminismes sociaux et Liberté humaine*, PUF, Paris, 297p.

Four global types of archaic structure, pp. 200–2.

GUSSMAN, B., 1953, 'Industrial Efficiency and the Urban African', *Africa*, 23, 2, April 1953, 135–44.

Productivity per unit of labour in Southern Rhodesia is the lowest in the Commonwealth. Causes: lack of a public voice, low rates of pay, unsatisfactory living conditions, crushing official controls (up to fourteen passes required), the impossibility of improving their social situation whatever they earn; urban workers constitute a nomadic community and continue to maintain links with their homes.

GUTKIND, P., 1975, 'The View from Below: Political Consciousness of the Urban Poor in Ibadan, Western Nigeria', *Cahiers d'Etudes Africaines*. No. 57, vol. XV (1).

How the poor proletariat see class relations.

HAILEY, Lord, 1938, *An African Survey*, OUP, London.

[A reference work, colonial in spirit, dealing with all the African problems. Periodically updated and re-edited . . . a document.]

HALLAM, R., 1974, 'The Production of Poverty', *Economy and Society*, 3, 4, November 1974: 451–66.

Critique of bourgeois notions of 'income', 'consumption', 'poverty'

172

References cited

in terms of dialectical materialism and the production of the forces of production.

HALPERN, J., 1967, 'Traditional Economy in West Africa', *Africana Bulletin*, 7, 91–112.

1968, 'The Roots of Agricultural Changes in Precapitalist Africa', *Acta Poloniae Historica*, 18, 120–9.
[Exaggerates 'demographic pressures' and underestimates the effects of trade.]

HARRINGTON, M., 1962, *The Other America*, Harmondsworth, Penguin Books, 186p.
The other face of North American prosperity: fifty million poor!

HASWELL, M. R., 1953, *Economics of Agriculture in a Savannah Village*, Colonial Office, London, No. 8, 141p.
Social organisation of labour resources in a Gambian village.

HARRIS, M., 1959, 'Labour Migration among the Mozambique Thonga: Cultural and Political Factors', *Africa*, 29, 1, January 1959, 50–65.
Sixty per cent of the men are labour migrants.

HERITIER, F., 1973, 'La Paix et la Pluie', *l'Homme*, XIII, 3:121–38.
Inequality between lineages and birth of a power 'through renewing lineage relations'.

1974, 'Univers féminin et destin individuel chez les Samo', *La Notion de Personne en Afrique Noire*, CNRS, Paris: 243–54.
Of man's need to take possession of 'the woman's wild fruit' and at the same time escape the fate she may inflict upon him by asserting law and culture and 'civilisation' against her.

HERMAN, E.-J., 1975, 'La Contre-Révolution des revenus', *Le Monde Diplomatique*, 253, April 1975.
The enduring inequality of incomes in the United States.

HEUSCH, L. de, 1955, 'Valeur, Monnaie et Structuration sociale chez les Nkutschi (Kasai, Congo belge)', *Revue de l'institut de sociologie*, 1, 1955, 1–26.
'Copper money', 'symbolic of woman', circulates as 'a claim' between kinship groups.

1958, *Essais sur le symbolisme de l'inceste royal en Afrique*, Institut d'Ethnologie Solvay, Bruxelles, 268p.
An attempt at a psycho-analytical analysis.

HIERNAUX, J., 1973, 'Some Ecological Factors Affecting Human Populations in Sub-Saharan Africa', in HOSWELL and BOURLIERE (eds), 1973, 534–46.
Ecology must take into account the past of each people.

HODGSON, G., 1974, 'Marxian Epistemology and the Transformation Problem', *Economy and Society*, 3, 4, November 1974, 357–392.
The relation between value and price: the debate isn't over.

HOPKINS, A. G., 1973, *An Economic History of West Africa*, Longmans, London, 337p.
[A welcome handbook, though very marginalistic.]

HOWELL, C. F. and CLARK, J. D., 1964, 'Acheulian Hunter-Gatherers of Sub-Saharan Africa', in HOWELL and BOURLIERE (eds), 1964.
'Methods of supplying meat must have varied considerably even within the limited range offered by the cultural level of the late pleistocene.'

173

References cited

HOWELL, C. F. and BOURLIERE, F., (eds), 1964, *African Ecology and Human Evolution*, Methuen, London, 666p.

HOYT, E., 1956, 'The Impact of a Money Economy on Consumption Patterns', *Annals of the American Academy of Political and Social Sciences*, May 1956, 12-22.
> Urban wages are established by reference to the subsistence costs of a single man. Cash crops have caused nutritional standards to fall.

HUBER, H., 1969, 'Le Principe de réciprocité dans le mariage Nyende', *Africa*, London, 39, 3, July 1969, 260-74.
> 'Sister' exchange and promises of marriage.

HUGON, Ph., 1968, *Analyse du sous-développement en Afrique noire: l'exemple de économie du Cameroun*, PUF, Paris, 325p.
> 'The wage level (in local industry) has no real influence on manufacturing cost', as it is so low.

HYAMS, P. R., 1970, 'The Origins of a peasant Land Market in England', *The Economic History Review*, XXVIII, I, April 1970, 18-31.
> Due to the importance of the family, land is transferred through inheritance, marriage and through other ways connected to kinship. How does it enter the market? Where does the money which buys it come from? Suggests that usurers play a role.

HYMER, S. H. 1970, 'Economic Forms in Pre-Colonial Ghana', *Journal of Economic History*, XXX, 1, March, 33-50.
> 'Development' without expropriating land.

INTERNATIONALE COMMUNISTE, 1934, *Manifestes, Thèses et Résolutions des quatre premiers Congrès mondiaux de l'Internationale communiste 1919-1923*; Bibliothèque communiste (reprinted in facsimile), Maspero, 1970, 216p.

ISICHEI, P. A. C., 1973, 'Sex in Traditional Asaba', *Cahiers d'Etudes Africaines* (52), XIII, 4, 682-700.
> Sexual repression.

IVANOV, Yu., 1973, *Labour Migration and the Rise of a Working Class in Tropical Africa*, Third Session of the International Congress of Africanists, Addis Ababa, 34p. roneo.
> Decline in the conditions for the production of cheap labour-power due to rotating migration in East Africa.

IZARD, M., 1975, 'Les Captifs royaux dans l'ancien Yatenga', in MEILLASSOUX (ed.), 1975, 281-96.
> Matrimonial redistribution by the king.

JACQUES-MEUNIER, D., 1949, 'Greniers collectifs', *Hesperis*, XXXVI, 1-2, 97-138.
> The family granaries are contained within a single 'tribal' building (the *agadir*), sacred, guarded, and managed by a small council of owners. Ways of dealing with agricultural contingencies (a good harvest being exceptional) and with the threat of theft.

JAULIN, R., 1966, 'La Distribution des femmes et des biens chez les Mara', *Cahiers d'Etudes Africaines* (23), VI, 3, 419-63.
> A precise study of matrimonial and food reciprocity, salted with structuralism.

[1970], *La Paix blanche*, Union Générale d'Edition, 1974, 2 vols.
> [A militant work opposing ethnocide, but weakened by its exoticism. Imperialism is reduced to a cultural weakness of 'whites'.]

174

References cited

1973, *Gens de soi, Gens de l'autre*, UGE, Paris, 439p.
> For the article by S. Pinton on the organisation of the Motilone collective house.

KAGAME, A., 1968–9, 'La Place de Dieu dans la religion des Bantu', *Cahiers des Religions Africaines*, 2, July 1968, 213-22; 4, January 1969, 5-11.
> By procreation, man perpetuates the human race: this is his religion.

KAHN, J. S., 1974, 'Imperialism and the Reproduction of Capitalism', *Critique of Anthropology*, 2, Autumn 1974, 1-35.
> 'Wages (in Indonesia) do not equal the total cost of the reproduction of labour-power.'

KANE, F. and LERICOLLAIS, R., n.d. [1975], *L'Emigration en pays soninké*, 22p. roneo.
> 'The function of Soninké emigration is to produce a labour-power which is exploited in France. However, for several years, the drain has been such that it is unlikely the situation can stabilise like this.'

KING, K. K., 1973, *Blacks in the White Highlands: Some Aspects of Squatting in Kenya*, University of Birmingham, CWAS, 19p. roneo.
> The Kenyan policy of the combined exploitation of both land and labour.

KIRK-GREENE, A. N. M., 1956, 'Tax and Travel among the Hill Tribes of Northern Adamawa', *Africa*, 26, 4, December 1956, 369-79.
> Seasonally the men migrate to work several hundreds of kilometres away as labourers, etc., to earn the money to pay taxes and the cost of marrying (selling in the market provides another means). Long-lasting migrations (four years) to the large towns.

KOHLER, J.-M., 1971, *Activités agricoles et Changements sociaux dans l'Ouest-Mossi*, ORSTOM, Mémoire No. 46, 248p.
> A careful description of the social organisation of production.

1972, *Les Migrations des Mossi de l'Ouest*, ORSTOM, Paris, Travaux et Documents No. 18, 106p.
> 'Migration maintains the infrastructure of local production at the lowest levels [. . .] The damage inflicted by migration on the dynamism and initiative of the population is even more serious than the loss which results from the departure of young labour.'

KORN, F., 1973, *Elementary Structure Reconsidered: Lévi-Strauss on Kinship*, Tavistock, London, 168p.
> A methodological critique of Lévi-Strauss' structuralism.

KRADER, L., 1972, *The Ethnological Notebooks of Karl Marx*. Ven Gorcum, Assen, 454p.
> [A faithful reproduction of Marx's reading notes (on Morgan, Phear, Maine, Lubbock) but difficult to use. An important introduction on the place of ethnology in Marx's and Engels' work.]

KULA, W., 1970, *Théorie économique du système féodal*, Mouton, Paris, 173p. *An Economic Theory of the Feudal System: Towards a Model of the Polish Economy 1500-1800*, tr. L. Garner, New Left Books, London, 1976.
> [One of the best works on the subject. Many interesting ideas, though his theoretical analysis is often nearer to marginalism than historical materialism.]

LABOUR ADVISING BOARD OF LAGOS, 1945, 'Industrial Conditions in Nigeria', *Africa*, 15, 3, July 1945, 165.

References cited

The 'sweatshop system' in the clothing industry is worse than during the British Industrial Revolution. Without payment, children work nights and Sundays. Employees work six nights in a row without a break until they fall asleep, etc.

LACLAU, E., 1971, 'Feudalism and Capitalism in Latin America', *New Left Review*, 67, 19-38.

One of the first discussions of the articulation of modes of production.

LAULAGNET, A.-M., 1967, *Les Schémas de la reproduction chez Marx*, Problèmes de planification, 9, Ecole pratique des Hautes Etudes, VIIe section, Paris, 47p.

Marx worked out his analysis of reproduction schemas within a framework of interesting abstract ideas and hypotheses, particularly in the short term.

LAURENTIN, A., 1960, 'Femmes nazakara' in PAULME, D., (ed.), 1960, 121-72.

Differences in status and conditions among women in the Nzakara sultanate.

LANGE, O., 1958, 'Le Marxisme et l'Economie bourgeoise', *Cahiers Internationaux*, April–May 1958, 95, 79-86; 96, 85-92.

The historical and ideological role of bourgeois economic theory.

LECOUR-GRANDMAISON, C., 1972, *Femmes Dakaroises*, Annales de l'Universite d'Abidjan, Serie F, tome IV, 253p.

The union of business and marriage among Lebou women of Dakar.

LEE, G., 1971, 'Rosa Luxemburg and the Impact of Imperialism', *The Economic Journal*, London, December 1971, 81, 847-62.

1972, 'An Assimilating Imperialism', *Journal of Contemporary Asia*, 2, 1, 15p.

Dependent economies are incapable of reproducing themselves.

1973, 'The Logic of Surplus-Value', unpublished, 25p. roneo.

[A discussion containing some confusion but through which some of the unresolved problems of 'labour-value' are revealed.] 'The total surplus-value of a society is determined within a single sector, the means-of-subsistence sector, in which, incidentally, the labour of woman as wife–mother is predominant.'

LEE, R. B. and DEVORE, I. (eds), 1968, *Man the Hunter*, Aldine Publishing Company, Chicago, 415p.

A basic text. Useful ecological data.

LEIRIS, M., 'L'Expression de l'idée de travail dans une langue d'initiés soudanais (Dogon)', (Le Travail en Afrique noire), *Présence Africaine*, No. 13, Le Seuil, Paris, 69-84.

'Work is conceived solely in terms of the good which results from it socially.'

LENIN, V. I., 1907, *Le Développement du capitalisme en Russie*, Editions Sociales (n.d.), Paris, 758p. *The Development of Capitalism in Russia*, F.L.P.H., Moscow/ Lawrence and Wishart, London, 1957.

The development of the internal market.

1913, 'Le Capitalism et l'Immigration des ouvriers', *Oeuvres complètes*, 19, 488-91. 'Capitalism and Workers' Immigration', *Collected Works*, IX, 464-7, F.L.P.H., Moscow/Lawrence and Wishart, London, 1964.

Quoted by Balibar, 1973.

References cited

[1916], *L'Impérialisme, Stade suprème du capitalisme*, Editions Sociales, Paris, 1952, 127p. *Imperialism, the Highest Stage of Capitalism*, Lawrence and Wishart, London, 1947 (eds.).

The immigration and exploitation of the colonial proletariat encourages the creation of a privileged group among the workers in exploited countries.

LEROI-GOURHAN, A., 1964-5, *Le Geste et la Parole*, Albin Michel, Paris, 323p.

An intelligent but non-historical materialism.

LEURQUIN, Ph., 1960, *Le Niveau de vie des populations rurales du Ruanda-Urundi*, Nauwelaerts, Louvain, 420p.

The royal economy; the colonial impact; the problem of famine; 'buying money'; the human limits to production.

LEVI-STRAUSS, C., 1967, *Structures élémentaires de la parenté* (Second edition), Plon, Paris. *The Elementary Structures of Kinship*, revised edition tr. J. H. Bell and J. R. von Sturmer, ed. R. Needham, Tavistock Publications, London, 1969.

1958, *Anthropologie Structurale*, Plon, Paris, 454p. *Structural Anthropology*, tr. C. Jacobson and B. G. Schoepf, Allen Lane, London, 1968.

LIZOT, J., 1972, 'L'Ethnologie du deshonneur', in *Le Livre blanc de l'ethnocide en Amérique* (R. Jaulin, ed.), A. Fayard, Paris.

A critique of Biocca (1968). Denies the importance of violence among the Yanoama, while recognising deaths following raids represent 24% of adult male mortality. Does not cite Chagnon, 1968.

LUAS, 1970, 'Le Travail: la main-d'oeuvre immigrée est une bonne affaire', *Front*, No. 3, reproduced in Union Générale les Travailleurs Sénégalais en France (UGTSF), 1970, pp. 82-95.

LUXEMBURG, R., 1913-15, *l'Accumulation du capital*, Maspero, Paris 1967, 2 vols. *The Accumulation of Capital*, tr. A. Schwarzchild, introduction by Joan Robinson, Routledge and Kegan Paul, London, 1951.

LUXEMBURG, R. and BUKHARIN, N. (1915), *Imperialism and the accumulation of Capital*, ed. and intr. K. J. Tarbuck, tr. R. Wichmann, Allen Lane (The Penguin Press), London, 1972.

McLOUGHLIN, P. F. M., 1963, 'Using Administration Reports to Measure Rural Labour Markets. Darfur-Sudan', *Bulletin of the International African Labour Institute*, 10, 1, February 1963, 15-41.

In the long term, the cost of living in Darfur is increasing at a rate two or three times faster than the increase in nominal wages. To maintain equivalent living standards, more time must be spent in the labour market.

MAINE, Sir H., 1861, *Ancient Law*, OUP, The World's Classics Series, London, 285p.

MALINOWSKI, B., 1927, *Sex and Repression in a Savage Society*, Routledge, London, 285p.

'Sociability develops through the extension of family ties and from no other source' (p. 185). Questionable.

1944, *A Scientific Theory of Culture and Other Essays*, Galaxy Books, OUP, New York, 1960, 228p.

The 'reproductive principle of integration' raised to the same level as territory, race, physiology, etc.

References cited

MAQUET, J., 1962, *Les Civilisations noires*, Marabout Université, Brussels and Verviers, 320p. *Civilisations of Black Africa*, revised and tr. by J. Rayfield, OUP, London, 1972.
[A clear and well documented argument based on a restricted materialist perspective.]

MARIE, A., 1972, 'Parenté, Echange matrimonial et Réciprocité', *L'Homme*, XII, 3, 5–46; 4, 5–36.
A comparison in depth between matri- and patrilineal systems. Society builds itself around modalities of control over human energy. [Structural] contradictions of matriliny. Patriliny is based to a greater extent on the principle of reciprocity. New relations of production detach kinship from social relations and structuralism has to give way to historical materialism.

MARSHALL, L., 1957, 'The Kin Terminology of the !Kung Bushmen', *Africa*, 27, 1, January 1957, 1–24.
Kinship above and before all!

MARTIN, J.-Y., 1970, *Les Matakam du Cameroun*, ORSTOM, Mémoire No. 41, 215p.
Among the Matakam bridewealth sanctions only the movement of wives, not that of progeny. The delineation of matrimonial areas.

MARX, K., (1857–8), *Pre-Capitalist Economic Formations*, (translated by J. Cohen with an introduction of E. J. Hobsbawm), Lawrence and Wishart, London, 1964, 153p.
Extracts from *Grundrisse*.

(1857–8), *Des formes antérieures au mode de production capitaliste*, (translated by E. Balibar), n.d., 33p. roneo.
Extracts from *Grundrisse*.

(1857–8), *Fondements de la critique de l'économie politique*, Anthropos, Paris, 1969, 2 vols: translation into French of *Grundrisse*.

(1857–8), *Grundrisse*, (translated by M. Nicolaus), Penguin Books, London, 1973, 898p.

(1859), *Contribution à la critique de l'économie politique*, Editions Sociales, Paris, 1957, 309p.

(1859), *A Contribution to the Critique of Political Economy*, tr. S. W. Ryazanskaya, edited, with an introduction by Maurice Dobb, Progress Publishers, Moscow/ Lawrence and Wishart, London, 1971.

(1866), *Un chapitre inédit du Capital*, U.G.E., Paris, 1971, 319p.

(1867), *Le Capital*, Editions Sociales, Paris, 1950, 8 vols.

(1867), *Capital*, Lawrence and Wishart, London, 1970, 3 vols.

(1895), *Les Luttes de classes en France (1848–1850)*, Editions Sociales, Paris, 1952, 144p. *Class Struggles in France (1848–1850)*, Lawrence and Wishart, London, 19 .

MARX, K. and ENGELS, F., 1846–95, *Correspondance*, Lawrence and Wishart, London 19 .

MARX, W. J., 1941, *Mechanisation and Culture: the Social and Cultural Implications of a Mechanised Society*, Herder, New York, 243p.
The effect of cash cropping on peasants in the United States. The decline in the terms of exchange. Specialisation compels the farmer to give up some of his activities and therefore to buy more on the open market, so that, despite the increase in productivity of his

References cited

labour, he still has to work as long as before to earn the money he needs to buy what he used to make himself. Mechanisation benefits large agricultural corporations, which cannot function without a floating labour force. [The American farmer as a victim of colonisation.]

MASEFIELD, G. B., 1950, *A Short History of Agriculture in the British Colonies*, Clarendon Press, Oxford.

MATTELART. A., 1969, 'Une lecture idéologique de l'Essai sur le principe de population', *Americana Latina* (Rio de Janeiro), 12, 4, October-December 1969, 79-114.
Malthus' theory is the prototype of bourgeois ideology, of its juridico-political mechanicisms and the pseudo-scientific basis of its dominance. It prepares the way for the sociology of *status quo* characteristic of anglo-saxon functionalism. It lives on an integrationist and participationist model of development. [A model study.]

MAUSS, M., 1924, 'Essai sur le don', in *Sociologie et Anthropologie*, P.U.F, Paris, fourth edition (1968), 145-279. *The gift: Forms and Functions of Exchange in Archaic Societies*, tr. I. Cunnison, introduction by E. E. Evans-Pritchard, Routledge and Kegan Paul, 1954 (etc.).
[A questionable interpretation of Boas' material and of the latter's questionable interpretations, but the starting point of new thinking about 'primitive' economics.]

MEILLASSOUX, C., 1960, 'Essai d'interprétation du phénomène économique dans les sociétés traditionnelles d'autosubsistance', *Cahiers d'Etudes Africaines*, 4, 38-67; Eng. tr. in SEDDON, 1978.

MEILLASSOUX, C. (MUNZER, T. and LAPLACE, E.), 1961, *L'Afrique recolonisée*, E.D.I., Paris.

MEILLASSOUX, C., 1962, 'Social and Economic Factors Affecting Markets in Guroland', *Markets in Africa*, in P. BOHANNAN and G. DALTON (eds), Evanston, Ill., Northwestern University Press, 1962, 279-98; the French translation in MEILLASSOUX, 1977.

1964 (third edition), *Anthropologie économique des Gouro de Côte d'Ivoire*, Mouton, Paris, 382p, 17 maps, index, bibliography.

1968, 'Ostentation, Destruction, Reproduction', *Economies et Sociétés*, II, 4, April 1968: 760-72 (in MEILLASSOUX, 1977).

1968b, *Urbanisation of an African Community: Voluntary Association in Bamako*, American Ethnological Society, Monograph No. 45, University of Washington Press, 1968, 165p., index, bibliography.

MEILLASSOUX, C. (ed.), London 1971, *The Development of Indigenous Trade and Markets in West Africa* (introduction). Oxford University Press, London, 444p. - bilingual edition.

1972, 'From Reproduction to Production', *Economy and Society*, I, 1972, 93-105.

1973, 'On the Mode of Production of the Hunting Band', in P. Alexandre (ed.), 1973.

1973a, 'Are there Castes in India?', *Economy and Society*, 2, 1, February 1973, 89-111.

MEILLASSOUX, C. (ed.), 1975, *L'esclavage en Afrique précoloniale*, Maspero, Paris, 582p.

1977, *Terrains et théories*, Paris, Anthropos.

References

1979, *Les derniers Blancs; le modèle Sud-Africain*, Maspero, Paris, 311p.

1980, *Les effets de l'apartheid sur les familles rurales Sud-Africaines*, FAO, Roma, 210p.

MERCIER, P., 1965, 'Les Classes sociales et les Changements politiques récents en Afrique noire', *Cahiers Internationaux de Sociologie*, XXXVIII, January–June 1965, 143–54.

The ruling group takes advantage of the limited development of social classes to deny their existence.

MERLIER, M. 1962, *Le Congo, de la colonisation belge à l'indépendance*, Maspero, Paris, 355p.

The development of social classes, and in particular of the proletariat. A well researched and cogent analysis of the successive forms of labour exploitation practised under Belgian colonialism.

MEYERS, J. T., 1971, 'The Origins of Agriculture: an Evaluation of Three Hypotheses' in STRUEVER (ed.) 1971, 101–21.

The contribution of archaeology.

MIDDLETON, J., 1960, *Lugbara Religion*, OUP, 276p.

The hierarchy within the domestic community.

1974, *Les Lugbara de l'Ouganda: religion et société*, Conférences à l'Ecole Pratique des Hautes Etudes, VIe section (Centre d'études africaines), Paris, 21p. roneo.

Egalitarian ideology among domestic communities.

MIDDLETON, R., 1962, 'A Deviant Case: Brother–Sister and Father–Daughter Marriage in Ancient Egypt', *American Sociological Review*, XXVII, 5, October 1962.

During the Roman occupation, marriages between brothers and sisters were fairly frequent in Egypt, probably so as to protect the patrimony. Contests the idea that the prohibition on incest is universal and argues its relativist nature.

MINCES, J., 1973, *Les Travailleurs étrangers en France*, Le Seuil, Paris, 476p.

[A descriptive, well-informed study. Contains transcriptions of many interviews, but the analysis dwells on the immigrant's psychology rather than upon the objective conditions of his situation.]

MOORE, G., 1968, 'The Imagery of Death in African Poetry', *Africa*, 38, 1, January 1968, 57–70.

The dead remain part of the living community: they nourish life and make renewal possible.

MORGAN, L. H,., 1877, *Ancient Society*, World Publishing Company, New York, 1963, 569p.

MOROKVASIC, M., 1974, *Les Femmes Immigrées au travail*, Colloque européen sur les problèmes de la migration, Louvain, January 31st-February 2nd 1974, roneo, 35p.

[Documented study.]

MOSCOVICI, S., 1972, *La société contre nature*, U.G.E., Paris, 444p. *Society Against Nature: the Emergence of Human Societies*, Harvester Press, Hassocks, 1976.

A Naturalistic discourse on evolution.

MUKHERJEE, R., 1956, *The Problem of Uganda*, Akademie-Verlag, Berlin.

The labour problem. A pioneer work on over-exploitation.

MURCIER, A., 1973, 'L'Afrique du Sud victime de l'apartheid', *L'Expansion*, No. 67, October 1973, 48.

References

Is the 'reserve of black labour' becoming exhausted?

MURY, F., 1904, *La Main-d'oeuvre aux colonies*, Imprimerie des Congrès coloniaux français, 12p.

NADEL, S. F., 1942, *A Black Byzantium: the Kingdom of the Nupe in Nigeria*, OUP, London, 420p.

The family organisation of production and the distribution of the product. The re-formation of functional families. . . .

1947, *The Nuba: an Anthropological Study of the Hill Tribes of Kordofan*, OUP, London, 527p.

A 'typical' domestic economy and its transformations. Bilineal but gynecomobile. Wage-earning work was undertaken exclusively to pay taxes.

NAVILLE, P., 1957, *Le Nouveau Léviathan*, I: *De l'aliénation à la jouissance*, M. Rivière, Paris, 514p.

Contemporary support for Marx's and Engels' thesis through the capitalist practice of labour exploitation.

N'DONGO, S., 1972, *La 'Cooperation' franco-africaine*, Maspero, Paris, 136p. [A bitter and disillusioned critique of the sham aid from French governments to Senegal.]

1974, *Voyage Forcé*, Maspero, 224p.

[The political itinerary of a migrant worker and the path to class consciousness.] Senghor, famine, emigration, and repression in Senegal.

NEEDHAM, R. (ed.), 1971, *Rethinking Kinship and Marriage*, ASA Monograph No. 11, Tavistock, London, 276 (and cxvii) p.

1974, *Remarks and Inventions: Skeptical Essays about Kinship*, Tavistock, London, 181p.

NETTL, J. P., 1966, *Rosa Luxemburg*, OUP, London, 2 vols.

NICOLAI, A., 1974a, 'Et le poussent jusqu'au bout', *Connexions*, 10, October 1974, 75-108.

A project to relaunch dialectical materialism.

1974b, 'Anthropologie des économistes', *Revue économique*, XXV, 4, July 1974, 578-610.

Marxist sociology of knowledge used to criticise contemporary 'economic science'.

NINNE, J., 1932, *La Main-d'oeuvre indigène dans les colonies africaines*, Jouve et Cie, Paris, 245p.

OBREGON, A. Q., 1974, 'The Marginal Role of the Economy and the Marginalised Labour Force', *Economy and Society*, 3, 4, November 1974, 393-428.

An explanation of capitalism in terms of management problems.

OLIVIER de SARDAN, J.-P., 1969, *Système des relations économiques et sociales chez les Wogo (Niger)*, Mémoires de l'Institut d'Ethnologie, III, Institut d'Ethnologie, Paris, 234p.

Marriage, core of social reproduction

1975, 'Captifs ruraux et Esclaves impériaux du Songhai', MEILLASSOUX (ed.), *L'Esclavage en Afrique précoloniale*, Maspero, Paris, p. 99-133.

Matrimonial relations and class relations.

OPPENHEIMER, H. F., 1954-5, 'The Human Aspect of South Africa's Gold Mines', *Progress*, London, 44, 245, winter 1954-5, p. 139-44.

In favour of desegregation and training of black labour [as a way of

References

recruting a qualified labour force which is cheaper than its white counterpart]. The point of view of anglo-saxon capitalism in South Africa.

ORDE-BROWN, G. St J., 1930, 'The African Labourer', *Africa*, 13, 1, January 1930, 13-29.
  Recommends preserving traditional communal structures to forestall pauperism, prostitution, alcoholism, etc. Social excuses for the exploitation of labour.

1941, *Labour Conditions in West Africa*, London, 149p.
  Detribalisation, juvenile delinquency, labour conditions, the cost of living, food supply, housing, education, etc.

ORGANISATION des NATIONS UNIES, 1957, 'Problèmes sociaux que pose l'urbanisation dans les régions économiquement sous-développées', *Rapport sur la situation sociale dans le monde*, 123ff.
  Cities gather in rural poverty.

PALLOIX, C., 1970, 'A propos de l'échange inégal. Une critique de l'économie politique', *L'Homme et la Société*, October–November–December 1970, 5-34.

PAULME, D. (ed.), 1960, *Femmes d'Afrique noire*, Mouton et Cie, Paris, 281p. *Women of Tropical Africa*, tr. H. M. Wright, Routledge and Kegan Paul, 1963.
  [Reference work.]

PEARSON, H. W., 1957, 'The Economy has no Surplus: Critique of a Theory of Development', in K. POLYANI, 1957.
  'Surplus' is institutional.

PERHAM, M. (ed.), 1946, *The Native Economies of Nigeria: being a study of the economies of a tropical dependency*, by D. Forde and R. Scott, Faber, London, 312p.
  Informative, descriptive.

PINTON, S., 1973, 'Les Travaux et les Jours', in JAULIN, 1973: 135-76.
  Features of the daily life of the Bari-Motilone Indians.

POLANYI, K., ARENSBERG, C. M., PEARSON, H. W. (ed.), 1957, *Trade and Market in the Early Empires*, Free Press, New York, 382p.
  How to distinguish different modes of economic circulation in history and anthropology.

POLANYI, K., 1968, *Primitive, Archaic and Modern Economics*, edited by G. Dalton, Doubleday, New York, 346p.
  A collection of articles.

POLLET, E. and G., 1968, L'Organisation sociale du travail agricole chez les Soninké (Diahunu, Mali)', *Cahiers d'Etudes Africaines*, VIII, 4(32), 509-34.
  Analyses the relations of production in domestic agriculture.

POLLET, E. and WINTER, G., 1971, *La Société Soninké*, Institut de Sociologie, Bruxelles, 566p.
  [Accurate fieldwork and an important contribution to theory.]

PONS, V. G., XYDIAS, N., CLEMENT, P., 1956, 'Effets sociaux de l'urbanisation à Stanleyville (Congo belge)', in FORDE (ed.), 1956.
  The minimum wage, calculated for an unmarried man, was not being paid to 70% of the labour force.

PONTIE, G., 1973, *Les Guiziga du Cameroun septentrional*, ORSTOM, Paris, 264p.

References

Inter-rural migration.

POWESLAND, P. G., 1954, 'History of the Migration in Uganda', in
RICHARDS (ed.), 1954.
Chronic shortage of labour in Rwanda until the 1928 and 1943
famines. The colonial economy dependent upon immigration.

RADCLIFFE-BROWN, A. G., 1956, *Structure and Function in Primitive
Society*, Cohen and West, London, 219p.
The 'corporate group', its ritual and patrimonial unity.

RAYNAUD, E., 1965, 'Le Sous-Emploi rural dans les pays en voie de développement' *Etudes Rurales*, 18, 37–68.
'The assumption that transfers of surplus labour from the agricultural sector to other sectors of the economy are desirable [. . .] is
valid only for countries already industrialised [. . .] such transfers in
developing countries are destructive.'

RAYNAUT, C., 1975, 'Un Aspect de la crise des sociétés agricoles de l'Afrique sahélo-soudanienne: le cas de la région de Maradi (Niger)', in
COPANS (ed.), 1975, vol. 2, 5–43.
Groundnut cultivation given up and the family economy transformed under the influence of commercialisation of food production.

READ, M., 1942, 'Migrant Labour in Africa and its Effects on Tribal Life',
International Labour Review, 14 (6), 605–31.

REBOUL, C., 1972, *Structures agraires et Problèmes de développement au
Sénégal*, I.N.R.A., Paris, Travaux et Recherches, No. 17, June 1972,
163p.
'The traditional mode of production is gradually losing its autonomy, to the point where, like self-consumption, it is becoming the
very condition for development of the market economy.'

1975, *Causes économiques de la sécheresse au Sénégal*, I.N.R.A., Paris,
59p. roneo.
Critique of Senegal's economic policies; self-sustenance and market
production; the capitalist effects of the 'socialist' law on national
property; the growing social and regional inequalities.

REICH, W., 1932, *L'Irruption de la morale sexuelle*, Payot, Paris (translated
1972), 240p. *The Invasion of Compulsory Sex-morality*, tr. W. and D.
Grossman, Souvenir Press, London, 1972.
How marriage with matrilineal cross-cousins introduces 'patriarchy'
in the ruling classes and inter-lineage exploitation. [A Marxist and
psychoanalytical re-interpretation of Malinowski.]

1933, *Psychologie de masse du fascisme*, La Pensée Molle, 1970, 150p.
The Mass Psychology of Fascism, Penguin Books, Harmondsworth,
1975.
The ideological function of the patriarchal family.

RETEL-LAURENTIN, A., 1974, *Infécondité en Afrique noire (Maladies et
consequences sociales)*, Masson, Paris, 196p.
In spite of pre-conceived ideas, fecundity is low in many parts of
Africa; this seriously impedes economic development and social
structures.

REY, P.-P., 1971, *Colonialisme, Néo-Colonialisme et Transition au capitalisme*, Maspero, Paris, 526p.
'Capitalism develops at the expense of the lineage system, but also

References

thanks to this same lineage system [. . . whose class relations it reinforces] it also maintains and increases its domination.'

1973, *Les Alliances de classes: 'sur l'articulation des modes de production'*, *suivi de 'Materialisme historique et luttes de classes'*, Maspero, Paris, 221p.

Are there 'transitional modes of production', formed through alliances between ruling classes?

1975, 'L'Esclavage lignager chez les Tsangui, Punu et les Kuni du Congo-Brazzaville', *L'Esclavage en Afrique précoloniale* (Ed. MEILLASSOUX), Paris, Maspero, 1975, pp. 509-20.

RICHARDS, A., 1939, *Land, Labour and Diet in Northern Rhodesia. An Economic Study of the Bemba Tribe*, Oxford University Press, London.

Nutrition deteriorates under the influence of white civilisation. Vulnerability to famine. The imbalance aggravated by recruitment of men for the mines.

1954, *Economic Development and Tribal Change: a Study of Immigrant Labour in Uganda*, Heffer, Cambridge (Revised ed., Nairobi, 1973).

A detailed sociological study. An important historical chapter. Migration was brought on by taxes, forced labour and famine. In 1950 they were up to 75% towards the rural areas where different forms of land tenure were practised. Nutritional standards fell in areas of emigration. Migration to towns on the increase.

RIVIERE, P. G., 1974, *Some Problems in the Development of Traditional Shifting Cultivators of Tropical Forest of South America*, S.S.R.C. Symposium on 'The Future of Traditional Primitive Societies', Cambridge, December 1974, 23p. roneo.

The ecological constraints on proto-agriculture.

RODBERTUS, K., 1865, 'Zur Geschichte der römischen Tributsteuern', *Jahrbücher für Nationalökonomie und Statistik*, IV, 1865.

RUYLE, E. E., 1973a, 'Slavery, Surplus and Stratification on the Northwest Coast', *Current Anthropology*, 14, 5, December 1973, 603-31.

Labour exploitation in *potlatch* societies.

1973b, 'Mode of Production and Mode of Exploitation: a Neglected Aspect of Marxist Theory', American Anthropological Association Symposium on Marxist Theory in Anthropology, I-XII-1973.

'Mode of exploitation' brings us back to the class struggle while the idea of 'mode of production' merely confronts abstractions.

1974, 'On the Origins of Social Classes and the State-Church', *Explorations in Political Economy*, 73rd annual meeting of the A.A.A., November 1974, 14p. roneo.

The exploiting classes draw towards them a greater flow of social energy. The State is the result of demographic pressure. . . !

SACHS, I., 1966, 'La Notion de surplus et son application aux économies primitives', *L'Homme*, VI, 3, July–September 1966, 5-18.

A study of statistical correlations, left unexplained, between surplus and population, taking no account of the problem of training the producer. No distinction is made between the production of subsistence goods and of unproductive goods.

SAHLINS, M., 1968, 'La Première Société d'abondance', *Les Temps Modernes*, 24, 268, October 1968, 641-80.

No social progress has been made since the age of the hunter.

184

References

1972, *Stone-Age Economics*, Aldine-Atherton, Chicago, 348p.
> In quest of theoretical rigour, but continues to confuse several non-capitalist modes of production.

SAMUEL, M., 1978, *Le prolétariat africain noir en France*, Maspero, Paris, 262p.

SAUER, C. O., 1969, *Agricultural Origins and Dispersals: the Domestication of Animals and Foodstuffs*, M.I.T. Press, Cambridge, Mass., 175p.
> Ecological constraints and their probable influence on the development of agricultural societies.

SAUTTER, G. et al., 1957, *Structures agraires et paysages ruraux: un quart de siècle de recherches francaises*, Annales de l'Est, Nancy, Mémoire No. 17, 188p.
> The diversity of methods of cultivation and soil use.

SCHAPERA, I., 1947, *Migrant Labour and Tribal Life*, OUP, London, 248p.
> A pioneer study. The migrant worker is kept economically dependent upon his community.

SCHMITZ, J., 1975, 'Pour une démographie de la force du travail', MS., typed, 16p.
> A theoretical view close to the one put forward in this book.

SCHNEIDER, H. K., 1964, 'A Model of African Indigenous Economy and Society', *Comparative Studies in Society and History*, 7, 1, October 1964, 37–55.
> Bridewealth and cattle. (The author treats cattle as a form of money.)

1970, *The Waki Wanyaturu (Economics in an African Society)*, Viking Fund Publications, 48, Wenner-Gren Foundation.
> A classical interpretation, in terms of the search for profit, of an agro-pastoral economy.

SEDDON, D. (ed.), 1978, *Relations of Production: Marxist Approaches to Economic Anthropology*, Frank Cass, London, 414p.

SERVOLIN, C., 1972, 'L'Absorbtion de l'agriculture dans le mode de "production capitaliste"', in *L'Univers politique des paysans dans la France contemporaine* by Y. Tavernier and C. Servolin (eds), Armand Colin, Paris, 41–77.
> The organic role of petty commodity production in the development of French capitalism.

SMITH, M. G., 1952, 'A Study of Hausa Domestic Economy in Northern Zaria', *Africa*, 22, 4, October 1952, 333–47.
> Family budgets and incomes.

SOUTH AFRICA (UNION of), 1944, *Report of the Witwatersrand Natives Wages Commission*, Pretoria, Govt. Printer (U.G. No. 21), p. 61.
> Studies the recruitment system, incomes and budgets. Incomes are inferior to needs. Recommends higher wages and 'radical' measures to improve conditions in the Reserves.

SOUTHALL, A. W., 1954, 'Alur Migrants', in RICHARDS (ed.), 1954, 141–61.
> Decline in the economic and social conditions of production among the Alur.

1956, *Alur Society: a Study of Processes and Types of Domination*, Heffer, Cambridge.
> The process by which members of one dynasty come to dominate several domestic societies.

References

SPERBER, D., 1968, *Le Structuralisme en anthropologie*, Le Seuil, Paris, 122p.
> 'For other anthropologists the human spirit is capable of acquiring everything; for structuralist ones it is capable of engendering everything.' [A personal and critical account of the ideas of Lévi-Strauss.]

STILLMAN, C. (ed.), 1955, *Africa in the Modern World*, University of Chicago Press.

STAVENHAGEN, R., 1972, 'Agrarian Structures and Underdevelopment in Africa and Latin America', *Strategies for Economic Development*, I.D.E.P., I.D.S., I.E.D.E.S., Conference at Dakar in September 1972, 22p. roneo.
> Modes of exploitation of the Latin American and African peasantry are compared, in the past, present and foreseeable future.

1973, *Sept thèses erronées sur l'Amérique latine*, Anthropos, Paris, 207p.
> Preliminary statements for any discussion about development.

STEWARD, J. H., 1968, 'Causal Factors and Process in the Evolution of Pre-Farming Societies', in LEE and DEVORE, 1968, pp. 321–34.

STRUEVER, S. (ed.), 1971, *Prehistoric Agriculture*, Natural History Press, New York, 733p.

SURET-CANALE, J. (ed.), 1967, 'Premières Sociétés de classes', *Recherches Internationales*, 57–8, January–April 1967, 344p. [Rediscovery of the 'Asiatic mode of production' by official Marxism.]

1964, *Afrique noire: l'ère coloniale, 1900–1945*, Editions Sociales, Paris, 637p. *French Colonialism in Tropical Africa, 1900–1945*, tr. T. Gottheimer, C. Hunt, London, 1971.
> [Reference work.]

SWIFT, M. G., 1957, 'The Accumulation of Capital in a Peasant Economy', *Economic Development and Cultural Change*, 5, 4, July 1957, 325–37.
> Malaysia. Rice growing and rubber producing peasantry. Low investment possibilities. Money not yet a reserve of value.

TARDITS, C., 1960, *Les Bamiléké de l'Ouest-Cameroun*, Berger-Levrault, Paris, 139p.
> *Knap* marriage.

1973, 'Parenté et Pouvoir politique chez les Bamoum', *L'Homme*, XIII, 1–2, 37–49.
> The 'provisioning king-father' in an 'economy of largely distributive character'.

TERRAY, E., 1969a, *Le Marxisme devant les sociétés 'primitives'*, Maspero, Paris 177p. *Marxism and 'Primitive' Societies: Two Studies*, tr. M. Klopper, Monthly Review Press, New York, 1972.

1969b, 'L'Organisation sociale des Dida de Côte-d'Ivoire', *Annales de l'Universite* F.1, 2, 375.

THION, S., 1969, *Le Pouvoir pâle*, Editions du Seuil, Paris, 317p.
> The anatomy of the economic system based upon apartheid, maintaining an unqualified, mobile labour force which is subject to permanent and organised structural unemployment. South African imperialism.

THOMAS, L. V., 1970, 'La Croissance urbaine en Afrique noire et à Madagascar', *C.N.R.S., Colloque de Talence*, September–October 1970, 117–38.
> Estimates unemployment in the capitalist sector.

References

THOMPSON, E. P., 1963, *The Making of the English Working Class*, Penguin Books, London, 958p.

TINLEY, J. M., 1942, *The Native Labour Problem in South Africa*, University of North Carolina Press, Chapel Hill, N.C., and Milford, London, 281p.

The importation of labour from the British and Portuguese colonies.

TONNIES, F., (1887), *Communauté et Société*, Paris, 1944, Community and Society, tr. and ed. C. P. Loomis, Routledge and Kegan Paul, London, 1955.

TROTSKY, L. D., 1932, *History of the Russian Revolution*, tr. M. Eastman, Gollancz, London,19.

The law of combined development in underdeveloped countries.

TURNBULL, C. W., 1965, *Wayward Servants: the Two Worlds of African Pygmies*, Eyre and Spottiswoode, London, 390p.

The hunting and gathering mode of production illustrated by observation of the Mbuti, both in the forest and in contact with Bantu farmers – by a 'culturalist'.

UNION GENERALE DES TRAVAILLEURS SENEGALAIS EN FRANCE (UGTSF), 1970, *Le Livre des travailleurs africains en France*, Maspero, Paris, 197p.

The legal, economic and health situation of migrants in exile from Senegal.

VAN DER HORST, S. T., 1942, *Native Labour in South Africa*, OUP, London, 340p.

The desires of Europeans, to make use of black labour and keep it at a distance, conflict. White workers' fear of black competition and ways of forestalling such a situation (unions for qualified whites only; migratory black labour, control of workers' movements). Weaknesses of the South African economy. Soil exhaustion. Necessity to increase the buying power of blacks.

VILAKAZI, H. W., in RUYLE, 1973a.

On the political exploitation of kinship ideology.

WAAST, R. (n.d.), 'Développement des sociétés occidentales malgaches au XXe siècle', manuscript, roneo, unpublished, 71p.

The history of economic, social and political relations engendered by colonialism between aristocratic classes, lineage communities and the successive forms of capitalism.

1974, 'Les Concubins de Soala', *Cahiers du Centre d'Etudes des Coutumes, Université de Madagascar*, 1974, 7–46.

How Malagasy women turn their dependence into a weapon against men in order to domesticate them in their turn.

WATSON, N., 1959, 'Migrant Labour and Detribalisation', in J. Middleton (ed.), *Black Africa; its peoples and their Cultures Today*, Macmillan, London, 1970, pp. 38–48.

[Good review of almost all the social problems.]

WATSON, R. A. and WATSON, P. J., 1971, 'The Domestication of Plants and Animals', in STRUEVER, 1971, 3–11.

WEIL, P. M., 1970, 'Mandinke Fertility, Islam and Integration in a Plural Society', American Anthropological Association, San Diego, November 19-22, 18p. roneo.

A women's association against sterility. 'Symbolically, the associa-

References

tion deals with food production and child production as being the same.'

WILSON, F., 1972, *Labour in the South African Gold Mines, 1911–1969*, CUP, Cambridge, 217p.

WILSON, M. (HUNTER, M.), 1936, 1961, *Reaction to Conquest: Effects of Contact with Europeans on the Pondo of South Africa*, IAI, OUP, London, 582p.
>   The degradation of Bantu society under the effect of wage-employment.

WINTER, E. H., 1955, *Bwamba Economy; the Development of a Primitive Subsistence Economy in Uganda*, East African Studies, No. 5, Kampala, 44p.
>   The opening of a domestic economy to cash cropping. Calculation of the labour time of women and men. Advocates the lowering of the price of coffee so as to make the Bwamba work harder.

WODDIS, J., 1960, *Africa; the Roots of Revolt*, Lawrence and Wishart, London, 285p.
>   Migration in southern Africa of adult men is for short, recurrent contracts; the men travel over long distances; migrations cause unbalance in the village economy; they hold back workers' organisation and maintain village solidarity.

1961, *Africa: the Lion Awakes*, Lawrence and Wishart, London, 301p.
>   [A militant and well-informed work about the exploitation of Africa and Africans.]

WOLPE, H., 1970, *Class, Race and the Occupational Structure in South Africa*, 21p. roneo (revised version of a paper delivered at the World Sociology Conference, Varna).
>   'The racial barrier in the economy may be the result of political decisions, but it still defines relations between social classes. Apartheid is as much "economic" as "political".'

1972, 'Capitalism and Cheap Labour-Power in South Africa: from Segregation to Apartheid', *Economy and Society*, 1, 4, 425–56.
>   [A key article.] The economic foundations of the racist and segregationist ideology and of its transformations.

(1974?), *The Theory of Internal Colonialism; the South African Case*, Department of Sociology, University of Essex, 25p. roneo.
>   Racism is not based upon ethnic differences but upon the 'conservation-destruction' relations of exploitation which characterise South African capitalism.

WOODHAM-SMITH, C., 1962, *The Great Hunger*, New English Library, London, 429p.
>   History of the Irish Famine of 1845–9. The resistance to emigration.

Index

Index

'extraction economy' 8, 14, 27, 66;
see also bands, hunter-gatherer;
economy, primary types; hunting-
gathering

family, 3, 18, 43, 83, 87, 143–4,
160; function of *xiii*, 47, 60, 99,
108, 141–4, 154
famine *ix*, 139, 140
fascism 121
father, concept of 47, 80, 86, 150;
see also elder
fertility; and population size *xii*, 12,
13; and women exchange 61–2
fertility cults 38
feudalism *xiii*, 96, and capitalism
104, 110, 157
filiation 19–22, 23ff; 38–9, 47, 48,
76, 77; male 43, *see also* patriliny; and incest 12
fishing 147
food: collection of 14; distribution
of 58–60, 130, 139; and human
energy 15, 50–1, 52, 151; as product 51, 52–5, 66, 129–30; preparation of 78, 153
food-aid 130, 150, 159
France 120, 121, 122, 123, 124,
136, 158, 159
'free labourers' 97, 99, 102, 104,
123, 143; *see also* labour-power

gardens, function of 108
Germany 109, 124, 125; *see also* Nazi
Germany
Ghana 92, 118, 150
gifts, function of 152
Great Britain 133
group, social 12–13, 33, 45–6, 81;
see also bands
Guro 46, 150
gynecostatism 24, 25, 28, 31, 33,
75–6

Hawaii 11
Haute-Volta 118
hierarchy 5, 42, 47; *see also* anteriority; class
historical materialism *viii*, *xi*, *xii*, 9,
19, 49

household 8; function of 27, 58–9;
see also family
human energy *xi*, 27, 46, 50–1, 59,
71, 149; in agriculture 34, 39,
55–6; as *E* 56, 151, 111, 113;
reproduction of 15, 45–6, 51–7;
see also labour-power
hunting, and kinship 25, 27, 28–30
hunting-gathering, and agriculture 8,
9, 14–15, 26–30, 39; *see also*
bands, hunter-gatherer

ideology; function of 45, 82, 93,
120, 121, 157; of power 86–7
immigrants 107, 116, 124, 155; status of 120–3, 129, 131–2, 135–6;
see also labour, migration of;
migration
imperialism 105, 138ff, 99, 105;
and domestic community 51, 87,
95; and exploitation 97–8, 140,
159
incest 11–12, 146
incest prohibition 10–11, 12, 45, 146
infanticide, female 17, 29
inheritance 78, 142
institutions, social *xiii*, 29, 38, 43,
59; in capitalism 108; *see also*
family; marriage; social product;
social security
Ivory Coast 118

Japan 109
juniors (young men) 79–80; *see also*
anteriority; authority; domination,
social; father; elders; hierarchy

kinship *xi*, 3, 20, 145, 150; importance of 5, 18–22, 31, 44, 48, 60,
86; theories of *viii*, 10–11, 18–
19; *see also* consanguinity; family;
lineage
Kukuya 81, 84

labour: division of 3, 6, 20–1, 37–
8, 78, 149; exploitation of *x*, 35,
91–5, 99, 105–6, 112, 120–3,
127–8, 133, 135–40, *see also*
labour-power, labour-rent; land
and 14–15, 34, 39, 92–3, 104,

AUTHOR INDEX

Index

Index

196

QUOTES BEGIN HERE, THEN CONTINUE ON FRONT PAGES

Human reprod as production; labour power XI, XIII

Categories of liberal econ's - can only negatively describe what dom comm is not 4

Aim - identify distinct modes of prod. 7, 96
 Polanyi 5   Specifically, domestic mode of prod 84
 Sahlins 6, 7   See adr. domm. comm III 96 (87)
                    ALL OTHER ECON'S HAVE BEEN BUILT ON THE DOM MODE OF PRO

Incest taboo - arises when control ans marriage becomes an element of pol. power 12

Kinship theory has confused 2 kinds of relas; 1) adhesion — (char of herds) 2) kinship 14-19, 21, 27, 38
                (agriculturalists)
Has also confused mating (quest for a wife) and filiation (quest for offspring) 19.

Power / knowledge 22
 Gynecostatic vs. Gynecomobile systems 24, 25, 33, 76
Contradiction of domestic rela's of prod. & reprod 28 -
matrilin forms of organiz tend to corr. w/ planting agric, while patrilin forms corr w/ cereal agric 25, 26
              proto agric.
Power based on war (to acquire ♀) 28-30 → agric.
to maintain suff # of ♀) 30°, 33, 43   civil power (age

Dw of civil lineage power & extended kin grps is hampered in planting soc's 31

permanent contradiction in gynrostatic systems - leads either to disappearance, violent reprod or intrid of patrilin 31, 43
 Therefore, mobility of ♀ is preferable 43
Advanced domestic comm - alliance supplants viol as means of securing ♀ 33, 43

Defining adv. dom comm & the (units of prod. to which it cor-responds 34, 35-38

Cereal agric is corr w/ adv dom comm 34

 Use of term property for land in dom comm's is inapprop.
Prop arises only w/ market system. Proper term is patrimony. 36

All insti's & social rela's in adv dom comm are dominated by & organiz around reprod 38

↓ Notion of filiation thus dev's 39   Use for
* It is subord. only to prod. 39 (48)   Tamby
Main char's of domestic agric. comm 40 (42)   / andlos
                                                        SCOTT-
Heir of elders is due to cycle of advances & returns in agric. & class
is manifested in cycle of prestation & redistrib 41, 42, 77 —
Rela's of prod in dom agric comm (42) gits & sts 79-81, 83, 84, 86
Rel's of reprod "   But not class relas bute
                               " 42-49 Reprod is not a nat
marriage - to estab. rules of filiation 43   Su trntpgi
solution to demographic hazards threatening grp (43) is
bilateral & multilateral exchange of ♀ 44
W/ exogamy their power shifts to control over ♀ 44, 45, 77 (82) —